D1605872

What does it mean to grow old?

What Does It Mean to Grow Old?

Reflections from the Humanities

Edited by Thomas R. Cole
and Sally A. Gadow

Duke University Press   Durham 1986

Publication of this book was supported by a grant
from the Diebel Foundation.

The Diebel Memorial Volume

In Honor of

DONNY RAE DIEBEL, M.D.

April 27, 1945–July 25, 1971

Contents

Acknowledgments

We would like to thank Sheila Keating and Kathleen Stephens for their indispensable help and patience in arranging the Aging and Meaning Seminar and in preparing the manuscript for publication. To Robert Kastenbaum, our gratitude for his participation in the seminar, in particular the presentation of his own commissioned play, *Ump*.

We would also like to thank Richard Rasche for his persistent and careful work in verifying the bibliography that appears in the appendix. Finally, we are grateful to Mrs. Glenella Diebel for establishing a fund in memory of her son to help support publications of the Institute for the Medical Humanities at the University of Texas Medical Branch at Galveston.

Foreword

The culture of aging and the aged is a distinctly modern phenomenon. Until very recently in our society, to reach three score
and ten was the exception. Now it is the rule. Time was when to
ask after the meaning of growing old or being old would have
seemed absurd. Today the question is becoming urgent.

It is commonplace that questions about meaning are prompted
by change. While frontiers are being pushed back, a certain im-
patience with considerations of meaning prevails. But now that the
expectation of physical life has been extended and further extension seems imminent, we are bound to ask: What for? What are
the purposes of more life? Assuming that longer life is not an absolute good, what sort of old age is desirable? What sort livable?
Old people themselves do not speak with one voice but they are
nonetheless the best source of answers to these questions.

Arnold Toynbee wrote in his seventy-eighth year, "The ordeal
of which I am most conscious at this stage is that of having to draw
in my horns." Necessity looms large in the writings of the old.
Physical energy is less plentiful than earlier in life. Resilience
wanes. Both physically and spiritually one has to work at what
once came effortlessly. As Emerson, at sixty-one, noted, "The grief
of old age is, that, now, only in rare moments, and by happiest
combinations or consent of the elements, can we attain those en-
largements and that intellectual *elan*, which were once a daily gift."

Having to acknowledge one's limits is not an unalloyed evil.

Hemingway's old fisherman says to his young companion, "I may not be as strong as I think . . . but I know many tricks and I have resolution." His luck has lagged but not his determination. His eyes, though almost blind, are "cheerful and undefeated." He knows his limits and within those he has staying power. The proverbial and admirable wisdom of old age may be misnamed. Perhaps wisdom is a judiciousness seasoned by years that emerges from the necessity to measure one's days.

"I still have my health and my wits," writes Toynbee, "and, so long as my wits do not fail me, my curiosity will not." Losing one's wits is dreaded as a death-in-life, the premature death of the spirit. Nor is health a good in itself but rather a precondition for living well. Freud, in his mid-fifties, confided in a letter to Pastor Pfister, "What would one do if ideas failed or words refused to come? It is impossible not to shudder at the thought. Hence, in spite of all the acceptance of fate which is appropriate to an honest man, I have one quite secret prayer: that I may be spared any wasting away of my ability to work because of physical deterioration."

What are the essential ingredients of a livable old age? Health? Work? Companionship? Intimacy? What else, and in what combination? These were among the leading questions about aging that prompted the work in this volume.

There were other questions—about meaning. Do we make meaning, or do we discover it? Both surely, but perhaps the balance is tipped more toward discovery in youth and toward discernment as one ages. In an important sense, the meaning of a life can be fathomed fully only from the end of that life looking back. Old age is a time for recapitulating, connecting part to part, re-membering.

Now that the great cultural systems of participatory meaning have largely lost their compelling power, such recollecting and drawing together are left to individuals. Are there patterns in these individual efforts—in, say, family rituals or the routines of neighborhood life? If there are commonalities in observers' accounts of such rituals and routines, or in autobiographies authored by the old—if old age makes sense "from the inside," whether individually or in concert with others both young and old—then we need to recognize and articulate this implicit meaning. I have in mind, for example, the sorts of reflections one finds in Ronald Blythe's *The View in Winter*, but also contemplative fiction such as A. G. Mojtabai's *Autumn*. Such articulations are valuable guides to the uncharted land of long life.

It is hard to avoid extremes in thinking about what old age means. To be old is to be wise—or foolish. Is there no middle ground? No appreciation of complexity and continuity? Is the doddering foolishness of old age different in kind or only in degree from the brash foolishness of youth? "You must bear with me. Pray you now, forget and forgive. I am old and foolish." Lear's folly is not a product of his eighty-odd years but of fondness gone awry.

Another extreme is that of facile celebration of the joys of aging. The poet comes close to this in Whitman's "Youth, Day, Old Age and Night":

> Youth, large, lusty, loving—youth full of grace,
>   force, fascination,
> Do you know that Old Age may come after you with
>   equal grace, force, fascination?
>
> Day full-blown and splendid—day of the immense
>   sun, action, ambition, laughter,
> The Night follows close with millions of suns, and
>   sleep and restoring darkness.

Yet surely the grace of old age not only measures up to ("equals") the robust grace of youth but exceeds it. There is a gracefulness of character that accrues only after long rehearsal, and there is a givenness (the theologian's grace) that is beyond promise and recompense. This last, when acknowledged and internalized, yields equanimity.

In early 1983, with the generous support of the Sid W. Richardson Foundation, the Institute for the Medical Humanities invited thinkers from the humanities, law, medicine, and the social sciences to train their attention on the relation of aging and meaning. Each participant drafted a paper which was then formally critiqued by a fellow participant at a working meeting in Galveston. (The single exception was a one-act play, *Ump*—a searching character study of an ebullient, hesitantly introspective, aging enforcer of rules and arbiter of baseball disputes—written by project participant Robert Kastenbaum and performed by the playwright and University of Texas Medical Branch faculty.) Papers were subsequently rewritten by their authors and edited by the project directors. Throughout the course of this project, the editors' perspectives on aging and meaning have remained in creative tension. In Thomas Cole's view, aging must be understood within an intersubjective web of

cultural meanings that are embedded in social relations and practices. For Sally Gadow, the meaning of aging is to be found in individual subjectivity. These differing approaches, held together by
the editors' shared commitment to the problem of aging and meaning, shape the volume and give it its critical edge.

   This volume represents a significant advance in the new humanities scholarship on aging. Initiated in the mid 1970s, this work
is informed by a sense that much gerontological research and practice tacitly incorporates the social values responsible for ageism
and the declining status of old people. In retrospect, the earlier
"human values" approach suffered from a diffuseness inevitable in
the absence of a common culture. Cole and Gadow invite us to explore the problem of aging and meaning within this historical context of declining collective beliefs.

                                                        Ronald A. Carson

What does it mean to grow old?

Part One

The tattered web of cultural meanings

Introduction For at least the last sixty years Western observers have sensed an impoverishment of social meaning in old
age. In 1922 G. Stanley Hall noted that modern progress both
lengthened old age and drained it of substance.[1] During the 1930s,
Carl Jung observed that many persons found little meaning or purpose in life as they grew older.[2] In 1949 A. L. Vischer wondered
whether "there is any sense, any vital meaning in old age."[3] Fifteen
years later, Erik Erikson argued that, lacking a culturally viable
ideal of old age, "our civilization does not really harbor a concept
of the whole of life."[4] Summarizing a large volume of research in
1974, Irving Rosow claimed that American culture provides old
people with "no meaningful norms by which to live."[5] And more
recently, Leopold Rosenmayr claimed that the position of the elderly
in Western society "can only be reoriented and changed if viable
ideals, 'existential paradigms,' become visible and receive some social support."[6]

Unfortunately, important insights such as these remain unde-
veloped, marginal to the study of aging. Gerontological research
and scholarship have been dominated by a positivist focus on biomedical and social conditions of aging—generally in the hope of
altering them. Popular faith in scientific progress and commitment
to control over the physical world find clear expression in mainstream gerontology's reified conception of aging as an entity, the
"meaning" of which equals the sum of its empirical descriptions.

Of course, meanings are always present implicitly in the study of aging; yet they are rarely brought into focus. (See the appendix, "Aging and Meaning: A Bibliographical Essay.") Hence we have been slow to understand our current predicament: the absence or inadequacy of shared meanings of aging and old age, and the bewildering multiplication and uncertain vitality of new meanings. But in the last quarter of the twentieth century, three broad historical trends have converged to compel us to address these questions: the ideological and fiscal crises of the welfare state; the democratization of longevity and rapid progress of biomedical technology; and the cultural crisis of the secular therapeutic ethos,[7] which followed the decline of a relatively unified Christian belief system.[8] In this context, the quality of our ideas about the meaning of aging has considerable implications for medical ethics and practice, psychotherapy and the education of older people, research on the biology of aging and the prolongation of human life, public policy, and religious and spiritual life.

But what is meaning? Why does it matter? Why does the relationship between aging and meaning demand rigorous intellectual inquiry? Will this inquiry serve more than academic and professional needs and interests? The materials included here begin to address these questions.

Meaning is a notoriously vague concept, used in various senses and applied to an infinite number of things. As Robert Nozick has demonstrated, there are at least eight different, though interrelated, modes of meaning. Meaning can refer to: external causal relationship; external referential, semantic, or symbolic relation; intention or purpose; lesson; personal significance; objective meaningfulness; intrinsic meaningfulness; and total resultant meaning, or the entire web of the preceding modes.[9] While Nozick's conceptual analysis is important for clarity, it cannot (as he acknowledges) provide an objective, predefined formula capable of fully grasping the meaning of meaning. As self-defining and self-interpreting animals, we human beings must enter into our own webs of meaning in order to understand ourselves.[10]

In contemporary culture these modes of meaning are generally used in one of two ways: as a generalized theory of language or as an intuitive expression of one's overall appraisal of living. Theoretically, many philosophical, cultural, and psychological writers stress the centrality of meaning and meaning systems in human experience. Existentially, meaning refers to lived perceptions of coherence, sense, or significance in experience. The concept of meaning, then, contains a crucial ambiguity, what Herbert Fingarette terms a "point of intersection from which one may move either into living or into theories about living. The existential questions about meaning are part of a process of generating a new vision which shall serve as the context of new commitment; the scientific questions about meaning are part of a process of developing a logical, reliably interpretable, and systematically predictive theory."[11]

As Fingarette has shown, the generative power of meaning as a concept derives from this seminal ambiguity, which allows one to connect the world of public understandings with the inner struggle for wholeness. At its best, for example, psychoanalysis exploits this ambiguity by using the language of meaning both scientifically to interpret a patient's problems and existentially to encourage personal movement toward new, more integrated meanings. On the other hand, orthodox, mechanical versions of psychoanalysis reduce individual experience to preconceived theoretical meanings—thereby stifling spiritual growth instead of nurturing it.[12]

The new inquiry into aging and meaning must attend to both kinds of meaning, as well as the connections between them. For example, which public and scientific meanings nourish and which impoverish the existential search for meaning in aging? Existentially nourishing views of aging, I believe, must address its paradoxical nature. Aging, like illness and death, reveals the most fundamental conflict of the human condition: the tension between infinite ambitions, dreams, and desires on the one hand, and vulnerable, limited, decaying physical existence on the other—between self and body. This paradox cannot be eradicated by the wonders of modern medicine or by positive attitudes toward growing old. Hence the wisdom of traditions which consider old age both a blessing and a curse. Or, as Ronald Blythe says, "Old age is full of death and full of life. It is a tolerable achievement and it is a disaster. It transcends desire and it taunts it. It is long enough and far from long enough."[13]

In the past the courage and understanding needed to face this ambiguous reality were often nourished in religious and philosophical traditions which counseled resignation and/or spiritual transcendence. In our own world, spirituality, contemplation, and concern for the virtues pale beside the pleasures of consumption, the activist pressures of the marketplace, and the promises of modern science and medicine.

These themes are touched on in several of the following essays. Harry Moody suggests the profound implications that flow from the seemingly academic issues of meaning and aging. Numerous practical decisions in professional ethics and public policy rely on the cultural and theoretical meanings we give to aging. The bureaucratization of the life cycle, the displacement of the search for meaning onto old age, the trivialization of leisure, the covert ideology that underpins the study of life span development—all call for philosophical study and public engagement in the search for more human meanings of old age.

William May argues that one of the most pervasive and insidious ways of demeaning financially or physically dependent old people is to place them in the hands of caretakers and bureaucrats guided by a philanthropic ideal. "Like a bustling cold front that moves in and stiffens the landscape," he writes, the knowledgeable, empowered professional handles the passive elderly client—without risking the real reciprocity required of a truly human relationship. Against this prevailing tendency to reduce the aged to moral nonentities, May calls not for a one-sided ethic of caregiving but for renewed cultivation of virtues and ideals that might guide moral and spiritual life in old age.

Of course, rethinking appropriate norms and obligations in old age is no excuse for shirking responsibility to those in need. As Christine Cassel contends in the second half of this book, our health care system attends poorly to those elderly who suffer from multiple and chronic diseases. Current efforts to reduce medical costs, combined with the dubious assumption that old people use "more than their share" of health care resources, prompt Cassel to inquire into the meaning of health care for the aged in a just society.

The question arises: do we allow the marketplace to serve as the moral and social arbiter of the status of older people, or do we locate the rights and responsibilities of the elderly within a larger vision of the political community? W. Andrew Achenbaum touches on this question in his discussion of the economic and political meanings that have characterized the Social Security system since the 1930s. He points out that social security is based less on financial arrangements or demographic ratios than on an intergenerational covenant whose principles are often ambiguous and misunderstood. Echoing Alasdair MacIntyre's contention that the nature of political obligation becomes systematically unclear in a society without a genuine moral consensus, Achenbaum calls for renewed debate over the goals and principles of welfare state programs in an aging society.

In a similar vein, Robert Burt reconsiders recent legal reform designed to uproot age discrimination. Burt challenges the traditional American assumption that employment decisions based on individual merit are more just than those built on age-based criteria. He points out that while opponents of mandatory retirement argue that it represents a preference for youth, their insistence that the elderly be allowed to demonstrate their continuing vitality endorses the same value premise. Hence, some elderly are permitted to free themselves from stereotypes of economic worthlessness while others are forced to endure them with a vengeance.

My own essay argues that the attack on ageism, which currently passes for an enlightened view of aging, is both conceptually and existentially inadequate, as well as politically dangerous. I suggest that ageism and its critics have more in common than is generally realized; their history reveals the relentless hostility of liberal capitalist culture toward decay and dependency. This ideologically rooted hostility may be the single most intractable obstacle to developing more socially just and spiritually satisfying meanings of aging.

Thomas R. Cole

Harry R. Moody

The Meaning of Life and the Meaning of Old Age

Editor's Introduction. In his wide-ranging philosophical essay, Harry R. Moody reminds us that timeless questions ("The Meaning of Life and the Meaning of Old Age") do not have timeless answers. All thought is historically conditioned—that is, related to changing structures of power and patterns of culture. This insight encourages Moody to analyze contemporary philosophical discussions of meaning in light of our modern "therapeutic" culture, the triumph of scientific professionalism, and the bureaucratized life-cycle of late capitalism. In doing so, he uncovers the ideological nature of life span developmental psychology's assumption that apolitical, value-free science benevolently improves society and enhances individual autonomy.

But this deconstruction does not leave Moody wringing his hands, either with glee or despair. Rather, it clears the way to pursue more philosophically sound, politically and existentially honest, and socially just answers to the questions of "The Meaning of Life and the Meaning of Old Age." Combining traditional values of contemplation, myth, and spirituality with a radical critique of trivialized leisure in old age, Moody points us toward the intersection of life review and autobiographical consciousness. Here perhaps, transcendent meanings meet the existential and social experience of individuals; here we may renew our understanding of the "gifts reserved for age."

T.C.

I approach the question of meaning in old age as a philosopher, yet not exclusively from a philosophical point of view. Alasdair MacIntyre has suggested that every philosophy presupposes a sociology, so it is just as well to be explicit about how social structure is related to ideas. If MacIntyre is right, then the examination of a seemingly remote or metaphysical question—"What is the meaning of life?"—may have extraordinary implications for how we think about the social system, about ethics and politics, even about the daily activities of our lives. It may prove to be the key to how we can think about the problem of meaning in the last stage of life.

I begin my inquiry by trying to make clear how we can succeed in thinking about the meaning of life and I conclude that we inevitably invoke some image of life as a whole, of the unity of a human life. Contemporary psychological systems appeal to some such idea but it is rarely made explicit. We live in a culture dominated by the therapeutic outlook, a world that looks to psychology rather than to traditional disciplines of religion or philosophy to find meaning in life. In practice, the perspective of psychological man tends to reinforce a separation between the public and private worlds, a separation that is a dominant feature of our society.

As we trace the origins of these psychological ideas, their ancestry reaches back eventually to Greek and Roman thought. We know that in time a suppressed dimension of ancient philosophy—the appeal to a principle of divine transcendence—eventually triumphed in the form of religion. Yet both ancient and medieval civilizations took for granted that the contemplative mode of life represented the highest possibility for human existence. By contrast, the modern world, since the seventeenth century, has favored a life of activity over a life of contemplation. This fact is fundamental to understanding the modern horror of old age, which is a horror of the vacuum—the "limbo state" of inactivity.

In twentieth-century philosophy the older problem of the meaning of life for a time disappeared, but when it resurfaced it was assumed that the solution must lie in some form of privatism: the meaning of *my* life. Modern philosophy has rejected any appeal to transcendent sources of meaning. Further, the modernist wish is to maintain that life in old age *can* have meaning even if life as a whole does not. The traditional answer was quite different. The traditional answer amounted to what Philibert called a "scale of ages" or a hierarchy of life stages in which late life was a time for unfolding wisdom and spiritual understanding. But any such positive image of old age depends on a cultural framework wider than the individual.

That cultural framework is what is missing today. The modernization of consciousness coincides with the modernized life cycle, with its sharp separation among the "three boxes of life" (education, work, retirement). This segmented life course undercuts any sense or meaning that belongs to the whole of life. The search for meaning is displaced from otherworldly to this-worldly concerns, then finally compressed into late life and brought under the domination of professions and bureaucracy. The result has been a covert ideology of life span development which lacks any rational foundation for shared public values whereby the idea of development might make sense. In the end, the empirical science of life span development must turn to the humanities and to cultural traditions if we seek to reconstruct a narrative unity to the human life course.

As soon as we begin to explore the question of meaning in old age, we come up against an obstacle presented by the forms of thought that prevail in our time. How are we to understand "meaning" in life? It is characteristic of modern thought to separate three levels of meaning: the individual, the collective, and the cosmic. That separation is what defines the present situation and throws up an obstacle to the inquiry.

That separation has a history of its own. After the Enlightenment, the cosmic sense of meaning began to atrophy. In its place came belief in a collective sense of meaning that absorbed into it-self both the individual and the cosmic senses of meaning: the idea of progress through history. Then in the twentieth century, the collective sense of meaning in turn has weakened, leaving us with an exclusively individual preoccupation with the meaning of life. Religious and metaphysical systems have lost credibility, belief in social justice and human progress has become doubtful, and the best advice appears to be Voltaire's prescription: "Cultivate your garden." In other words, retreating to a private sphere of meaning is the best we can hope for in a disordered and meaningless world. We have gone the way of Candide: we can hope at best to cultivate our gardens, but those gardens have now shrunk to the size of win-dowboxes.

This retreat to privatism is an unsatisfactory solution to ques-tions about the meaning of life and the meaning of old age. Pri-vatism, what Christopher Lasch has called "the culture of Narcis-sism," is unsuited to provide any abiding sense of meaning that transcends the individual life course. That absence of enduring meaning creates a special peril for old age when the temptations of narcissistic absorption are greater. The psychology of narcissism—the self-reflexive center of psychological motivation—has emerged as a dominant problem for modern man.[1] The heart of the problem is that in the modern age, at just the moment when the meaning of old age is in question, the cultural fabric itself unravels to the point where "the center cannot hold." Things fall apart and the search for meaning turns inward to escape from collapsing institu-tional norms. But in a therapeutic culture can late-life narcissism find satisfactory resolution apart from any binding institutional norms?[2]

The bankruptcy of privatism becomes all too evident in old age. But by that point individuals alone cannot invent meanings to save themselves from despair. The exercise itself invites the humor of Samuel Beckett and others who have seen the problem for what it is. We have shrunk the question of meaning down to its lowest denominator, the psychological meaning of *my* life. But it turns out that any serious inquiry even in that direction brings us quickly to a wider collective and historical level: the survival and meaning of the human species.

Finally, we cannot consistently sustain a sense of meaning without situating our collective enterprise in a wider cosmic setting. The philosophical questions are all connected, regardless of how we come to answer them. The levels of meaning—individual, collective, and cosmic—must be connected. As we become increasingly an aging society, the collapse of a coherent framework for meaning in old age becomes a more pressing social and cultural problem. It cannot be resolved without clarification of the philosophical issues, and it is to these issues that I now turn.

I have suggested that we can distinguish between three levels of meaning in life: the meaning of my life, the meaning of human life, and the meaning of the cosmos. In each case we could add the phrase "as a whole." Ordinarily, human beings act as if they understand quite well the range of meanings that life can in fact possess. But when we add the qualifying phrase, "life as a whole," then we are clearly talking about something else, something out of the ordinary. It is this larger or global sense of meaning that comes to attention at times of crisis and particularly when the *limits* of a life come into view: for example, in the shock that surrounds death and bereavement. These moments, which Jaspers called "limit situations" (*Grenzsituationen*), are the familiar signposts of modern literature and existential philosophy. Characteristically, in literary expression or philosophical reflection, as soon as we begin to reflect on the meaning of life *as a whole,* we quickly reach the boundaries of language itself, as Wittgenstein noted: "The solution of the problem of life is seen in the vanishing of the problem. Is this not the reason why those who have found after a long period of doubt that the meaning of life (*Sinn des Lebens*) became clear to them have then been unable to say what constituted that meaning?"[3] But, contrary to Wittgenstein's contention, the problem of the meaning of life has *not* vanished. On the contrary, with the emergence of an aging society, it seems certain on demographic grounds alone that more and more people will be confronted with the "limit situation" of old age in which the whole of life itself may be put into question. My purpose here is to examine how that question is intelligible, in both cultural and philosophical terms.

At certain times in life, we tend to ask questions about the meaning of life *as a whole.* In mid-life crisis or in autobiographical reflection in old age, what is at stake is a sense of the meaning (or lack of meaning) of my life.[4] This is the psychological version of the question of meaning that is most familiar today. But we must also distinguish a second sense of this problematic question about the meaning of life. This is the concern about the meaning of the entire human situation, the meaning of human existence or human history *as a whole.* This concern is alive today in fears about the threat of nuclear war and the future of the human species. Here obviously is something more than individual concern alone. For old age, that collective concern can be felt as disillusionment with the collective goals and efforts of earlier years. All earlier goals presupposed an image of the future.[5] But in old age that imagined future has now become history. The results are likely to be different from what was anticipated, and effort often gives way to disillusionment. Struggles to create a more just world, for example, run up against a mood expressed in Ecclesiastes: "I saw that under the sun the race is not to the swift, nor the battle to the strong, nor bread to the wise, nor riches to the intelligent, nor favor to the men of skill; but time and chance happen to them all." The pessimism of Ecclesiastes is not uncommon in old age. In our time, doubts about progress and the advance of social justice have become endemic. In old age, this questioning about the meaning of human life as a whole may be unavoidable.

Finally, we come to the widest possible question about meaning in life: the meaning of human existence in the cosmos, the meaning of life and death. These are the questions of traditional philosophy and religion. The questions may be greeted by the cry of Ecclesiastes, "All is vanity"; or by faith in an inscrutable reality beyond understanding, a faith expressed for example in the Book of Job; or again by belief, as we find in works by Aristotle and Spinoza, that human existence is part of an order of nature that makes our human life intelligible at a cosmic scale. Note that I have not stressed here the question of belief in immortality or life after death. This is of course a vital question, but I am concerned at the moment to bring out alternative responses to what is a more fundamental question about *cosmic* meaning: does our human existence have an ultimate significance in the universe as a whole?[6] This is a level of meaning wider than either individual or collective concern. Nonetheless, we can presume that any answer to this wider question of the meaning of the cosmos or of human life as a whole will have implications for the psychological or personal question of the meaning of *my* life.

Any question about the meaning of life finally comes back to intuitions about wholeness: the unity or wholeness of an individual life, the unity of the human species, the unity of the universe as a whole. As we approach the completion of any task—building up a new business, writing a book, leaving one job for another—it is inevitable that we think of the task *as a whole*. We ask the question,

"What did it mean?" It is as if we were on a ship or a plane leaving a city and then, at a certain distance, we look back and see the city as a whole for the first time.

But the analogy fails, as Kant noted in his *Critique of Pure Reason*. When I ask questions about the unity or totality of myself or my life, I am still within my life, not outside it, not able to see it as a whole. The same point holds true for the human species or human history, in which we live our lives, and again, at the widest possible scale, for the universe as a whole. Thus, argues Kant, it is a logical error to think that we can form intelligible concepts of the self or of the universe as a whole. But we cannot resist the impulse to seek such concepts, despite the fact that we can never grasp the metaphysical totality of things.[7]

Kant's critical observation opens up a different kind of question about the search for meaning over the course of human life. The question is transformed into a phenomenological inquiry into the different forms of meaning. How are the three levels of meaning—individual, collective, and cosmic—bound up with one another? What is the shape of this question about the meaning of life in old age and how is the question related to the status and social meaning of old age itself? How have these relationships changed historically over time, and what are the possibilities for rediscovering old age as a period of life in which the search for meaning has a legitimacy and even a broader social importance?

The question of meaning in old age, after all, is not merely an academic inquiry; it has implications for the quality of life in old age in our world today. Old age is the period of life when the shape of life as a whole comes into view, or when it is natural, at any rate, to try to see things in a wider scale. Totality may be metaphysically unattainable but the drive toward totality, the search for meaning, appears at a point when the task of life is about to be completed. In Hegel's phrase, "The owl of Minerva takes flight as the shades of dusk are falling."

Is it permissible to use the word "task" in speaking of this search for meaning? Even life span development psychology cannot avoid the language of developmental "tasks" for different life stages. It is just here that old age is in a precarious position, for the task of the final stage of life is in some way bound up with the *completion* of life as a whole. Old age is not simply one more stage but the final stage, the stage that sums up all that went before. Here we cannot avoid thinking of life *as a whole*. But can we speak of a task for life as a whole without some larger philosophical concept of meaning? And without this larger intuition about life as a whole, what sustains the integrity of the last stage of life?

Inevitably, we find ourselves caught up in an image of the *normative* life cycle. But what the social sciences have lacked is a philosophical legitimation for such covert appeals to the idea of a normative life cycle. In the work of our most prominent exponent of such a theory—Erik Erikson—such covert ethical appeals command widespread public admiration.[8] Erikson's ideals evoke in us a numinous image of something we desperately want to believe in: the unity of the life course, the integrity of the life cycle. In Erikson's work developmental psychology becomes a vehicle of hope.

Yet at the crucial moment, the moment when we need to justify the purposes that give meaning to life, the psychology of life span development falls apart conceptually. Fundamental questions are left unanswered. How are life stages, after all, to be distinguished from one another? What about the contrasting roles of fate and freedom in the developmental cycle? By what sleight of hand do we deduce values from the empirical data of psychological change?

The implications of this conceptual incoherence are, unfortunately, quite serious. The failure to articulate a philosophical notion of meaning across the life span means that practical activities such as psychotherapy, which are based on normative theories of life span development, cannot be fully successful. I believe, too, that questions of meaning are of the utmost importance for practical decisions in ethics and public policy. Without reflection on these metaphysical questions we will inevitably lose our direction when we try to think about very specific matters in gerontology: for example, the ethics of suicide and euthanasia, cognitive development over the life span, reminiscence and life review, late-life education, adult counseling and psychotherapy. Practice and theory both depend upon certain shared normative grounds. The attempt to cut loose the problem of meaning from its philosophical presuppositions cannot succeed. Our concepts of life span development must instead retrace the path through the philosophical tradition out of which they emerged.

When we speak of *meaning* of life in old age we may intend several very different things. These multiple meanings become clear as we retrace the history of the search for meaning in the philosophical tradition. Questions about the meaning of life reach back to the earliest period of Greek philosophy. It was Socrates who framed the question in concise form: "The unexamined life is not worth living." Socratic questioning in turn found an answer in the Platonic doctrine of man and the cosmos. For Plato, the answer was *wholeness:* the balanced functioning of all the powers of the human soul, powers guided by the light of reason reflecting a divine cosmos. The Platonic answer was matched by a system of education for life span development where each stage of life would prepare the way for the final vision.

For Aristotle, too, integration of self over time was the touchstone. Aristotle's term *eudaimonia* is variously translated as "happiness," "self-realization," or, in a more global context, "living well."[9] The Aristotelian view sees a good life in old age as a culmination of dynamic elements operating over an entire life span: One is happy when one has the good fortune to have access to all those elements (friends, sufficient wealth, good character) required for living well. The *meaning* of old age, then, would be found in just that immanent pattern of activity that allows the human being to exercise those powers which belong to human nature.

Viewed in this naturalistic fashion, the metaphysical questions of the meaning of life cannot be separated from the natural structure of the entire life span. It is not isolated moments of pleasure but the fulfillment of an entire course of life that determines whatever happiness or meaning a life can have. Consequently, happiness in old age remains precarious. "Call no man happy until he is dead," the Greeks said. In other words, meaning is contingent on the circumstances of life. Beyond this, we are compelled to say on these premises, the question of the meaning of life cannot even arise. To Aristotle the question would not even make sense. The Aristotelian understanding of meaning in old age is thus not far from what Freud meant when he remarked that the moment a person begins to question the meaning of life, he is already sick.

The difficulty with the classical Aristotelian account of virtue and *eudaimonia* is that it appears to make human fulfillment excessively dependent on the force of external circumstance. That limitation was the point of departure for the philosophical movement known as Stoicism, which took its inspiration not from Aristotle but from the ethical example of Socrates. For the Stoics, the meaning of a human life could be understood only as self-integrity and self-possession: living in accordance with one's nature. How can this ethical self-integrity be reconciled with the loss of self entailed by death?[10]

It is a fact of our nature that we grow old and die. From the Stoic point of view, then, the natural human life cycle must be accepted and lived out in full self-possession. Each stage of life has its own integrity and hence its own meaning. Such a stance enables us to bear the existential pain of aging: the facts of perishing, loss, the disappearance of the past. How are these losses to be reconciled with the goal of living well in late life? It is here that the Stoic view of the role of pain and suffering takes on its importance. Rational suicide remains one possibility, but the supreme ethical demand is always for rationalistic self-control.[11]

The Stoics were the first philosophers to offer a coherent response to the philosophical problem of aging. The most influential account along these lines appeared in Cicero's *De Senectute*, where old age acquires a meaning identified with the achievement of total self-possession, ego-integrity, and wisdom. In our psychologically oriented culture, the terms "ego-integrity" and "wisdom" evoke immediately association with Erik Erikson's Eight Ages of Man.[12] I have given this picture of the Stoic perspective on aging precisely to stress the ways in which Erikson's own psychology, on its normative side, is finally only a restatement of Stoic ideals. In the last stage of life, in old age, Erikson finds a distinctive polarity between ego-integrity and despair. To resolve that polarity, and to achieve wisdom, argues Erikson, constitutes the task of the last stage of life. Erikson's virtue of ego-integrity, like Freud's courage in the face of suffering during his last illness, reveals that behind psychoanalytic theory stands an ancestry of Stoic philosophy.

The psychoanalytic approach to the meaning of old age is a naturalistic view of human fulfillment. It is a balanced view in that there is no room for overconfidence; nor is there any recourse to pessimism or appeal to divine grace. Reason, or ego-strength, belongs to our nature just as much as instinctual conflict. To find a balance between reason and instinct promises a state of equilibrium or "living in accordance with our nature," which is the opposite of repression. Achieving this wisdom of self-possession may require a lifetime of discipline, but wisdom alone retains the strength to offset the inevitable losses of old age without retreat to narcissism or despair. Old age, then, in both the Stoic and psychoanalytic view, is not the metaphysical "completion of being" but simply the final test of the human being's hold on the reality principle.

In the Roman world the lofty idealism of Stoic ethics was felt by some to be unsatisfying, in part because it seemed to enclose human consciousness too narrowly within the boundaries of all-controlling reason. But the Stoic ideology of self-contained consciousness also embodied a deeper despair about the integrity of the wider social order. The Roman concept of citizenship had decayed. For the elite who were attracted to Stoic ideas the sphere of meaning had shrunken to a smaller, more manageable scale. Transcendence became impossible; self-mastery was everything. But the claims of transcendence would not remain long suppressed. We know that the historical outcome of the conflict of ideas in antiquity was the triumph of a religious view with the coming of Christianity. For a thousand years and more, the symbols of transcendence would provide an answer to the meaning of life.

Transcendence can mean many different things. Peck, speaking of old age, has pointed to a polarity between ego-preoccupation and ego-transcendence. Ego-preoccupation represents the temptations of narcissism in old age: withdrawal of feeling for others or for concerns that go beyond individual or personal existence. By contrast, ego-transcendence means living for the sake of causes or objects that lie beyond the self.[13]

Peck speaks of ego-transcendence in a purely descriptive, psychological sense. But the object or cause of transcendence can be understood in either humanistic or religious terms. In both cases, the object is a source of meaning that allows me to make sense of my life because that object is what survives my death. Ego-transcendence may be understood either as a kind of secular immortality or as faith in a transpersonal cosmic reality (salvation).

The concept of transcendence as secular immortality is discussed by Lifton[14] where it signifies the capacity of the individual ego to project its concerns onto a social institution or aesthetic object that survives individual extinction and thereby confers meaning on the temporal striving of finite individual existence. This level of meaning corresponds to the collective, historical sense of meaning described earlier. My life means something because I am part of a human enterprise larger than myself.

In addition to this humanistic sense of transcendence, one can recognize the search for meaning as an encounter with what transcends not only the finite ego but even the human history itself. It is this encounter with absolute Reality that the historical religions speak of in the language of salvation or deliverance: *moksha, samadhi, 'irfan,* or other terms denoting the experience of transcendence.[15] The language has its origin in the experience of a numinous reality encountered in contemplative consciousness.[16] Indeed, cosmic transcendence cannot be understood apart from the experience of contemplation or detachment from the world of activity.

Cultures differ in their appreciation of the virtues of contemplation versus activity, but there is no question that modern culture prizes activity to the degree that the idea of contemplative receptivity has become almost unintelligible.[17] This failure to understand contemplation poses a grave problem in the process of growing old today. Without some feeling for the virtues of silence, inwardness, patience, and contemplation, it is impossible for us to understand what ego-transcendence in old age might ultimately be about. We can only form a distorted image of it and call it "quietism" or "disengagement." The next move is then to retreat to secular immortality (i.e., living on through our actions) as a version of transcendence more acceptable to the activist temperament of modernity.

A vigorous defense of an activist style of growing old is offered by Simone de Beauvoir in *The Coming of Age*, where she warns about what must be done in order to escape the existential vacuum of late life:

> The greatest good fortune, even greater than health, for the old person is to have his world still inhabited by projects: then, busy and useful, he escapes both from boredom and from decay. . . . There is only one solution if old age is not to be an absurd parody of our former life, and that is to go on pursuing ends that give our existence a meaning—devotion to individuals, to groups or to causes, social, political, intellectual or creative work. In spite of the moralists' opinion to the contrary, in old age we should wish still to have passions strong enough to prevent us turning in upon ourselves.[18]

Old age, in this view, is not a time for wisdom or summing up. It is a time for continual engagement.

Simone de Beauvoir's existential view of old age, while perhaps extreme, is not really far from the view that prevails among the enlightened upper middle classes who articulate the dominant values in our society.[19] The style of activist aging seems to embody our preferred solution to the problem of aging. It is a widely shared image of ideal old age and is entirely coherent with dominant social institutions and with the activist ethos of the modern age itself.[20] Here a remark by Schuon is appropriate:

> According to an Arab proverb which reflects the Moslem's attitude to life, slowness comes from God and haste from

Satan, and this leads to the following reflection: as machines devour time modern man is always in a hurry, and, as this perpetual lack of time creates in him reflexes of haste and superficiality, modern man mistakes these reflexes—which compensate corresponding forms of disequilibrium—for marks of superiority. . . .[21]

It is common for young or middle-aged people today to feel exactly this sense of superiority toward the elderly: old people are slow-moving, not modern, even throwbacks to an earlier era. So we can easily feel a sentimental pity toward the old when they are unable or unwilling to share those reflexes of haste and superficiality which have become our daily habits. In our common desire to help the elderly, what we secretly wish is to prolong the haste which excludes us from even a moment of quietness and contemplation. We find the quietness of the old, even their very presence, disturbing, as if it were a repudiation of all that we hold dear. Old age, like death, is an indictment of that fantasy of agitation which the young and middle-aged take to be the meaning of life. Old age appears only as a limbo state, an absence of meaning in life.

Activity as a refuge from the limbo state of aging: this formula is the preferred solution to the problem of late-life meaning in the modern world. A cursory glance at the academic literature of gerontology will turn up the familar advice that we find in the popular literature of the organized old age associations, such as the American Association of Retired Persons' magazine *Modern Maturity*. The formula is always the same: keep busy, keep active. This formula is both a sociological statement about institutional life and a philosophic world-view. What we now need is a philosophical critique of how this formula came to achieve its almost hypnotic power over the culture at large. To carry out that critique requires some further examination of philosophy and meaning. It will be clear that philosophy in our time has in fact defined a point of view about the meaning of life that is completely coherent with the dominant institutions of our society. This philosophical point of view must now be the center of our inquiry.

Twentieth-century philosophy has offered an ambivalent response to questions about the meaning of life. On the one hand, existential philosophers such as Heidegger and Jaspers have pointed to features of modern society that prompt individuals to experience their lives as meaningless.[22] In this view, old age is the stage in life when individuals are forced to confront an existence that has been meaningless all along. Old age is the time when we discover the emptiness and self-deception behind goals and values that were taken for granted. The central preoccupation of existential philosophy, broadly understood, is to understand how it is possible for human beings to live an authentic existence in a world where traditional meanings are no longer convincing. While existential thinkers differ in their answers, they agree on the importance of the question of the meaning of life.

By contrast, Anglo-American analytic philosophers for many years dismissed the question of the meaning of life as illegitimate. An extreme point of view, developing largely under the influence of logical positivism, held that the phrase "the meaning of life" was meaningless. Following a line of critical thought initiated by Kant, questions reaching beyond empirical knowledge were viewed as attempts at metaphysics. But in recent years this hostility to metaphysical questions has diminished and become less doctrinaire. At the same time there are few who are willing to return to traditional underpinnings of confidence in the meaning of life. Thus the philosophical tendency is to reaffirm traditional questions of global meaning while at the same time avoiding the traditional answers, generally religious or metaphysical, that have been given to the question of the meaning of life.

Recently, this question has again emerged as important.[23] In the first half of the twentieth century analytic philosophers banished the question of the meaning of life from rational discourse. In recent years some prominent analytic philosophers[24] have suggested that questions about the meaning of life are intelligible and in fact important. Finally, a few philosophers[25] have questioned whether academic philosophical thinking is itself somehow debarred from coming to grips with the full existential depth of the question of ultimate meaning in life.

The force of philosophical argument in our time is to drive a wedge between meaning for an individual life and any wider sense of meaning that could have a rational foundation. The connection between the two levels appears increasingly arbitrary, thus reinforcing the split between the public and private worlds. Modern thought characteristically maintains that objective elements of meaning beyond the self—the meaning of life as a whole—are not a necessary or sufficient condition for the subjective sense of meaning, the meaning of the individual life. In other words, modern thought tends to insist that even if the universe as a whole or human history as a whole lacks meaning, nonetheless *my life* can have a meaning.

Existentialists express this idea in a mood of radical anxiety and see it as the necessity to choose, once and for all, the final meaning of our lives in every one of our actions. By contrast, ordinary people go about their lives pursuing projects and hobbies that give their lives meaning in a purely private sense. That private pursuit of meaning today is often irreligious, and increasingly often people lack confidence in any grand historical design. Perhaps, in the age of nuclear weapons, they even lack faith in the collective future of mankind. In short, neither the universe as a whole, nor human history as a whole, inspires confidence in total or objective meaning.[26] Consequently, people go about their business pursuing a form of meaning that is increasingly privatized. In old age, as time runs out, the final question remains to be asked: what did it all mean?

Old people commonly encounter this question in moments of autobiographical reflection and reminiscence about the past. This fact has given rise to the growing literature surrounding the concept of "life review," originally introduced by Butler[27] as interpretation of the phenomenon of reminiscence in old age. But the appeal of the idea of life review does not come from its scientific or explanatory status. The vogue among gerontologists for life review ("reminiscence therapy") and oral history springs from many sources. At bottom, though, the attraction of these ideas represents a wish to find in the experience of old people elements of strength and positive affirmation. Yet this positive impulse bears in it a danger of degenerating into mere wish-fulfillment and sentimentality, where the concept of life review becomes a kind of ersatz spirituality in humanistic costume.

Butler speaks of the life review as an effort by the older person to sum up an entire life history, to sift its meaning, and ultimately to come to terms with that history at the horizon of death. The gerontological literature on life review makes it clear that a wide variety of professionals in gerontology identify the life review as an opportunity for the elderly to find meaning in life through autobiographical consciousness.[28] In sum, the normative underpinning of life review involves an appeal to ethical, philosophical, even spiritual values. It incorporates a specific view, recast into psychological language, of where meaning in old age will be found.

Are there standards, then, or criteria, by which a life review could be judged successful? How are we to know whether an act of reminiscence is a discovery of final meaning or perhaps just another "metaphor of self" constructed for obscure purposes, or even a new form of self-deception? It is here that the philosophical literature turns out to be illuminating. A good example of the style of recent philosophical thought is the essay by Kurt Baier, "The Meaning of Life."[29] In that discussion Baier attempts to analyze and refute the widespread conclusion that human existence is meaningless: a conclusion supported, in different ways, by both existentialist and positivist thinking. But this pessimistic conviction of meaningless existence, Baier argues, arises from too strict a standard in the first place. That strict standard holds that human existence would be meaningful if and only if: (1) the universe is intelligible; (2) life has a purpose; and (3) all men's hopes and desires can ultimately be satisfied. But Baier adopts a more modest stance toward the meaning of life: the familiar privatism or subjectivism that characterizes the modern mind and that Baier expresses so well:

> People are disconcerted by the thought that *life as such* has no meaning . . . only because they very naturally think it entails that no individual life can have meaning either. They naturally assume that *this* life or *that* can have meaning only if *life as such* has meaning. But it should by now be clear that your life and mine may or may not have meaning (in one sense) even if life as such has none (in the other). Of course, it follows from this that your life may have meaning while mine has not.[30]

In the act of individual life review, then, I may discover that *my* life can have a meaning even if life in general is meaningless. In fact, Baier's three conditions for meaning can be transposed from the objective or cosmic level to the level of individual autobiography. Instead of asking about the meaning of life as a whole, I may ask about the meaning of *my* life. And this latter form, in an acutely felt way, is how the question of the meaning of life is often understood in late-life reminiscence. When the question of meaning is transposed to the level of autobiography, what we have in effect is a set of conditions for inquiring into the intelligibility of life review.

Following Baier, we may suggest that a successful resolution of the old age life review signifies that: (1) my life is intelligible; (2) my life has a purpose; and (3) my hopes and desires ultimately can be satisfied. These conditions amount to causality, teleology, and happiness. Stated in this way, we not only make transparent the philosophical presuppositions of life review but we also link those presuppositions to older philosophical questions about the nature of causality, teleology, and happiness. The three conditions are the covert normative underpinning for life review.

Presumably, a life review that, in fact, arrived at the fulfillment of all three conditions would be successful in the sense that the person would have achieved self-knowledge or wisdom, ego-integrity, and self-actualization. What is the opposite of these? Clearly enough, lack of intelligibility, lack of purpose, lack of happiness. A person might, however, possess one or two of these three but lack a third. For example, Montaigne's later years were filled with a profound sense of self-knowledge and self-acceptance, yet the purpose of his life, as embodied in his earlier idealistic Stoicism, was largely unfulfilled.[31] In some ways, Montaigne's final philosophy is best understood as an affirmation that man is most himself when he lives without purposes that extend too far into the future.

It is revealing that Montaigne, unlike Augustine or Rousseau for example, does not engage in life review or autobiography. He refuses temptations of totality. Instead, Montaigne writes a journal, a collection of *Essaies* (*essayer*: to try, to attempt, to experiment). For Montaigne, in other words, there is no summing up, no final perspective point from which to "see life steadily and see it whole." To see life at all is to see it at a particular moment, from a glance, over one's shoulder, so to speak. The wholeness of the self eludes intelligibility. Still less can the entire movement of existence be said to have a purpose in Montaigne's world-view. This characteristic relativism and fluidity give Montaigne's *Essays* a quality we inescapably call modernity.

What then do we make of the search for the meaning of life at the level of individual autobiography? Simply this: that there are at least three distinct threads woven into the concept of "the meaning of my life." These are the three conditions identified earlier: that my life be understandable, that it be purposeful, and that it be happy. We can imagine a life to be happy without being either purposeful or intelligible, and vice versa. We can also imagine all three conditions obtaining at once. This last combination would be the "strong" condition for meaningfulness, but weaker conditions are also acceptable. In short, I argue that the concept of "the meaning of my life" is a multivalent concept, a set of "family resemblances" (Wittgenstein's phrase) weaving together interrelated but distinct ideas.[32] It follows that we cannot say that my life altogether lacks meaning if any single condition is unfulfilled. But what if all three conditions fail to be fulfilled? If my life lacks intelligibility, lacks a purpose, and is miserable, then it seems unavoidable to say that it is meaningless.

In alluding to Wittgenstein's concept of "family resemblances," what I suggest is that, philosophically speaking, there are a variety of "languages," "metaphors," or "world hypotheses" that constitute a plurality of conceptual paradigms for looking at the meaning of life through autobiographical consciousness.[33] Within each of these conceptual paradigms, the life review can be judged according to values of truth, authenticity, integrity, and so on. But each of the conceptual paradigms remains incommensurable with the others. Let me briefly characterize four of these paradigms: the psychological, the spiritual, the literary, and the philosophical.

The dominant presupposition of our time is the reductionism of psychology. In psychological autobiography we reduce life review to a causal-psychological process. We see the process at work in gerontology and the human service professions of social work and psychiatry, where the concept of the old age life review was vindicated. Psychological autobiography is the taken-for-granted psychological reductionism that comes as second nature in our epoch: the "age of suspicion," as Nietzsche shrewdly called it. Psychological autobiography was dominant in the milieu where the term "life review" was first used. It remains the dominant system of interpretation. Under that species of pan-psychologism, the task of facilitating life review is easily assimilated into some variety of psychotherapy. Accordingly, the criterion for success of life review is understood to be adaptation, mental health, or some other standard of psychological functioning.

In spiritual autobiography life review is seen as the path to salvation or deliverance. This understanding of the meaning of reminiscence goes back at least to St. Augustine's *Confessions*, which is still the paradigmatic source even for autobiographies that reject Augustinian assumptions, such as those of Rousseau or Sartre. The distinctive factor in spiritual autobiography is that an individual life story is depicted as a stage on which a universal, spiritual drama is enacted in memory. On this stage for memory, universal myth and individual historicity coincide. Like parallel lines that meet at the horizon, individual lives lose their separateness at the "still point" of eternity. Spiritual autobiography discovers in each of these parallel lives a transcendent coincidence of destiny. All differences of individual existence are finally absorbed at the horizon of divine truth. Time and memory are taken up in eternity and the act of reminiscence becomes an act of prayer or meditation. This form of spiritual autobiography may also overlap with a psychotherapeutic understanding of life review, as in some schools of humanistic psychology where "self-actualization" substitutes as a secularized version of salvation.

The literary or artistic form of autobiography arises when we see life review as a manifestation of artistic creativity. This form of the autobiographical consciousness is celebrated by James Olney as the power of metaphor.[34] But vindicating life review as a form of creative invention of the self means that the criterion of truth in autobiography loses its earlier transparency as self-discovery or self-disclosure. In modern literature no such naive version of self-disclosure is possible. Instead modernism is obsessed by the dialectic of sincerity and authenticity.[35] We live our lives as ongoing narratives, stories we make up as we go along through the life course. The possibility that those life stories—or "metaphors"—might have the freedom of fiction or myth-making opens up a dizzying prospect of creativity. And that prospect in turn leaves us looking for clues for the interpretation (hermeneutics) that must go hand in hand with the creative act of self-expression (poetics). In place of the unmediated vision of traditional self-knowledge, literary autobiography moves toward a more radical "deconstruction" of the self. We find ourselves in the landscape of postmodernism where the objectivity of self-knowledge is eclipsed in favor of pluralism. In the postmodern world, meaning is to be found only in a fictive version or metaphor of the self.[36] The duality of appearance and reality in autobiography has collapsed, to be replaced by the search for a new taxonomy of metaphors elicited from the linguistic forms in which autobiographical acts occur. Whether any transcendent form of truth can be salvaged here remains to be seen.[37]

In philosophical autobiography the status and truth-claims of the autobiographical consciousness emerge as central or problematic in their own right. Philosophical autobiography is found preeminently in those autobiographical works written as philosophical treatises or, alternatively, in first-person life stories written by great philosophers (such as Augustine, Montaigne, Rousseau, Kierkegaard, and others). These works of philosophy undercut any

reductionist attempt to convert them into psychological epiphe-
nomena because the works incorporate in their own logic and
rhetoric all the problematic philosophical questions that reductionism itself fails to address: namely, the status of time and memory,
our knowledge of other minds, the intersubjectivity of language,
and the nature of the self. What characterizes philosophical autobiography is that such acts of personal narrative include both questions and answers to these perennial philosophical questions.[38] A
philosophical autobiography need not be autobiography written
by a philosopher. Rather, it is found whenever the activity of life
review turns back on itself to reflect on its own purposes and
assumptions.

Psychological, spiritual, literary, and philosophical autobiography are genres of autobiography that all have their counterparts
in life review, whether written or not. The same "deep structures"
of meaning are apparent in old age reminiscence as well as in refined works of autobiographical writing. The attractiveness of life
review lies in its covert appeal to those same deep structures of
meaning. We want the last stage of life to possess this resonance
of meaning that reassures us of the integrity of the life cycle in a
world where values are in flux.

Life review, the autobiographical consciousness, and the developmental psychology of life stages: these are our modern ways
of structuring human time, the time between birth and death.
Clearly there are some life cycle transitions, such as infancy,
maturation, puberty, senescence, and death, which are rooted in
biological rhythms. But beyond this, the structure of human time
is fluid and the meaning of aging is ambiguous, subject to interpretation. As long as the time of the life course is anchored in
cosmic time, then the human life cycle and the cosmic cycle will,
so to speak, "reverberate" with one another. Traditional *Homo
religiosus* experiences time as an individual rhythm contained in a
larger cosmic process: a ripple in the midst of a vast ocean of existence.[39]

For modern man, there is no such coincidence between individual, collective, and cosmic time. The time of the human life
cycle is irreparably shattered by the historical fact of modernity.
That discontinuity severs the ties between these levels of meaning
and makes meaning at each of these levels problematic and open to
multiple interpretations. Psychological, spiritual, literary, and philosophical autobiography represent alternative modes of interpreting the life course. But to be committed to any one of these modes

is already to take up a commitment to a certain framework of meaning. Once the framework is given, only certain questions can be asked. It is characteristic of the modern situation that these alternative commitments or interpretations of the life course lie before us, not as a given but as matters of choice. And any choice is susceptible to infinite revision, opening up a plurality of life worlds. With that vast expansion of choices, a chasm opens up. This is the chasm between the certitude of any wider, shared meaning and the condition of open-ended individual choice that can at any time call all commitments into question. It is this chasm which constitutes the situation of modernity.[40]

Traditional societies contain dual, even contradictory images of the movement of aging: a downward movement toward debility and death and an upward movement toward unifying knowledge. The first movement is an invariant motion of organic existence while the second movement represents the possibility of old age as a period of wisdom and plenitude.[41] Let me stress as strongly as possible that this traditional doctrine is not meant to be an account, even disguised, of the actual position of power or status of the aged in society, still less of any alleged veneration accorded to the aged. It is a statement about meaning, not about social structure. In Puritan America, for example, only the well-to-do elderly were venerated, and there is evidence of competition or intergenerational conflict revolving around property and power. Nevertheless, Puritan America, like other traditional societies, incorporated a keen sense of the dual movement of aging: of the dialectic between spiritual strength and physical frailty that was confirmed in the religious tradition.[42]

What is important about such traditional doctrines of old age is not how they support the social status of the aged in society but how they furnish individuals with a cultural framework for finding meaning in their experience. In this view, the elderly are not held to be morally superior but rather further along on a journey of life, with life seen as a movement of lifelong fulfillment whose consummation is found only in death and the afterlife. The sufferings of old age, in the traditional view, are seen against the wider background of the cosmos. The loss of that wider perspective is partly what deprives aging of meaning.[43]

But that element of the cosmic scale concerns only the negative aspects of growing old, the inevitable losses and suffering. In many traditional societies these were balanced by a more positive view of human development. It is this positive movement that

Philibert calls "the scale of ages." By this term he means a ladder of life span development that individuals *may* ascend by way of spiritual perfectibility or growth in grace and wisdom. But such a spiritual ascent does not necessarily serve to protect the power position of the elderly. In some cases, the opposite may be true. In ancient Hindu doctrine, for example, the concept of *ashramas* (life stages of later life) would demand renunciation and the abandonment of power roles, not their protection.

Still less does spiritual development—movement up the scale of ages—serve to protect the individual against the downward movement, which includes the natural ravages of old age such as the loss of loved ones and the prospect of our own death. Wisdom does not prevent suffering but allows us to find meaning in it. As the poet Louise Bogan said: finally, we want life to be understandable. But if the traditional doctrine did not provide worldly compensations, it did promise a consolation for the inevitable losses. The modernist concept of the self contains no such potency toward spiritual fulfillment; it holds only an image of ceaseless flux and change, terminated by death.

The question of meaning in old age may signify at least two different things. First, does old age as a stage of life have a special meaning; and second, is old age that time of life when the full meaning of life itself is to be understood? These two different senses of meaning in old age cannot finally be separated. They coincide in the image of old age as a period of wisdom. We *want* the old to be wise, even if we aren't certain any more what wisdom might mean. Inasmuch as we ascribe wisdom to old age, then we expect those who are wise to understand the meaning of life.[44]

Since Aristotle, wisdom has been understood in a twofold sense: the knowledge that belongs to right action and the knowledge that belongs to right understanding.[45] If wisdom is seen as an ingredient of action, then the wise are those who have lived in harmony with life's true meaning or purpose: those who know how to live well. If wisdom is seen as an ingredient of understanding, then the wise are those with the widest and deepest insight into the nature of things. In both cases, whether wisdom belongs to contemplation or to action, we naturally look to the old ones for such wisdom. Wisdom is seen as an intellectual attribute, and the wise are those who, by definition, understand the meaning of life. Thus the meaning of old age as a period of life seems intrinsically bound up with the larger question of whether life as such has a meaning and whether we can know that meaning.

But today we feel that human beings can find no such objective meaning to the existence of human life in the cosmos. Existentialists may despair of this predicament while secular humanists cheerfully propose projects to improve our condition. All are agreed on a basic premise: human life as such has no meaning other than the purposes that we give to it by our values and actions while we live. The traditional concept of the meaning of life is a delusion to be rejected. In the cosmic scheme, human existence is meaningless, and on the stage of history every generation is on its own. We can learn nothing from the old. We give our lives whatever meaning they will have by the projects we choose.

This stance toward life of course deprives old age of any particular epistemological significance. We may owe the elderly decent treatment, but they can teach us nothing. Insofar as life in itself is felt to be meaningless, those who have lived longer will be no closer than younger people to an imaginary destination called "the meaning of life." Like the two characters in *Waiting for Godot,* we are in a position of merely accumulating more years in waiting. But the waiting brings us no closer to a goal that cannot exist. We live, we die; we are on our own, young and old alike.

The final paradox of the modernist ambivalence toward old age can be seen in the ideology and technology of medicine. Through biomedical technology all possible effort is expended to keep elderly patients alive as long as possible. Thanks to the triumphs of public health and general affluence, an increasing proportion of the population now lives to experience the last stage of life—old age—which has itself been drained progressively of meaning. At the moment when the meaning of old age vanishes, we find that enormous economic resources are expended to prolong lives which have been deprived of any purpose. This paradox is apparent to anyone who works among the elderly in our society. As Jean-Pierre Dupuy notes, the contradiction informs our despair over the meaning of old age:

> The histories of pain, illness, and the image of death reveal that men have always managed to cope with these threats by giving them meaning, interpreting them in terms of what anthropologists call "culture." Today, however, the expansion of the medical establishment is closely connected with the spreading of the "myth" that the elimination of pain and the indefinite postponement of death are not only desirable objectives but that they also can be attained with the increased

development of the medical system. A problematic arises: how do we give meaning to something that we seek to eliminate by all means? This issue is linked up with a more general characteristic of industrial—or postindustrial—societies, namely, that entire aspects of the human condition are becoming meaningless.[46]

Historians are divided on how far modernization in itself has led to a devaluation in the status or power-position of old age in comparison with other age groups.[47] What seems clear, nonetheless, is that modernization has led to a devaluation in the meaning of old age. Modernization has created distinctive social and cultural stresses on the position of old age in society, stresses that are experienced subjectively as a feeling that life in old age is meaningless. Among historically minded students of aging there is recognition that the collapse of subjective meaning so often experienced in late life is a result of modern social policy: for example, the growth of retirement and the rise of bureaucratic systems in the human services.[48] There are some features of the culture of modernism, such as the diminishment of traditional community in favor of an isolated self, that have distinctly negative implications for old age. Then there are other features of modernism—preoccupation with time consciousness, for example—that are congenial to a recovery of a sense of the meaning of old age. In short, a central question to be examined is the connection between *meaning* and *modernity* with respect to human aging.

Modernization is not simply a matter of industrialization, technology, or changes in social institutions. It also signifies, in Peter Berger's words, a "modernization of consciousness."[49] The modern world reinforces a separation between the public and private world. When one belongs to the society of job-holders, one participates in the public world; but upon retirement the older person enters the invisible world of private existence. For the well-to-do that private existence may be richly dedicated to pleasure or entertainment, but most elderly people find it difficult to anchor the self in a wider public world. In short, the dichotomies of public versus private and work versus leisure become transposed onto the life course itself.

The modernization of consciousness signifies a fundamental plasticity of the self—Lifton's "Protean Man"—infinitely open to change and transformation.[50] This Faustian image of the self is central to the project of modernism and its Promethean effort to overcome all limits.[51] The self is to be continually remade as new meanings are discovered or created. This process of perpetual remaking is what constitutes the modern project and the modern version of the meaning of life: to be always on the way, never to arrive. The significance for aging in the modern project is not merely its heroic or Promethean aspiration, which goes back to Leonardo, Michelangelo, and the spirit of the Renaissance. Heroic aspirations themselves have meaning only against a background of relatively stable tradition. But now tradition itself is in question. The cultural significance of the modern project lies in its conscious repudiation of tradition-as-limit.[52] There is no enduring set of traditions serving as a limit for the meaning that life can have. Consequently old age, as the natural limit of life, is rejected along with those traditions that took such limits for granted.

Gerald Gruman has described the "modernization of the life-cycle."[53] The modernized life cycle is characterized by a twofold development, unprecedented in history: first, the separation of life into separate stages and age-groups; and second, the displacement of meaning into old age. It is the simultaneous convergence of these two trends that imperils the sense of meaning in late life. The shape of the life cycle in modern societies itself entails a displacement of the search for meaning into the last stage of life. This is a double displacement—from the afterlife into the last stage of life on earth and then from all earlier stages into the final stage. Since the cosmic sense of meaning has weakened, the image of fulfillment takes on the tone of secular ideologies. The most important of these is the displacement of free time and leisure into late life, supported by the spread of an ideology of retirement. The twofold development of the modern life cycle sets the stage for the contemporary problem of the meaning of old age.

One aspect of this development is the truncation of the life cycle. By truncation I mean division of the life course into the "three boxes of life," namely youth, adulthood, and old age, into which the social order allocates the three domains of education, work, and leisure.[54] The problem with this truncation of the life cycle is that it deprives us of any image of the unity of a human life, as Alasdair MacIntyre notes:

> Any contemporary attempt to envisage each human life as a whole, as a unity, whose character provides the virtues with an adequate *telos* encounters (an) obstacle. . . . The social obstacle derives from the way in which modernity partitions

each human life into a variety of segments, each with its own norms and modes of behavior. So work is divided from leisure, private life from public, the corporate from the personal. So both childhood and old age have been wrenched away from the rest of human life and made over into distinct realms. And all these separations have been achieved so that it is the distinctiveness of each and not the unity of the life of the individual who passes through those parts in terms of which we are taught to think and feel.[55]

The second aspect of the development of the modern life cycle is the dual displacement of meaning. By dual displacement I mean first, the displacement of leisure/contemplation/meaning from the rest of adulthood into old age and second, the displacement of death/finitude/judgment from the afterlife into the present life. The modern distaste for contemplation is accompanied by a nostalgia for leisure, a wish to escape from haste, and a sentimental image of retirement as the "Golden Age" of life. Late life becomes the period when, freed from alienated labor, the "real self" can be fulfilled, as in the ideology of retirement. The modern world relentlessly projects meaning into the future. Thus work, savings, and deferred gratification are all strivings after a goal located in the future—in old age. But upon arriving at old age, there are many who would agree with Yeats's comment, "Life is a preparation for something that never happens."

Second, the dual displacement transposes the last judgment from eternity or afterlife into time. We see that displacement in the modern cult of death and dying, in "death education," in the submerged spirituality of life review as the final opportunity for meaning in life.[56] We are urged to "accept" death as a part of life but we lack any cultural resources that might make acceptance possible.[57] Religious ideas of transcendence have not entirely disappeared. Instead, they have been transposed from the hope of salvation to the self-actualization promised by humanistic psychology, from the encounter with God to a new goal of freedom from anxiety. Medieval paintings once offered a deathbed scene with angels wrestling for the soul of the departing believer. Today the dual displacement brings the last judgment into the nursing home and the intensive care unit. Under the dual displacement, the problem of meaning falls under the dominion of thanatology and gerontology, a new priesthood of professionals.

Both the truncation of the life cycle and the dual displacement of meaning are now reinforced by bureaucratic and professional institutions whose power and ideology are of great importance for the problem of meaning in old age. The institutions of the school, the workplace, and retirement have become bureaucratically or-dained means of enforcing the "three boxes of life" for purposes of the political economy. The truncation of the life cycle is required by the economic system because our current economy cannot pro-vide employment for both the young and old. To get around that problem without challenging the basic structure of society, it is more feasible to disguise or displace free time under the names of "education" and "retirement." These phases of life then become longer and longer, as work is compressed into middle adulthood.

Unlike the situation in traditional societies, where myth and symbol shape the "rites of passage" over the life course,[58] the shape of the life course today is more and more subject to profes-sional expertise of specialists in this or that segment of the life course. Just as scientific management of human beings is needed to provide a smooth flow of labor in the assembly line, so a smooth flow of age groups is maintained by professional management for the different stages of life. The truncation of life stages is ordained not by nature but by the planning and control needs of the larger society. There is, accordingly, a need to manage the periodic crises of different life stages: adolescence, mid-life crisis, pre-retirement planning, and so on.

Unlike traditional laissez-faire capitalism, where competition is theoretically open-ended, late capitalism is monopoly capitalism in which the state plays a critical role in organizing labor markets, planning research and development, and organizing the social in-frastructure, including the system of education, old age services, and, in general, the broad spectrum of social welfare activities re-quired for existence in society.[59] Consequently, neither education nor retirement can be left to private decision-making or discretion-ary choice: both the first and the last stages of the life course are absorbed into the planning and control systems of society. Decisions now fall under the direction of specialized professions—child de-velopment, gerontology, adult counseling, industrial psychology, etc.—which in turn provide normative guidance for organizing the life course from birth until death. The rationale for management is provided by a covert ideology of normative life stages that is itself subject to changing interpretations.

The heart of the problem for management is clear. There is an ideological contradiction in the fact that the society is increasingly driven by two opposing demands: a cultural drive for maximum autonomy on the one hand, and an economic drive for efficiency and control on the other.[60] The progressive truncation of the life course promotes efficiency but contradicts individual autonomy. At points of life course transition or crisis, contradictions are exposed. It is the task of the ideology of life span development to mask these contradictions at every point.

The newest of these covert ideological interpretations is the good news from gerontologists that we are about to enter an "age-irrelevant" society.[61] Nothing could be further from the truth. But the proclamation of an end to the tyranny of normative life stages will be welcomed in a society where the denial of aging and death is still deeply rooted: "You're only as old as you feel." New interpretations of life span development end up proclaiming the American bootstrap ideology of self-determination ("Pull your own strings," "You're never too old to learn," etc.). But the distribution of opportunities for life span development is bound to forces of history, culture, and political economy. This contradictory relationship between political economy and the ideology of the life course stands unexamined by the professional ideologies of life planning and life span development. On the contrary, images of the life course furnished by the social sciences are held to be a form of "value-free" knowledge independent of human interests.[62]

The covert ideologies of life span development present themselves as apolitical, "scientific" conclusions devoid of value-commitments. Yet they inevitably share the dominant liberal ideology: improvement of society through applied scientific knowledge, which is eventually to lead to greater individual self-determination. In the ideology of gerontology, this liberal individualism is expressed in a refusal to accept age categories as a basis for social decisions (such as opposition to mandatory retirement). This refusal of the truncation of the life course is appealing. But the hope of breaking up the three boxes of life remains utopian as long as the relation between culture, ideology, and political economy stands unexamined. The liberal hope of maximizing individual opportunity in opposition to restrictive categories, including age, is another of the cultural contradictions of capitalism.[63]

Even a weakening of rigid truncation may not necessarily lead to a favorable outcome. As old boundaries are erased new forms of domination take their place. An age-irrelevant society is indeed taking shape, but not in the utopian form imagined. Both young and old are affected today. The rise of the "young old" is matched by the "disappearance of childhood."[64] Under the impact of television the idealized innocence of childhood is becoming a thing of the past. Both the innocence of childhood and the wisdom of age are relics of a pre-modern world. For young and old alike, sophistication and activity become the dominant style. In both cases, the early and late stages of the life course are absorbed into the endless present of perpetual young adulthood, now the dominant ideological image of the ideal worker-consumer.

Here the modern project of a boundary-less existence—the perpetual remaking of the self—comes full circle. In Auden's phrase, "we are all contemporaries," but only because history, including life history, has been abolished. We live in an information economy, a world where instantaneous media imagery juxtaposes past and future, fantasy and reality. In this world it becomes easy to believe that the self is only a metaphor, a choice to be discarded or refashioned at will. It is a worldwide Disneyland where the world of tomorrow and the antique past are equally available and equally unreal.

These remarks are critical of the covert ideology of life span development. But I do not conclude that scientific inquiry into life span development psychology lacks importance for a deepened sense of meaning in old age. On the contrary, the idea of life span development psychology is itself the great and indispensable myth of our time. For better or for worse, it remains our hope for some form of meaning embracing the whole of life. Further, the emergence of a new image of human development over the entire life span has the greatest importance today in providing an underpinning for movements of social change that could improve the quality of life for older people. Whether as ideology, myth, or science, we need some image of the whole of life.

But where will the cultural resources for this new image be found? I suggest that the future of life span development psychology may depend very much on concepts drawn from the humanities rather than on the biological models that have prevailed in the past.[65] Such a paradigm of life span development, we would argue, would be hermeneutic: that is, it would presuppose that acts of interpretation—specifically, self-interpretation—lie at the center of the developmental drama.[66] We would move, in short, "from system to story,"[67] away from cybernetic models toward a fully historical understanding of the stories by which we live out our lives.[68]

We would begin to see that there is no such thing as the "natural" human life course. The scientific project to discover such a natural pattern is misconceived and must end in mystification. Even the empirical discovery of uniform or fixed periods of stability and change—as Daniel Levinson and his associates report from clinical data—would become a problem of hermeneutical, not biochronological, significance.[69] Why, for instance, does it turn out to be the case that critical life transitions—the so-called "mid-life crisis," for example—are linked to round-number age-transitions— age thirty or age forty? There is no question that these age transitions are often important "marker events" in the psychological development of adults, as Levinson shows. But Levinson does not even offer an explanation for the numerical regularities he finds in these transitions.

An explanation for these periodicities will not be found in the model of the Periodic Table of Elements. The true explanation is to be found in the symbolic meaning of age numbers—the "developmental numerology" of our developmentally obsessed culture. An historical analogy makes the point clear. As the millennial year 1000 approached, all of medieval Christendom waited with fear and trembling for an apocalyptic end to the world. We may fully expect a comparable outpouring of mythic energy in our own time when the millennial year 2000 comes round—only a decade and a half away. But, obviously, no natural law dictates the upsurge of such collective feelings. Rather, these round numbers galvanize our collective imagination around dramatic temporal symbols. In the same way, approaching age thirty or forty or sixty-five can provoke anxieties of transition. But this developmental numerology demands a hermeneutical, not a positivistic, explanation. It opens up questions of *meaning*.

It is preeminently to the disciplines of the humanities that we turn for illumination of questions of meaning. The primary disciplines of the humanities—philosophy, history, and literature— are concerned with the "three C's": criticism, continuity, and communication.[70] Critical questioning (philosophy), the continuity of time (history), and the communication of shared meanings (literature) are all central in understanding the problem of meaning of old age. Analytic philosophy has approached questions of the meaning of life from a logical, atemporal standpoint, while literary criticism has incorporated the temporal depth of meaning into the study of autobiography. We need an approach to the hermeneutics of aging that can do justice to the time-bound nature of aging as well as to the timeless philosophical questions involved. I do not want to imply that the hermeneutic approach alone is adequate. Meanings and acts of interpretation are never purely subjective transactions occurring outside culture and history.[71] They are part of this larger context.

In recent years we have seen a rapprochement between life span development psychology and concern for spiritual growth.[72] An encouraging development has been the appearance of work that draws on the resources of spirituality.[73] The spiritual traditions have never accepted the idea that human fulfillment is the product of social roles or relentless activity in the world. Nor have they accepted the idea that the meaning of old age can be separated from the meaning of life as a whole. As I argued earlier, I believe that no assessment of the search for meaning in late life will be adequate without a reappraisal of the role of activity and contemplation in the modern world. There may well be gifts of understanding that are, in an existential sense, reserved for the last stage of life. In casting aside the values of contemplation from our benevolent desire to "do something" for the aged, we may have missed what is of still greater importance—namely, what the aged can give to us: a reminder, perhaps, of the finality of life, which could be a precious gift for those who can receive it.

William F. May

The Virtues and Vices of the Elderly

Editor's Introduction. Like Harry Moody, William F. May is skeptical of the organized benevolence of the professional aging enterprise. He is equally skeptical of professional ethicists, who generally seek to redress the unequal relationship between experts and their clients with a one-sided ethic of caregiving. This approach may actually compound the problem by conceiving the professional doctor, nurse, social worker, lawyer, minister, or teacher as *the* source of knowledge and morally informed power, and the patient or client as a passive beneficiary.

As a theologian and student of religious ethics, May makes two initial points. First, aging is fundamentally a mystery rather than a problem and therefore demands that we ask, "How does one behave towards it?" rather than, "What are we going to do about it?" Second, the Christian tradition specifically treats the subordinate person in the social order as a moral agent. The powerless are empowered as personally responsible moral beings.

Thus, taking old people seriously as members of the moral community means understanding their obligations as well as their rights. But what are these obligations? The absence of a contemporary consensus indicates the impoverishment of our cultural meanings of old age. Hence, May helps initiate the long overdue reconstruction of guidelines for moral and spiritual life in old age.

What are the "virtues that age calls for"? They are neither automatic nor restricted to old age and are achieved only through "resolution, struggle, perhaps prayer, and . . . perseverence." May suggests that courage, public virtue, humility, patience, simplicity, benignity, integrity, wisdom, and hilarity may take a special form in old age—offering instruction and inspiration to those not yet old.

T.C.

> Perhaps with full-span lives the norm, people may
> have to learn how to be aged as they once had to learn
> how to be adult. It may soon be necessary and legitimate
> to criticize the long years of vapidity in which a healthy
> elderly person does little more than eat and play
> bingo, or who consumes excessive amounts of drugs,
> or who expects a self-indulgent stupidity to go un-
> checked. Just as the old should be convinced that
> whatever happens during senescence, they will never
> suffer exclusion, so they should understand that age
> does not exempt them from being despicable.
>   One of the most dreadful sights . . . is that of
> the long rows of women playing the Las Vegas slot
> machines. Had Dante heard of it he would have
> cleared a space for it in hell.—Ronald Blythe, The
> View in Winter[1]

Ronald Blythe's scolding comment about the vices of some of
the elderly—gluttony, pill-popping excess, compulsive gambling,
prodigal wastes of time and money, and self-indulgent stupidity—
should not mislead the reader about the book he has written. *The
View in Winter* movingly depicts the lives of the elderly in an English village. Rigorous moral criticism of the elderly does not inevitably exclude them from moral community. Quite the contrary,
the failure to criticize them may subtly remove them from the human race. It pretends, in effect, that they are moral nonentities; it
treats them condescendingly as though they were toys. We will
take an important step toward re-entry into community with the
aged when we are willing to attend to them seriously enough as
moral beings to approve and reprove their behavior.

Not that the elderly are bereft of the give and take of criticism when they live within (or near) the home of one of their children. And many of the elderly have just that kind of contact. Some 18 percent of them live in the same household with one of their children at any given time; almost 80 percent have seen a child within the last week. But these figures mislead. Other of their children may live at great distances. To that degree, these children (and grandchildren) do not have much rough-and-ready contact, or moral give and take, with aging family members.

Increasingly, the elderly depend upon persons—professional caregivers, planners and designers of facilities for the elderly—who function at some emotional distance from them. Caregivers, planners, designers, and even recent critics of these two groups—professional ethicists—can unwittingly exclude old people from the human race by consigning them to a state of passivity, moral and otherwise.

This essay, then, will cover first some of the ways in which professionals (with emotionally distanced responsibility for the elderly) tend to slight them morally; the second part will offer a tour of the horizon of the virtues and vices germane to the moral life of the aged.

Professional caretakers loom especially large in the life of the elderly. An old *New Yorker* cartoon graphically displayed this point by changing the relative size of significant others at different stages in a person's life. In childhood, the mother, of course, dominates. Then the father grows in scale. In youth, friends expand at the expense of mother and father until they at length fade before a single romantic partner and mate. Coworkers and children fill the middle years but eventually diminish as the nest empties and the retirement dinners take place. When at length the mate sickens and dies, perhaps the doctor, the nurse, the lawyer, or, for some, a clergyman figures prominently in the final scene. It exaggerates, to be sure (since the data show heavy reliance on family members for care), but the cartoon reminds us that in advanced age the professional looms large as a source of security and sanctuary. Appointments with the physician become red letter days on the calendar around which time gets organized. How professionals treat the elderly acquires an even greater significance since professionals often represent and symbolize for the elderly their treatment at the hands of the society at large.

Professionals, of course, vary greatly in their habits of respect for the elderly. Some intervene with a powerful sense of solidarity with their patients and clients. Others behave condescendingly. But

the professional relationship itself inherently reflects a power imbalance between professionals and clients, and tempts the insensitive to condescension. This imbalance shows up etymologically.
The lawyer as "advocate" literally *speaks for* his client. The word
"client," on the other hand, means "auditor," that is, a troubled
person who needs a mouthpiece working on his behalf. The word
"patient" similarly denotes passivity. The sick must yield not only
to the ravages of disease but also to the heroic measures of the professional and the aggressive action of drugs, knife, and burning
iron in the body. This power imbalance compounds, often quite
automatically, as younger professionals deal with the elderly. Professionals of all stripes who handle the infirm and the aged display
their health and youth—often quite unwittingly—like a bustling
cold front that moves in and stiffens the landscape.

Idealistic members of the helping professions do not easily
escape the potential for estrangement. The professional ethical
ideal of philanthropy reflects and reinforces rather than redresses
the original imbalance in the relationship. The conscientious professional defines himself or herself as a relatively self-sufficient
monad who draws on knowledge-based power and bestows bene-
factions on clients. Clients appear before the professional in their
neediness, exposing their illness, their crimes, their ignorance, or
their age, for which the professional as doctor, lawyer, social
worker, nurse, minister, or teacher offers remedy. Idealistic professionals tend to define themselves as benefactors, others as relatively passive beneficiaries. Thus they tend to obscure for themselves the degree to which professionals actually receive from their
clients not only money, but in a sense, their vocation. This reciprocal dependency once obscured, a gulf opens between benefactor
and beneficiary. Philanthropy isolates. As Ronald Blythe comments,
"The old do not want outreach, they want association."[2]

Planners and designers, in the nature of the case, function at
a distance from the elderly, whether as analysts of the social security system or as designers of total institutions. Numbers inevitably
take the place of faces. Counting means more than countenance.
The elderly disappear behind the numbers and eventually behind
the walls of the institutions developed to solve the problem of their
care.

Statistically, the consignment of the elderly to nursing homes
today appears inconsequential. Less than 6 percent of the elderly
reside in such facilities. The figure, however, misleads. Although
only 6 percent live there at any given time, almost 80 percent will

spend some time in a nursing home, and many will die there. Often the prospect shadows the last years of life. Moreover, I am convinced that the percentage of those who *fear* ending up in a nursing home far exceeds the percentage of those who spend some time there.

The nursing home occupies the same place in the psyche of the elderly today that the poorhouse and the orphanage held in the imagination of Victorian children. Even those who never set foot in these facilities fear them as fate. The deprivations these institutions impose hardly argue for their dismantling. They have their place. But planners must give serious thought to their design, particularly to what might be called the moral significance of turf.

Before the twentieth century, physicians and nurses ordinarily came to the patient's home to deliver their services. Only the poor went to the hospital. Now, rich and poor alike end up in the professional's domain. The very architecture of the hospital and the nursing home tends to reflect and serve the convenience of the staff and the machines that dominate the institution. Disease has already disabled the patient; now, strange noises, rhythms, and procedures in the hospital further enfeeble and baffle. Patients are removed from the familiar setting where they feel in charge; strangers assume control. Not surprisingly, the elderly balk, even more than the sick, at entering total institutions. The stakes are so much higher for them. Sick people go to the hospital because they have no alternative and they hope to come out alive. But the elderly usually move to the care center permanently and irreversibly. It smacks of death. The institution swallows them up; its limited room prevents them from bringing many of their valued possessions and other tokens of identity. The new location often removes them from their communities. It condemns them to a kind of premature burial.

Successively and progressively, impairment, old age, immobility, and death restrict space. The world at large shrinks to a single room and ultimately to a casket. Ordinarily, people live in a number of different environments—home, workplace, streets, parks, gardens, and sidewalks. The bedroom is only part of a total world, often a sanctuary from it. But, for the immobile or the impaired, the world contracts to a single room. Designers of total institutions take on an awesome responsibility. They create for residents not just a fragment but the whole of their perceivable world. Meanwhile, the psychic life of the elderly also shrinks, with an increasing preoccupation with the body and its troubles. Physical space and psychic space tend to contract together. The design of humane institutions that gives moral scope to the elderly requires sensitive reflection on the shape of the older person's perception of his or her body and the contracting world it inhabits.

The body has a threefold meaning for a human being. First, and most obviously, it is an instrument for controlling the world: hands for working, feet for walking, tongue for talking. Illness and aging threaten us with a loss of control. Moving into an institution diminishes control not only because the elderly person moves to another's turf, but also because the shock of the move assaults the memory and, with it, the capacity to function. A man in his eighties living alone in long-familiar surroundings may live and care for himself competently despite a tattered memory. He turns off the gas jet seven or eight times after preparing his breakfast. He has enough memory left to know that he should turn off the gas, but not enough left to know whether or not he has done it. If, however, society denies this man enough supplementary services to sustain him in familiar surroundings, and locates him instead in a large institution with its architectural accommodation to staff rather than to residents, then his memory and competence can deteriorate precipitously. Sensitive institutional design alone will not eliminate such problems, but it should attempt to minimize the loss of control and the humiliation resulting from that loss.

Further, the body is a means of savoring the world—far beyond the reach of our controlling. The world pours in upon us through the sluice gates of the five senses: the glare of sunlight, wine on the palate, the hum of streets, a fragrance on the breeze, and the corrugated feel of tree bark. A move into a home for the elderly substitutes a functionally bland, salt-free environment for the variegated texture of the world that each of us has come to savor. (Yeats once complained about the formula H_2O: "I like a little seaweed in my definition of water.") Conscientious planners usually work hard to purge their buildings of the unpleasant smells that go with illness and old age. They also need to admit into the room/world of the elderly a few of the bona fides of sensuous life.

Finally, the body is a means of revealing ourselves to others. As the existentialists used to say, we not only *have* bodies, we *are* our bodies. Others know me through my countenance and gesture. Separate me from my body and I am divorced from my community. With old age this separation takes place increasingly, and in two forms. In some cases, the mind remains alert but the body sinks into ruin beneath it; in others, the body persists plausibly itself, but the mind abandons it. In the first instance, the alert experience their bodily defects less as imperfections than as stigmas. Indeed, since we *are* our bodies, the defects stigmatize not just the flesh but the whole person. Like the obese adolescent, the elderly can be tempted to a kind of angelism. One wishes for escape from the body altogether. One's body, and therefore one's self, no longer feels lovable, touchable, huggable, cherishable. This experience has implications for institutional design. It calls for respect for the body, respect for modesty, even for the modesty of the demented. And it reinforces the warrants for creating an attractive environment. A room functions as a kind of extension of one's body. People find the bedridden more approachable if the rooms they inhabit are attractive. They cast a sacramental aura. The peculiar slant of sunlight, the texture of the rug, and the comfort of a chair become means of sharing. When the elderly offer a chair to a visitor, in a limited way they offer and extend themselves.

Academic ethicists, of course, think of themselves as critics of the condescensions of the caretakers and the insensitivities of the designers. But often they contribute to the power imbalance between the professionals and the planners, on the one hand, and the elderly, on the other. Ethicists do so by concentrating exclusively on the ethics of care-givers and neglecting the ethics of care-receivers.

Understandably, moralists concentrate chiefly on the ethics of caretakers and planners because they deem them to be the new rulers of the West, the wielders of a knowledge-based power. Moralists take satisfaction in defining the limits of that power, usually by charging professionals and planners with paternalism. Ethicists thus think of themselves as champions of the patient's moral dignity by pure and simple appeal to the principle of autonomy.

Ethicists, however, do not adequately respect or protect the moral being of client/patients or residents of facilities if they simply clear out a zone of indeterminate liberty for them while remaining indifferent to its particular uses. A liberty merely patronized is a moral being denied. Respect for the patient demands more than giving him berth, licensing him to do, say, or be whatever he pleases. Respect must include an additional moral give-and-take, a sometimes painful process of mutual deliberation, judgment, and criticism, and an occasional accounting for one another's views and deeds.

But moralists will need to emphasize a different part of the field of ethics if they would illuminate the problems faced by the elderly. Modern philosophers and theologians have concentrated chiefly on moral dilemmas. They like to identify quandaries that the decision-maker faces and then search for moral rules and principles that will help to solve or resolve these moral binds. This view of ethics adjusts nicely to the task of criticizing professional decision-makers (lawyers, doctors, accountants, and the like). But it does not offer much help to patients facing the ordeals of sickness, legal crisis, infirmity, and fading powers. They need guidelines for action, to be sure, but more than that they need strength of character in the face of ordeals.

Ethicists must deal with problems not simply of *doing* good or *producing* good, but of *being* good. They must deal not simply with quandaries but with questions of character and virtue. Men and women do not function merely as agents turning out occasional decision-bits to solve problems, but also as authors or coauthors of their lives, shaping an extended narrative with its rhythms and alterations, its crises and its pauses, including, in addition to all else, the extremely important last chapter.

T. S. Eliot once pointed in the direction of this second moral sensibility. At the close of his lecture on a serious moral problem, an undergraduate rose to ask urgently, "Mr. Eliot, what are we going to do about the problem you have discussed?" Eliot replied, in effect, "You have asked the wrong question. You must understand that we face two types of problems in life. One kind of problem demands the question, 'What are we going to do about it?' Another presses the different question, 'How does one behave towards it?' " The first kind of problem demands relatively technical, pragmatic, and programmatic responses; the second kind poses a deeper range of challenges—hardy perennials—which no particular policy, strategy, or behavior will dissolve. In Gabriel Marcel's language, the latter type of problem resembles a mystery more than a puzzle, a ritual more than a technique. It requires behavior that decorously and appropriately fits the occasion.

Most of the deeper problems in life are of the latter kind: the conflict between the generations, the intricacy of signals between the sexes, the mystery of birth, and the ordeal of fading powers and death. "I could do nothing about the death of my husband," the wife of a college president once said to me. "The chief question I faced was whether I could rise to the occasion." The humanities, at their best, deal with such questions, but they do so less through the deliverances of casuistical philosophy and theology than through historical narrative, poetry, drama, art, sacred writing, and fiction.

In the health care professions, the dividing line between Eliot's two types of questions falls roughly between the more glamorous systems of cure and the humbler actions of care, the kind of care which those in extreme old age especially require.

Both kinds of moral challenge call for virtue. But in the second instance, the virtues supply us not merely with settled habits and dispositions to *do* what we ought to do, but with the impetus to *be* what we ought to be. B. F. Skinner, the behaviorist par excellence, has published a book on coping with old age, *Enjoy Old Age: A Program of Self-Management.* Skinner's book offers helpful little tricks for handling forgetfulness, impaired movement, appetite, and the like. The relentless determinist treats old age as a problem to be solved. He fails to address the challenges that come to us not simply as agents managing problems, but as authors and coauthors of our very being.

None of this self-definition comes easily. Inevitably the virtues (for any age group) must contend with adversity—not simply the objective adversity of conflict between principles in the moral life but also the subjective adversity of the temptations, distractions, and aversions that vitiate us. Virtues indicate not only those habits whereby we must transform our world through deeds but also those specific strengths that both grow out of adversities and sustain us in the midst of them.

A serious exploration of the moral status of the aged requires, then, some reflection on the specific adversities and virtues of age. Such virtues do not come automatically with growing old. Even limited dealings with the elderly quickly disabuse us of that sentimentality. Rather, the virtues grow only through resolution, struggle, perhaps prayer, and perseverance. Further, these virtues hardly appear only in the elderly. Some common human virtues—which men and women of all ages might do well to cultivate—simply take special form in the later years. When they do appear in the elderly, however, they can instruct and sometimes even inspire. Their example can encourage particularly the fainthearted among the young who believe that full human existence is possible only under the accidental circumstances of their own temporary flourishing.

The following sketch of the virtues deals only in passing and by implication with the vices. The too brief treatment of the vices runs the danger of adding to an already existent confusion. People often confuse physical infirmity with moral failing. When does the older person suffer from brain atrophy and when does he or she merely impose on others a self-indulgent stupidity? When does he betray the garrulousness of the self-important bore, and when the verbal incontinence of the impaired? In the following, I have vices not infirmities in mind; we only add to the suffering of the infirm when we confuse the two.

First on the list of virtues is *courage*. Westerners have too often restricted this virtue to the battlefield. But the soldier's prospect of death is uncertain; his separation from his loved ones but temporary. Not so for the aged who face the certainty of their end as well as losses that are anything but temporary. Thomas Aquinas defined courage as a firmness of soul in the face of adversity. An eighty-year-old unmarried woman resolutely faces her declining years; a widower suddenly takes his first steps alone after fifty years of marriage; an aged mother finds her children too busy to have her around. Courage is not fearlessness, a life free of aversions; it requires keeping one's fears, one's dislikes, one's laziness under control for the sake of *the* good as well as one's own good. Such courage need not take the more passive form of Stoic endurance. Indeed, David Gutmann has noted that the extremely old often evince a feisty, yeasty combativeness that characterizes the survivor.[3]

Sometimes this combativeness can (and ought to) carry beyond private life into the political arena. Heroes among the elderly include the old New Dealer Claude Pepper, and the intrepid Gray Panther Maggie Kuhn. In a nation given to interest-group politics, the elderly qualify as one of those interest groups whose needs ought to be met; they have a right to organize and press for their interests. Yet a democratic society cannot flourish if interest groups within it fail to perceive themselves also as publics within the larger public. What the Revolutionary thinkers called *public virtue*—that is, a readiness to make some sacrifices for the common good—distinguishes a public from a mere interest group. The Revolutionary thinkers saw this virtue as characterizing the very soul of a republic. Only a species of angelism would expect any and all groups to detach themselves wholly from questions of self-interest. Indeed, a republic requires that groups within it make their interests known, since such subgroups—the elderly included—are most competent to determine their own interests. At the same time, an intemperate pursuit of self-interest, unqualified by questions of the common good, eventually diminishes the stock of those public goods upon which all people, and the elderly particularly, depend (such as libraries, concerts, safe ways for pedestrians, parks, and gardens). Further, the unqualified pursuit of self-interest by the elderly can impose injustice on other groups in dire need who do not have the limited good fortune in this case of being old. Clearly, entitlement programs established on the basis of age alone can take away some resources desperately required by the needy of every age and can diminish the amounts available to the penurious among the elderly. The elderly need not alone submit themselves to the test of the common good, but neither should they be exempt from the obligations to public virtue.

Most people at sixty-five can look forward to a dozen years of good health, a few much longer. Most people require substantial care in the last six months to a year of their lives. Caregivers need the virtue of *humility* as an antidote to their arrogance of power. They are receivers as well as givers in the professional relationship. It goes without saying that care-receivers also need the same virtue. The progressive loss of friends, job, bodily prowess, and energy; the passing look on the face of the young that tells us we are old—these experiences assault one's dignity; they humiliate. All the care in the world will not overcome the sting of humiliation; only humility can. It bears remembering that the words for human, humility, and earth itself—humus—have the same root. God took the dust of the earth and breathed his spirit upon it and brought men and women into being: human, humus, beset by humiliation but destined for humility. Perhaps mid-life would not be so scary, so spoiled by pretension, so shadowed by the fear of failure, if we knew how to keep our feet in the soil of humility, not so afraid of the soil to which we shall return.

Patience does not inevitably characterize old age; advancing age and infirmity provoke anger, frustration, and bitterness. This virtue, moreover, becomes trivialized when we interpret it as a state of pure passivity. Patience is purposive waiting, receiving, willing; it demands a most intense sort of activity; it requires taking control of one's spirit precisely when all else goes out of control, when panic would send us sprawling in all directions. Such patience is even more active than that frenzied state of busyness that characterizes mid-life. Most of mid-life rushes by in a state of passive activity. Despite the appearance of great activity, our agendas are really set for us by the drift of things: the demands of others, the volume of work to be done, the day's schedule to keep up with. We tend to go on automatic pilot that gives only the illusion of great and heroic purposefulness. But sickness, sudden loss, protracted pain, or the curtailed movement of old age bring all this bustling to a halt and require us once again to become centered in the deepest levels of our lives as purposive beings.

The Benedictine monks used to talk about other marks—moral marks—of old age: *simplicitas* and *benignitas*.[4] *Simplicity* should mark the elderly, and not merely because memory lapses into its familiar, repetitive grooves, but because the pilgrim has at long last learned how to travel light. Old age hardly produces automatically the virtue of *benignity*, which the monks understood as a kind of purified benevolence. On the contrary, the *ars moriendi* of the late Middle Ages identified avarice as the chief besetting sin of the aged. The closer one gets to the final dispossession of death, the more fiercely one may be tempted to clutch one's possessions, holding, grasping, managing, manipulating. The hands have always symbolized the sin of avarice. It tempts those for whom insecurity is maximal, and mobility, except for the reach of the hands, minimal. Benevolence opposes the tightfistedness of avarice, not with the empty-handedness of death, but the openhandedness of love.

Some thinkers link—and, I think rightly—the virtue of *integrity* with an inclusive unity of character rather than with any part of the whole. Since character as a whole is a moral structure rather than a mere temperamental state, one needs, in addition to all particular virtues, a virtue that summarizes the inclusive structure when it is at one with itself. Like all other virtues, integrity must be acquired; it will not result from disposition alone or from an automatic ripening with age.

Integrity draws on the overlapping images of uprightness and wholeness. The image of uprightness reminds us that integrity has to do with moral posture—the perpendicular. It does not stoop to conquer. Integrity is tested at the outset of life for the ambitious in the forward scramble for admission to privileged schools, competition for grades, position, approval, and neighborhood. The upright professional refuses to put his nose to the ground, sniffing out opportunities at the expense of clients, customers, and colleagues; he will not bow before the powerful or knuckle under to external pressures.

Uprightness, in one sense, comes easier in old age. The years of warping ambition have passed, and a more powerful generation no longer lies ahead to intimidate and reward. The George Bernard Shaws, the Harold Ickeses, and the Maggie Kuhns symbolize an intrepid and upright old age, articulate and well-nigh fearless. Yet old age per se hardly bestows that uprightness. It is doubtful whether one derives from old age much more than one brings to it. Some elderly, to be sure, feel freer to speak out, less frightened than formerly of the opinions and reactions of others. But a person had best develop some measure of probity during the earlier years when the rewards for obsequiousness abound. The opinionated garrulousness of some elderly seems little more than a species of compensation for years of verbal servitude, rather than the forthrightness of integrity.

The virtue of integrity also signifies a wholeness or completeness of character, a roundedness, as it were—a self gathered up into a unity, not scattered or dispersed. Such wholeness of character does not permit a division or split between the inner and the outer, between word and deed. In this respect, the image overlaps with uprightness. Integrity makes possible the fiduciary bond between human beings. Persons of integrity, undivided and upright, do not say one thing while intending another. At one with themselves, they do not need to dissemble with others or deceive themselves.

No one recognized better than Augustine of Hippo that this rounded completion of the self which constitutes integrity does not come automatically with experience or aging. His *Confessions*— often called the first autobiography written in the West—deliberately retrieved and re-presented Augustine's own past not for the sake of amusement but as part of a mystic discipline. He needed to engage in a steadfast, often painful, retrieval of the self out of its scattered, dispersed, and squandered state to make possible its ascent to the divine. In Augustine's perspective, no self exists to commune with God without this re-collection, this integration; and this re-collection itself cannot take place, fully and freely, without the conviction of the forgiveness of sins. Forgiveness alone makes confession possible; it frees the confessor from the need to engage in fancy self-deception or even fancier ploys to impress others.

Some modern people, of course, find a partial and secular analogue for this movement toward wholeness and integrity through the discipline of psychoanalysis—which requires a painful retrieval of the past in the course of a final self-recovery. Those who cannot afford the luxury of such formal analysis must find their own makeshift ways of binding up their lives and healing memory. Thus the elderly informally engage in the moral work of autobiography. When it goes wrong, this reconnecting with the past deteriorates into a melancholy nostalgia, a profitless, endlessly repetitive and wistful, sometimes bitter, invocation of ghosts. When it works constructively, autobiography signals the aspiration for a completed life, where the ending rounds a corner and recovers the beginning. Fittingly, the analyst Erik Erikson defines integrity as "accrued ego integration,"[5] or more broadly as the integration of the self with its past. In attaining wholeness the self gathers and connects with its social, cultural, and ethnic heritage. A religious echo sounds in the few sentences Erikson wrote on the subject. He recognizes that wholeness—especially in the elderly—requires a reckoning with fate and death: fate accepted "as the frame of life," death "as its finite boundary."[6] Fate and death test the virtue because they constantly threaten the self with its dispossession; they would leave it empty rather than full. They oppress the self with what it has not accomplished or with the triviality of what it has accomplished; they turn all goods to ashes and disconnect the self from all its previously accepted meanings. Thus disgust and despair beset the self and unravel all its petty integrations.

In Erikson's judgment integrity alone, as a virtue, can hardly tame death and reduce it to the relatively quiescent boundary of human existence. Rather, death looms as the abyss that confounds all provisional meanings—unless the event can be set within the context of a transcendent meaning. Thus Erikson had to close his discussion of the virtue by linking the moral with the religious. He invokes the Tillichian phrase, "ultimate concerns," and closes his discussion of integrity and old age with a passing reference to the "great philosophical and religious systems."[7]

Many will shy away from this attempt to link integrity with religious conviction and especially with the explicitly theological. But even our ordinary associations with the virtue press beyond the purely self-referential and toward a standard that transcends the self. The completeness or roundedness of integrity differs from mere personal self-sufficiency. While referring to the self in its wholeness, integrity also points beyond the self toward the person, the ideal, the transcendent, that gives shape to the person's life. The virtue refers to the inclusive self, to be sure, but the self turns out to be ecstatic—pitched out beyond itself toward that in which it finds its meaning. Thus we instinctively say that a man has lost his integrity when his identity with those ultimate aims and purposes that grounded his life breaks asunder.

At this point, the topic of integrity requires a discussion of the role of ritual in the moral life, even though that discussion in a rapidly changing world must be highly speculative. Most people connect with the transcendent or express their "ultimate concerns" chiefly through ritual behavior. The rituals in question here do not refer simply to religious ceremonies officially associated with traditional denominations. They include official rites, to be sure, but more broadly they cover a whole range of repeated actions that conform to and represent the foundational events and patterns of meaning in a person's life. How one eats, cleanses oneself, greets one's fellows, rises to challenge, and shuts down the day—these repeated actions signal the way in which one connects with the ultimate. The virtues are habitual structures of character that derive from, flourish within, and give rise to these often repeated actions. The way an old woman, living alone, tamps down her anxieties at night ritualizes (or "makes present") her ultimate resources and also habituates her character.

Modern moralists tend to miss the connection between our daily rites and moral behavior because they concentrate on the aforementioned moral binds and quandaries—special situations in which we do not know what to do. They emphasize too much those moments of puzzlement when the individual, thrown outside of routine, appears to be without shape and form, poised neutrally between alternatives, uncertain as to which way to jump. They deal too little with those great overarching rhythms that pattern life. Moralists must reckon, to be sure, with breaks in pattern, but if they wish to reflect on life as it actually is lived, they must illuminate as well our habitual appropriations of work, bread, love, rest, and play.

On the whole, older women seem to sustain more successfully than elderly men the moral/ritual side of life. Pastors notice that widows often function better than widowers. Old men are much more inclined, once they have retired, lost a mate, or suffered a reduction in income, to withdraw or to allow their lives to dwindle to a minimal routine. Men reduce more readily to an abstract cipher, disconnected and noncommunicative.

Many reasons suggest themselves for these contrasting "performances" of older men and women. For some, it seems providential that women, who are biologically fated to live longer than men, adjust better than men to old age. Others note that women receive an earlier and clearer biological preview of aging—if not of mortality; menopause gives them a clear signal that the wheel of existence turns downward toward the ground, while men find ways to obscure in themselves whatever signals they receive. Women tend more often than men to associate aging and death with the corruption of bodily form; men, with a flagging vitality. The corruption of the body shows up relentlessly in the morning mirror; the failure of vitality overtakes in more elusive ways and is suppressed more easily in men—although the poet Eliot dispatches an entire civilization under the symbol of failing male power: "I am an old man in a dry month."

The sexes have differed until recently in yet another way that affects later performance. When their nests empty many women, while still in their middle years, have to face and adjust to the loss of their major vocation. A man usually does not suffer that trauma until much later, at retirement, when his resources and resilience may have declined. The massive shift since World War II of women into the outside work force will doubtless change this cultural contrast. A majority of women, like men, will now face a major adjustment at a much later age when coping grows more difficult and a new life and structure may become harder to mount.

Undoubtedly, we are much too close to these changes to assess long-range consequences. Suffice it to say that the contrasts between the sexes at the level of ritual life until recently have been striking. Middle and professional class men sought their basic life's meaning in and through the unilinear progression of a career. Once detached from that career, life lost its tang. Compensatory routines smacked of the trivial. Men who chronically complained about the corporation while they worked for it nevertheless prized retrospectively that identity. Upon retirement, they often found it more difficult than women to body forth their life in rituals, more cyclical than unilinear in their justifying source. Divorced from work, men often find themselves harder put to develop fitting habits of friendship, love, eating, conversation, art, celebration, and play. They frequently find it much more difficult than women to achieve, display, and share the virtue of integrity conceived as a rounded, full, and connected life.

Conventional thought emphasizes *wisdom* as a final, special virtue of the elderly. Age brings with it accrued experience, and, to the degree that one learns from experience, wisdom results—so older politicians have always proclaimed as they run for reelection. The related practical virtue of *prudence,* as the medieval moralists analyzed it, makes possible the aforementioned integrity. The medieval definition of prudence included three parts: *memoria, docilitas,* and *solertia.*

Memoria characterizes the person who remains open to his or her past, without retouching, falsifying, or glorifying it. Such openness, as we have seen, makes possible the wholeness of integrity. But *memoria* should not be confused with the propensity of many elderly people to wander endlessly in yesterday. Old age hardly offers this virtue automatically. Indeed, it tempts especially to the falsifications of nostalgia and remorse.

Docilitas connotes not the passivity of the English word "docility," but a capacity to take in the present—an alertness, an attentiveness in the moment. *Docilitas* signifies a capacity to be silent, to be still, and thus to take in. It helps keep the elderly connected to others. Garrulousness in old age sadly deprives old men and women of the present and of the presence of others. *Solertia* completes, if you will, the threefold temporal ecstasy of prudence. It signifies a readiness for the unexpected. Once again, old age hardly guarantees such openness toward the future. On the contrary, the lives of many older people harden into routines which make the unexpected always unwelcome. Others, though, learn how to "travel light," as I phrased it earlier in the discussion of simplicity. They learn to sit loose, as it were, to life, sometimes more so than the middle-aged who too often perceive themselves to be embattled fortresses beleaguered on different fronts by aging parents and wayward adolescents. The event of death, of course, symbolizes everything contingent and unexpected about the future. (In order to emphasize the uncontrollable intrusiveness of death, Muriel Spark, in her novel (*Memento Mori*) has death break in upon the residents of a nursing home through the device of telephone calls.) Readiness for the unexpected includes a readiness for death. The elderly at their best teach us that.

Erik Erikson links the traditional virtue of wisdom with detachment, an attitude that depends in part upon a store of experience. The inexperienced are prone to overreact or underreact. They do not know how to weigh and evaluate what has happened to them, and let themselves be engulfed by a catastrophe or overinvest in particular goods or outcomes. They do not yet know how to worry wisely or to love wisely. (For this reason, grandparents often seem wiser than their adult children in relating to the next generation. Many parents are inclined to drive their own ambitions through their children like a long stake. Grandparents often seem a little freer and sufficiently detached to enjoy and savor without bending the young to the warp of their own frustrated hopes.)

But one must not confuse detachment with the Stoic ideal of the passionless state. The Stoic ideal of apathy solved the problem of suffering by banking low the fires of desire. The Stoics urged the self to operate at the lowest possible wattage—to keep on, at most, a night light. Such a self suffers little because it risks little and loves not at all. It detaches itself from any and all things before the final extinction of death. The Stoic ideal evinced its own dignity in kings and slaves alike; it depended upon a rare, almost aristocratic, rational self-control and discipline. In the modern world we are more likely to see a mockery of such detachment in the behavior that a few managers of the very old impose on them. Some hard-pressed caretakers prefer to deal with people who are relatively passive, compliant, and yielding to the powers that be. They can manage the very old more easily if they are doped up, unobtrusive, unintrusive, and dozing. The Stoic argued for a clear-headed detachment; the unscrupulous manager reduces the elderly to a vegetable-like apathy.

The Biblical tradition grounds wisdom differently from the Stoic. It achieves some perspective on the human condition not through an all-encompassing detachment but through a primordial attachment. In the setting of Christianity, this fundamental attachment to the divine love sustains, but also orders and limits all other attachments and fears. It produces two virtues which, for want of better terms, we might designate Christian "nonchalance" and "courtesy." (I ought not call them Christian virtues—for the obvious reason that others besides Christians evince them. But it may be of some general interest to indicate the specifically Christian warrants for them.) Both virtues bespeak serenity—a metaphysical serenity in the case of nonchalance and a social serenity in the case of courtesy. Nonchalance betokens a capacity to take in one's stride life's gifts and blows; courtesy, a comparable capacity to deal honorably with all that is urgent, jarring, and rancorous on the social scene.

Neither virtue, at least as enjoined in the religious tradition at its best, expresses passivity. Pilgrims on the move should evince these virtues, those who are in but not of the world, those who know how to sit loose to the world. The virtues do not grow out of unattached indifference. Indeed, the politically active, prophetic theologian Reinhold Niebuhr recommended, in his later years, Romans 8 as the *classicus locus* for a Christian nonchalance. The passage does not, in the fashion of Christian Science or secular versions of optimism, solve the problem of suffering by denying the reality of disease, pain, aging, and death; it puts these destructive forces in the setting of a power that persists and endures in the midst of them. God ultimately encompasses the powers that dazzle and terrorize the heart; they are *real* but not *ultimate;* these powers do not speak the last word about the human condition: "neither death, nor life, nor angels, nor principalities, nor things present, nor things to come, nor powers, nor height, nor depth, nor anything else in all creation, will be able to separate us from the love of God. . . ."[8]

The Apostle Paul does not ground this nonchalance in a Stoic detachment, a final state of apathy that conveniently settles on the heart precisely at that late moment in life when the fires of desire seem to flicker and gutter. For the divine love which justifies nonchalance did not avoid or eliminate suffering and death, but itself experienced the full range of human need. As the Apostle's Creed says, Christ "suffered under Pontius Pilate, was crucified, dead and buried." He exposes the destructive powers that men and women fear in their final impotence will separate them from God. This love does not extricate men and women from the arena of human need, suffering, and death, but relieves this arena of its final terror. It locates the self, the beleaguered and fearful self, within the dynamics of giving and receiving. In allowing the self to sit loose to the world, divine love makes it easier for the self to meet its obligations within the world, without panicking before it or getting mired in it.

This metaphysical nonchalance leads to the social virtue of courtesy. Ties to others can deepen precisely because they have been lightened. A primordial tie makes other ties bearable. Men and women no longer need to rely on petty devices to crowd, force, outdo, upend, trump, and duck others. They can see the needs of others and their own in a more spacious setting that makes courtesy possible in the midst of pain, aging, suffering, and dying.

This more spacious setting makes sense of a final virtue which the Benedictine monks associated with old age, *hilaritas.* At first glance, hilarity seems out of place in the elderly. In fact, they are more clinically disposed than their juniors to depression. Anxiety over resources, grief over loss, insufficient exercise, broken sleep patterns, and diminished appetites precede and accompany depression. Yet the monks talk about *hilaritas,* a kind of celestial gaiety in those who have seen a lot, done a lot, grieved a lot, but now acquire that humored detachment of the fly on the ceiling looking down on the human scene.

Whatever special meaning hilarity may have for the monk in the monastery, it is hardly reserved for the monks alone. Children are blessed when their grandparents' lightness of spirit offers sunny relief from their parents' gravity. The year before his death, Yeats expressed this hilarity in "Lapis Lazuli," a poem that spreads out the whole human scene of "old civilizations put to the sword." The poem ends by focusing on two ancient oriental sages:

> Two Chinamen, behind them a third,
> Are carved in lapis lazuli,
> Over them flies a long-legged bird,
> A symbol of longevity;
> The third, doubtless a serving man,
> Carries a musical instrument.
>
> Every discoloration of the stone,
> Every accidental crack or dent
> Seems a water-course or an avalanche,
> Or lofty slope where it still snows
> Though doubtless plum or cherry-branch
> Sweetens the little half-way house
> These Chinamen climb towards, and I
> Delight to imagine them seated there;
> There, on the mountain and the sky,
> On all the tragic scene they stare.
> One asks for mournful melodies;
> Accomplished fingers begin to play.
> Their eyes mid many wrinkles, their eyes,
> Their ancient, glittering eyes, are gay.[9]

W. Andrew Achenbaum

The Meaning of Risk, Rights, and Responsibility in Aging America

Editor's Introduction. The welfare state has been hailed as a landmark in the development of citizens' rights and for its contribution to economic progress and efficiency. It has also been condemned for either protecting or destroying the rights of private property and for retarding economic growth. One thing is clear: the relatively good health and economic well-being of older people today rest almost entirely on welfare state programs in the Western capitalist democracies. In the United States, roughly 60 percent of the aged population would fall beneath the poverty level today without Social Security.

From somewhere near the center of the political spectrum, W. Andrew Achenbaum examines the history of Social Security. Since the system rests not on contractual financial arrangements but on a "political compact" whose principles are neither obvious nor eternal, Achenbaum seeks to "uncover prevailing themes, ambiguities, and contradictions in our way of thinking about the goals and limits" of public policy for the elderly. Tracing the concepts of "rights, risks, and responsibility" from the 1930s to the 1980s, Achenbaum suggests that the normative foundations of Social Security are "shakier" than we might suspect.

The fiftieth anniversary of Social Security, while certainly cause for celebration, leaves little room for complacency. The overall progress in reducing poverty among the aged has still left the "marginal" among the elderly (the very old, women, blacks, some

other ethnic minorities) as poor as ever. This has led some observers to suggest that need replace age as the criterion for future
entitlements. Others fear that such a strategy would lead to the dismantling of hard-won citizens' rights and a resurgence of the
power of capital. Achenbaum points out that the great expansion
of Social Security benefits in the 1960s and 1970s worked well
ideologically and financially for middle-class Americans. Yet it
also contributed to the disturbing trend toward a "no-risk" society
and, by the late 1970s, was implicated in economic stagnation and
the fiscal crisis of the state. Under these conditions, we are increasingly often compelled to make difficult policy decisions—to
clarify and debate what we mean by rights, risks, and responsibility in aging America.

T.C.

In his June 8, 1934, message to Congress, President Franklin Delano Roosevelt announced his intention to "undertake the great task of furthering the security of the citizen and his family through social insurance":

> I am looking for a sound means which I can recommend to provide at once security against several of the great disturbing factors in life—especially those which relate to unemployment and old age. I believe that there should be a maximum of cooperation between States and the Federal Government. . . . These three great objectives—the security of the home, the security of livelihood, and the security of social insurance—are, it seems to me, a minimum of the promise that we can offer to the American people. They constitute a right which belongs to every individual and every family willing to work. They are the essential fulfillment of measures already taken toward relief, recovery and reconstruction.[1]

Roosevelt's statement should be read carefully, for its simple, commonsensical language is as revealing in what it presumed and finessed as it is in what it actually said. Note that the President never really defined what "security" is—though apparently a home, a job, and social insurance provide some of the means of achieving it. By connecting his notion of "security" with the concept of "social insurance," Roosevelt moved toward identifying the cause of his concern if not his precise objectives. "Insurance" historically has been a vehicle for protecting people against hazards. While it may not restore life or property lost through negligence, injustice, or accident, it nevertheless does compensate potentially vulnerable women and men—and others designated as beneficiaries in our stead—for specific misfortunes. Thus, providing a measure of economic protection against "risks" was a major purpose of this intended "security" legislation. The risks the President had in mind were characterized in shorthand—"old age" and "unemployment." What precisely did he mean? That old age sui generis is hazardous? Or did he really intend to limit his attention to the physical and financial woes of late life? Similarly, did the President mean temporary unemployment or that caused by technological obsolescence? It is impossible to say on the basis of this text alone; his words must be interpreted in the context of the times.

And who should have a "right" to this measure of security, particularly against the "disturbing hazards" of old age and unemployment? Once again, the President was vague. At one point, he invoked the rights of a "citizen." At another point, he referred to the right of a *working* individual and "every family willing to work." Did this mean that everyone would be eligible for benefits, or only those in the labor force? To what extent would bonds of kinship with a worker covered under social insurance count in order to claim benefits under this legislation? The President left such thorny matters up to his experts to decide.

Roosevelt never questioned, however, where the responsibility for such an initiative lies: "If, as our Constitution tells us, our Federal Government was established among other things 'to promote the general welfare,' it is our plain duty to provide for that security upon which welfare depends."[2] Consonant with the New Deal's "three rs" (recovery, reform, and reconstruction), the President definitely believed that it was Washington's responsibility to provide for the well-being of the public. Yet what were his reasons for embarking upon such an initiative in 1934? Was the federal government just now acknowledging "its plain duty" to act on behalf of the people in this area? Was this vision of what government should do to promote welfare secondary to the President's commitment to do whatever he could to ensure economic recovery? Roosevelt never really addressed such issues—he wrote as if the concept of "responsibility" were so obvious that it required no justification.

Three ideas—"risks," "rights," and "responsibility"—thus were linked in Franklin Delano Roosevelt's declaration of the need for legislation to provide an unprecedented measure of "security" for the American people. In this essay I intend to trace the history of these three concepts, noting continuities and changes in their meanings from the 1930s to the present. I shall show that Social Security's policymakers from the very beginning sought to forge a delicate balance among several desirable—but not necessarily compatible—goals. They hoped to capitalize on inherent tensions and contradictions that traditionally have characterized the American creed. Legislators knew that they could not afford to ignore longstanding American values; they were also keenly aware that normative changes in a dynamic society were inevitable. Indeed, the meanings of terms that we use to describe basic features of the Social Security system have shifted during the past five decades.

I hope to draw two lessons from this exercise. First, insofar as maintaining a right and proper balance among risks, rights, and responsibilities remains a major concern of Social Security policymaking—and it does—the changing meanings of these three terms provide insights into the philosophical and cultural tenor of modern life in aging America. Since Social Security remains the foundation for all social programs for the aged and the aging, exploring how and why the normative foundations of this measure have changed over time can uncover prevailing themes, ambiguities, and contradictions in our way of thinking about the goals and limits of public policy. The real meanings of many seemingly self-evident ideas are mirrored in the ways we have adapted social insurance in the postindustrial era. This leads me to the second lesson: the normative foundations of Social Security are shakier than we might suspect. Indeed, it might not be an exaggeration to suggest that the illusions we harbor concerning the meaning of risks, rights, and responsibility under Social Security may pose greater concern than likely economic downturns, inevitable demographic pressures, and possible intergenerational rifts within the electorate. As we shall see, Social Security is based less on financial arrangements than it is a political compact resting on principles whose salience and perdurance the American people largely accept on blind faith.

Predictably, there was much debate over what should be included in the original Social Security bill. Edwin E. Witte, who chaired the Committee on Economic Security appointed to draft the legislative particulars, was primarily interested in designing a program of unemployment compensation. Some activists pressed for a modest health insurance plan, and had to settle for special programs for the blind and handicapped. Others hoped to expand aid to dependent children and assistance for maternity care.[3] But policymakers had little difficulty agreeing on the principal causes of "insecurity" afflicting Americans: "They are unemployment, dependency in old age, loss of the wage earner of the family, and illness."[4] Far from being isolated phenomena, these "major hazards of life" were considered unfortunate risks that directly or indirectly affected people at various junctures in their lives.

Debility, dependency and death are increasingly likely to occur in late life. They have been age-old features of the old-age story. Steadily after 1900, however, more and more Americans believed that the elderly's woes had a significance that transcended their individual ramifications. Demographic trends and economic conditions were making the plight of older men and women more visible as it became more acute.[5] The devastating effect of the Depression on the elderly's well-being underscored the extent to which old-age dependency had become a "social problem." The unemployment rate among the elderly exceeded rates for the population at large. Savings, insurance policies, and company pensions proved inadequate. Children, friends, and relatives who traditionally had borne a major part of the cost of caring for the needy elderly often found the task too onerous as they tried to meet the needs of their immediate families. Private charity and public old-age relief was rapidly becoming exhausted.[6]

As the Townsendites, black tenant farmers, desperate middle-aged sons and daughters, and older persons who had presumed themselves comfortably fixed all cried out for help, public officials knew that something had to be done: "Old-age dependency is definitely and positively one of the great tragedies of modern economic progress. . . . The only way [the elderly] can subsist and save themselves from penury, hunger, and want, is to join the great caravan that finally wends its way over the hill to the poorhouse."[7] How many elderly Americans actually needed assistance? The Committee on Economic Security assumed that at least 50 percent of the population over sixty-five was "dependent," a figure accepted by the 74th Congress.[8] The numbers of older people unable to find work and maintain their previous standard of living would probably continue to grow even after prosperity returned to the land. Commentators at the time pointed out, moreover, that young as well as old workers needed some assurance that their old age would not be troubled financially. Hence policymakers thought it necessary to address the future as well as the current dimensions of old-age dependency.[9]

Accordingly, the architects of Social Security instituted a two-pronged approach to the problem of old-age dependency. Congress initially appropriated $49,750,000 "for the purpose of enabling each State to furnish financial assistance, as far as practicable under the conditions in each State, to aged needy individuals."[10] Besides inaugurating a federal-state program of old-age assistance (Title I), an old-age insurance program (Title II) was established. Under the 1935 Act, employees in the commercial and manufacturing sectors (who then represented about 60 percent of the labor force) were to contribute .5 percent of the first $3,000 of covered wages into an Old Age Reserve Account; his or her employer would match that worker's payroll tax. Then, beginning in 1942, those past the age of sixty-five who had accumulated enough credits would be eligible to receive monthly checks based on their prior contributions.

Older Americans gained new rights through Social Security's old-age assistance and old-age insurance programs. But the precise nature of these rights depended both on the wording of Titles I and II and on the ways the law actually was implemented. Public relief in old age was no longer a gratuity that could be suspended when funds ran out. If an elderly person could prove that he or she met the age, residency, and needs requirement established by a state and approved by the federal board, then an applicant could receive the pension mandated in that jurisdiction. Eligibility rules, however, varied enormously from place to place. Nor was there any uniformity in the actual amount of assistance provided under Title I. In December 1936, for example, the average monthly allowance nationwide was $18.36; the average per recipient in California was $31.36—nearly ten times what it was in Mississippi.[11]

Similarly, the right to old-age insurance was narrowly defined. Policymakers intentionally allowed for considerable differences in benefits. Originally, only workers who had contributed to the system for a sufficient period of time were covered by the nation's retirement program. Benefits, moreover, were related to contributions which in turn reflected a recipient's covered work history and earnings record. More than cost considerations dissuaded policymakers from instituting a flat-rate retirement pension.[12] Thus both blue-collar and white-collar earners were assured that the traditional American reliance on self-help was not being abandoned. Employees would contribute to the best of their ability. Their em-

ployers would pay a matching tax. Government would ultimately
pay benefits to superannuated workers not as an act of paternalis-
tic generosity, but because such payments had in some sense been
"earned." America's social insurance program, according to this
view, was helping workers help themselves.

The notion that Washington should help individuals protect
themselves against the hazards of life was hardly unprecedented.
Under the Constitution, the federal government was responsible
for all matters affecting the commonweal not directly placed under
the jurisdiction of the states. Gradually, during the first 140 years
of the Republic, primary responsibility for defense, monetary matters, and public health became concentrated more and more in
the central government. Nevertheless, Social Security represented
Washington's first successful, sustained effort to move into the
welfare arena and deal directly with alleviating and preventing
the hazards associated with the modern political economy.[13] Since
the federal government *was* moving into relatively uncharted terri-
tory, advocates of this new Social Security legislation felt a special
need to emphasize that public intervention was merely reinforcing
a longstanding American commitment to the principle of mutual
responsibility.

Social Security, declared Congressman Wolverton during the
House debate, "recognizes the principle that, 'We are our brother's
keeper.' The mere recognition of this great fundamental principle
is in itself an outstanding victory."[14] By establishing a system of
relief for the aged poor along with orphans, the blind, and the
handicapped, Americans were demonstrating concern for some of
the neediest segments of the population. And by coordinating the
old-age insurance program with a system of old-age assistance, the
federal government was adopting a plan that "amounts to having
each generation pay for the support of the people then living who
are old."[15] Washington was committing itself to underwriting a
system of intergenerational income transfers that benefitted all age
groups. The aged would receive relief and future protection; their
middle-aged kin would be freed to devote their attention to their
children.[16] Why should the federal government, rather than (say)
a private insurance company, do this? The rationale offered by
Senator Lewis was indicative of the arguments made by those most
committed to the idea of social insurance: "It is the question of
faith. It is the controlling element in our conditions. Now, the Government supplies that element of faith. The private company has
to face a wall of distrust and break through it. . . . The Govern-

ment has no wall of distrust to meet. It can educate the public."[17] Only Washington, policymakers believed, had the requisite powers to influence and direct American citizens to do what was in their individual and collective best interests.

Lest such sentiments strike the present-day reader as excessively pious or hopelessly naive, I hasten to add that for all of their humanitarian impulses, the creators of the Social Security Act were pragmatic policymakers: "The vast amount of human suffering and the enormous relief costs, which inevitably will result in increased taxes, show conclusively the folly of failure to give thought to the security of men, women, and children."[18] Since taxpaying citizens could not "escape from the costs of old age," Social Security offered a "dignified and intelligent solution." Given the magnitude of the funds being committed in this initiative, it made sense to have federal officials assume ultimate responsibility for the program's direction. But no one presumed Titles I and II to be a *complete* solution. President Roosevelt, on signing Social Security into law, reminded the public that "we can never insure one hundred percent of the population against one hundred percent of the hazards and vicissitudes of life."[19] Furthermore, Social Security addressed existing woes and immediate hazards. It did not try to solve the underlying causes of structural unemployment or old-age pauperism. It neither relieved the individual of primary responsibility for his or her well-being nor diminished the importance of family members' duty to one another.

Not only did policymakers emphasize the limited nature of the protection being afforded by Social Security, but they also were quite explicit about the narrowly circumscribed nature of potential beneficiaries' rights. Social Security was hardly a get-rich-quick scheme; it certainly did not "soak the rich." Rather, it sought to give the aged a *floor* of protection, and a rocky floor at that: an acceptable standard of living could not be achieved by living exclusively on old-age assistance or retirement pensions. Perhaps more important, legislators noted that whatever rights to Social Security benefits workers had earned, their benefits were neither contractual nor transferable: "It must be remembered that this effort to create an old-age reserve account to take care of all persons in the future is not a contract that can be enforced by anybody. What we do here is merely to pass an act of Congress, which may be changed by any Congress in the future, and has in it nothing upon which American citizens can depend."[20]

The passage of the Social Security Act, therefore, constituted a cautious and open-ended attempt to deal with major hazards of modern America in an unprecedented manner. Roosevelt emphasized the need at the outset to avoid discrediting such "a sound idea—a sound ideal" by attempting to do too much too fast: "The place of such a fundamental [sic] in our future civilization is too precious to be jeopardized now by extravagant action."[21] The President had no doubts that history would vindicate his action, but a thorough study of social insurance in foreign countries had taught him and his advisors several key lessons. Experiences elsewhere demonstrated that actuarial and financial forecasts were often erroneous, because the scope and costs of such programs depended so directly on the prevailing state of the economy.[22] Accordingly, prudence dictated proceeding with Social Security in a step-by-step manner. The concept had to be tested on American soil, and critical tests arose almost at once.

The Committee on Economic Security had anticipated correctly that critics would challenge the constitutionality of a federally sponsored omnibus "general-welfare" package, including an old-age insurance program; the experts also expected the Supreme Court to uphold the fledgling Social Security system. On May 24, 1937, Justice Cardozo delivered the majority opinion in two landmark cases that vindicated the policymakers' faith. In *Steward Machine Co.* v. *Davis*, the Supreme Court ruled in a 5–4 decision that the method of collecting taxes for the state-federal unemployment compensation program (Title III) violated no constitutional principles; in *Helvering* v. *Davis*, the court did not comment on the wisdom of Title II, but it did hold that Congress had the right to address problems such as old-age dependency, that were "plainly national in area and dimensions."[23] These court decisions facilitated efforts at the federal level to expand the system.

An advisory council convened in 1937–38 recommended sweeping changes that were subsequently enacted as the 1939 amendments to the Social Security Act. Coverage under the program was expanded, and the first benefits were to be paid two years earlier, on January 1, 1940. The most important change was that the emphasis of Title II "shifted from the worker as an individual to the worker as breadwinner for the family group."[24] Significantly, in expanding the number of potential beneficiaries covered by Title II, Congress chose not to raise payroll taxes. Instead, the legislators decided to finance the old-age insurance program largely on a pay-as-you-go basis. If the funds generated through payroll taxes were not sufficient to cover the costs of benefits, then those who understood how the system worked expected the federal government to make up the difference. Policymakers were willing to underwrite additional protection for a greater proportion of the population (within limits) because they believed that in the long run this would benefit an aging society.[25]

The principle of mutual responsibility was the intellectual linchpin in the 1939 amendments that justified expanding rights in the process of helping Americans safeguard themselves against the risks of old age. Old-age dependency was not the only or even the most important hazard of modern life, but public officials were convinced that alleviating this risk would have a ripple effect throughout society, which would work to the advantage of all age groups. Providing more security in this area, it was hoped, would not only bolster public morale but also make citizens more security-conscious and thereby increase concern for protecting themselves and their children to the best of their ability.[26] And while the actual benefits a given individual might receive still bore a relationship to a covered worker's prior contributions, Social Security was envisioned more than ever as a system of intergenerational income transfers in which the payroll taxes and benefit levels were to be determined by the government in light of competing national priorities and existing economic resources generated by the country's productive capacity. Such a procedure made economic, political, and moral sense only insofar as the aging as well as the aged benefited from the exchange.

Having surmounted potential constitutional obstacles and having succeeded in expanding the scope of Title II even before the first old-age insurance benefit was paid, President Roosevelt looked forward to doing even more. Speaking before the Teamsters Union Convention on September 11, 1940, the President declared: "It is my hope that soon the United States will have a national system under which no needy man or woman within our borders will lack a minimum old-age pension that will provide adequate food, adequate clothing and adequate lodging to the end of the road."[27] In part, F.D.R. was echoing sentiments being expressed in other advanced industrial societies. The basic premise of the British Beveridge Report (1942), for instance, was that a major function of government is to guarantee "minimum economic security" for all citizens in order to make the nation itself more secure and productive. The President's own National Resources Planning Board went a step farther, and enunciated late in 1942 a set of "new freedoms" that it hoped would guarantee Americans freedom from fear and want and the right to reap the fruits of a liberal, democratic capitalist country.[28]

Although many political analysts and lawmakers were discouraged by the limited progress being made in the welfare arena during the war years, Roosevelt looked forward to a new era once the fighting ended. The President declared in his 1944 State of the Union address, "We have accepted, so to speak, a second Bill of Rights under which a new basis of security and prosperity can be established for all—regardless of station or race or creed." Roosevelt discussed eight rights, including the right to a good education and a useful, remunerative job, the right to an adequate wage and decent living in order to afford a decent home and adequate medical care, and protection from the financial fears caused by accidents, unemployment, and old age. He said, "All of these rights spell security . . . to new goals of happiness and well-being."[29] If Roosevelt's program were adopted, it would commit the government to provide, under the rubric of mutual responsibility, material as well as noneconomic rights to increasing numbers of citizens as Americans tried to cope with the hazards of modern living.

The federal government functioned increasingly often as a broker, mediator, and senior partner in the spheres of commerce, labor, industry, and agriculture in the depths of the Great Depression and in the course of winning a world war. The trend continued: More than ever before, policies and initiatives emanating from Washington were having a profound impact on ordinary citizens. Besides assisting veterans and their dependents with mortgages, job training, and college tuitions through the Serviceman's Readjustment Act, Congress approved several measures that increased federal involvement in the economy, thereby affecting workers' conditions in the marketplace.[30] The Employment Act of 1946, for instance, made full employment a national goal. By adjusting prevailing interest rates, amending the tax code, and raising the federal deficit ceiling, policymakers found that they could stimulate growth or cool the economy as circumstances warranted.

Similarly, in the social welfare arena, federal officials endeavored to increase the range and level of protection against major risks that threatened the financial well-being of most American individuals and households. Edwin E. Witte envisaged a program that "would provide 'cradle-to-grave' security, but in amounts not so large as to discourage industry and initiative, providing only a floor below which Americans would not fall, whatever catastrophe might strike them."[31] There were, however, mighty constraints in converting Witte's vision into reality. Social Security administrators and policymakers acknowledged that limited resources, competing priorities, and opposing philosophies required them to proceed with restraint. They never doubted, however, that they would eventually succeed. "To them, it was a matter of timing, not philosophy; of conditions, not a theory."[32]

Thus, pragmatically, Social Security advocates engaged in "the politics of incrementalism"—that is, they adopted the strategy of achieving broad policy objectives in a step-by-step manner.[33] To protect a greater proportion of the population against the risks of old-age dependency, policymakers worked toward including nearly every employee under the system. Compulsory coverage was extended in the 1950s and 1960s to agricultural and domestic workers, military personnel, and the self-employed. By the early 1970s, every major employment group (except federal bureaucrats) participated in the program, or could elect to do so. Furthermore, as coverage expanded, benefits were increased and requirements liberalized. Federal old-age assistance and insurance provisions as a consequence increasingly often became the basic—and in many instances, the only—means of support for a majority of older Americans.

While trying to improve the effectiveness of the existing federal Old Age Insurance (OAI) program, Social Security officials sought to realize many of the objectives initially discussed in the 1930s. Policymakers succeeded in creating new program initiatives whenever they could make a compelling case in a congenial political environment amidst favorable economic conditions. Hence, disability insurance was added to the Old Age and Survivors Insurance (OASI) program in 1956. Nine years later, Congress inaugurated two federally sponsored health care programs, largely to assist the old. Medicare provided hospital insurance for those eligible for Title II benefits and a supplementary, voluntary plan to help those over sixty-five cover some of their physicians' bills. It was hoped that Medicaid, which provides assistance to poor people of all ages, would make minimal medical attention accessible to the poor, frail elderly. The original Title II (OAI) hence gradually became OASDHI. Old-age assistance also was revamped. In 1972, Congress overwhelmingly voted to establish a Supplemental Security Income (s.s.i.) program, designed to replace the existing federal-state system of relief for the aged poor, blind, and disabled with an exclusively federally financed one that provided a minimal floor of protection nationwide. Many observers forecast that s.s.i. would become the basis of a comprehensive and adequate income-maintenance program available to all citizens.

By expanding the scope of protection afforded by Social Security to include the hazards associated with disability, illness, and insufficient income that nearly *every* American potentially faced, regardless of past or current employment status, legislative and executive officials were enlarging the meaning of risk: "The proper test of coverage is not the special nature of a worker's employment but the universal nature of risks he or she faces."[34] Building Social Security in an incremental manner nonetheless meant that *continuous* protection from womb to tomb had not yet been achieved. Financial constraints and political considerations limited just how much coverage was possible. Some reasonable guidelines needed to be adopted: "Social insurance must implement the concept of adequacy in the prevention of hardship, not by some single arbitrary estimate of need, but by relating a standard schedule of events that disturb the normal status and create a need."[35] The risks to be covered under Social Security thus were basically those that policymakers judged to be "normal" occurrences that might disrupt the predictable behavior and expectations of a significant segment of the population.

In this context, *chronological age* increasingly often became the index by which to measure the incidence of "risk" and to trigger society's response to the hazards of modern life. Sixty-five was the initial baseline used to determine eligibility for old-age insurance and assistance benefits.[36] Over time, Congress (typically following the advice of Social Security Administration officials) instituted other age-based criteria. Beginning in 1956, female employees with sufficient covered work experience could receive actuarially reduced retirement pensions between the ages of sixty-two and sixty-four; men were given the same option five years later. The 1956 amendments to the Social Security Act established fifty as the minimal age for eligibility for disability insurance benefits; once a disabled worker reached age sixty-five, he or she automatically qualified for old-age benefits. In addition, chronological age was a major determinant of eligibility for spousal and survivors benefits. Female dependents of retired-worker beneficiaries after 1956 could receive reduced benefits at age sixty-two. Effective in 1965, a divorced dependent who had been married to a beneficiary for at least twenty years could receive full benefits at age sixty-five and partial benefits beginning at age sixty-two; in 1977, the twenty-year requirement for duration of marriage was reduced to a decade. Widows could first receive survivors benefits at age sixty-five according to the 1939 amendments to the Social Security Act; subsequent amendments lowered the minimum age to sixty or sixty-two depending on other eligibility factors. Children were covered under the age eighteen, though a series of changes since the mid-1960s introduced some broader age-specific options: some "children" could receive benefits up to age twenty-two depending on whether or not that dependent was enrolled in school. Finally, even before it became fashionable to evince concern for the "frail" and "old old" elderly, special cash benefits and earnings-tests criteria were instituted for individuals and couples over the ages of seventy and seventy-two.[37]

Defining coverage against risks on the basis of age, from the perspective of policymakers, had more advantages than disadvantages. Administratively straightforward, this method avoided associating the stigma of "welfare" with many social adequacy programs substituting proof of attainment of a certain age for some means-testing formula. Yet age-based eligibility criteria created unavoidable holes in coverage. Insofar as the risks being covered were based on observations and politically sensitive judgments about people's "normal status," it was inevitable that those who deviated from the existing set of age-based norms would not be covered. Critics rightly noted that some workers became disabled before age fifty, and that many housewives became widows before the age of sixty. Policymakers were not oblivious to such possible inequities. Nevertheless, given the politics of incrementalism, they realized that they could not remedy everyone's situation at once. And since they were adjusting the rules to accommodate the needs and desires of "most" people—a perfect example is the decision to underwrite early retirement benefits as successive cohorts of workers chose to retire before the age of sixty-five—they felt justified in viewing age as a reliable measure of "normal" risk. In so doing, they helped to make modern America more bureaucratically age-conscious than ever before.[38]

Just as the range and nature of risks alleviated through Social Security expanded after World War II, so too one can trace the evolution of more and more elastic definitions of citizens' *rights* to federally guaranteed benefits. A very precise and deliberately narrow interpretation of rights continued to form the basis for entitlements in postwar America. Policymakers did not wish to undermine or supplant longstanding precepts with new and potentially countervailing principles: "Social security and private institutions for

economic security have not rendered unnecessary or valueless individual initiative, enterprise, and thrift. . . . Social insurance not
only is consistent with free enterprise, but is a bulwark for its con-
tinuance."[39] The right to achieve a measure of economic security
through the fruits of one's labor and the responsibility to preserve
one's standard of living were never meant to be vitiated by the
promise of benefits under social insurance.

"The guiding idea in American social insurance is that the
individual earns the right to benefit through payment of contributions by himself and on his behalf," observed political scientist
Gaston Rimlinger in 1961. "Nevertheless, the act of contributing,
while it has important political advantages, can only bind the government morally, rather than legally, to render specified benefits."[40] Rimlinger was emphasizing that the notion of "contract"
under Social Security had ideological rather than legal standing.
This indeed appeared to be the case. The Supreme Court held in
the landmark case of *Flemming* v. *Nestor* (1960), for instance, that
"to engraft upon the social security system a concept of 'accrued
property rights' would deprive it of the flexibility and boldness in
adjustment to ever-changing conditions which it demands."[41] The
justices by a 5–4 margin reaffirmed the logic of *Helvering* v. *Davis*
which stated that Congress had the right to "alter, amend or re-
peal" any aspect of Social Security law within constitutional
bounds. This meant that the promise of future benefits based on a
worker's prior contributions were not deemed to be contractual
rights.[42] To some, *Flemming* v. *Nestor* revealed the ominous side
of allowing an enlightened state to gain so much power that it
could legitimately disregard individual rights under the seemingly
benign rubric of "the public interest."[43] Indeed, it is important to
note that the Supreme Court's ruling occurred at a time when
scholars and public officials were taking another look at the socioeconomic obstacles and philosophical-legal justifications for taking
rights seriously as they tried to respond to and capitalize on the
civil rights movement sweeping the land.

This is not the place to rehearse the intellectual, sociological,
political, and economic forces that converged by the early 1960s to
usher in a period of national concern for redressing past inequities
and ensuring disadvantaged segments of the population access to
facilities and opportunities that most middle-class Americans took
for granted. Still, there can be little question that mounting public
pressure and acts of civil disobedience by the disenfranchised and
poor; an increasingly activist Supreme Court, a sympathetic Con-

gress, and an energetic executive branch; as well as a popular mandate from voters and rising prosperity, all led the federal government to launch a "war on poverty" as public officials boldly envisaged a "Great Society" in which the housing, health- and job-related, financial, educational, and psychological needs of all citizens could be satisfied: "An age attuned to the idea that a government has vast responsibilities for the material welfare and human rights of citizens can hardly share the founders' fear of strong national government."[44] Not since the New Deal had the broad powers of the central government been called upon—and utilized—to promote the rights of individuals to participate and prosper in the American way of life regardless of race, geography, or education.

The times demanded, and facilitated, bolder steps in protecting and advancing individuals' rights as American citizens than this nation has witnessed since the Founding Fathers debated the purposes of government. Nowadays, it has become fashionable to deride the Great Society for its intellectual contradictions, misjudgments, and biases, and to seize upon its failures and excesses in order to dismiss the significant achievements accomplished through government intervention in the fields of civil rights, education, and social welfare. To do so, however, is to miss the genuine commitment to advancing the well-being of disadvantaged individuals and groups that gave rise to the soaring expectations and self-confident presumption that money and justice made all good things possible.

The problems of older Americans received less media attention during the 1960s than did the plight of blacks and poor people in Appalachia, but it would be reasonable to claim that Washington promised to do more to advance the *rights* of the elderly than those of any other age group. To be sure, policymakers often explicitly or unwittingly defined and dealt with the elderly's needs and desires differently from the way they handled the demands and problems of those under the age of sixty-five. Nevertheless, in the "declaration of objectives" that constituted Sec. 101 of the Older Americans Act (1965), Congress made Roosevelt's vision of post-war America a matter of public law for senior citizens:[45]

The Congress hereby finds and declares that, in keeping with the traditional American concept of the inherent dignity of the individual in our democratic society, the older people of our Nation are entitled to, and it is the joint and several duty and responsibility of the governments of the United States . . .

to assist our older people to secure equal opportunity to the full and free enjoyment of the following objectives:

(1) An adequate income in retirement in accordance with the American standard of living.

(2) The best possible physical and mental health which science can make available and without regard to economic status.

(3) Suitable housing, independently selected, designed and located with reference to special needs and available at costs which older citizens can afford.

(4) Full restorative services for those who require institutional care.

(5) Opportunity for employment with no discriminatory personnel practices because of age.

(6) Retirement in health, honor, dignity—after years of contributing to the economy.

(7) Pursuit of meaningful activity within the widest range of civic, cultural, and recreational opportunities.

(8) Efficient community services which provide social assistance in a coordinated manner and which are readily available when needed.

(9) Immediate benefit from proven research knowledge which can sustain and improve health and happiness.

(10) Freedom, independence, and the free exercise of individual initiative in planning and managing their own lives.

The Older Americans Act was not limited to dealing with the financial and health hazards of late life. This measure presumed that *every* aspect of the elderly's daily life required public support. The Older Americans Act affirmed government's duty to advance "the inherent dignity of the individual" as public policy facilitated individuals' pursuit of "health and happiness." It is one thing, of course, to set objectives and quite another to execute the law so as to reach those goals.[46] Nevertheless, working toward advancing the rights of older people—rights that were theirs as individuals, as citizens, and in accordance with a "traditional American concept"—was now statutory law. Older Americans were "entitled" to basic social services and income support. In this context, the passage of Medicare and Medicaid, and the adoption of a wide range of community services and outreach programs, were clearly consonant with the principles of the Older Americans Act. The increase in average monthly Social Security checks, the passage of the Supplemental Security Income program and the automatic indexing of Title II benefits can all be interpreted as attempts to help reduce the elderly's vulnerability to rising inflation and thereby advance their economic "freedom."

By extention, if Washington were really serious about advancing the rights of older Americans through congressional action and judicial intervention, then a new basis for understanding the nature of rights in our society was taking shape. The nature of the national polity itself was being transvalued: "The national idea means something more than mere centralization of power. As the principle of community, it provides, along with the democratic idea, one of the standards by which governmental unification can be justified and by which it should be controlled and guided."[47] By committing itself to improving the quality of life of the aged, government ultimately would have to embrace the rights and needs of all citizens. And even though the precise nature of rights and entitlements remained a matter for Congress to debate and the courts to adjudicate, these political and constitutional facts of life did not relieve public officials of the need to look out for the interests of the poorest and least articulate members of society. Thus there arose a flurry of scholarly interest in delineating and guaranteeing the rights of welfare recipients to public benefits.[48]

Court decisions often helped to sharpen thinking. Perhaps the most significant Supreme Court case affecting the nature of rights under Social Security since *Nestor* v. *Flemming* was *Goldberg* v. *Kelly* (1970), which involved the case of a person whose AFDC benefits were terminated without giving the plaintiff the chance to appeal the decision. In this case, the Supreme Court held that "welfare benefits are a matter of statutory entitlement for persons qualified to receive them and procedural due process is applicable to their termination."[49] A fairly subtle but straightforward line of reasoning thus emerges from opinions rendered in these two cases at either end of the volatile 1960s. While the actual benefits under Title II of Social Security are not contractual, a citizen *is* guaranteed the right to due process—that is, to a hearing before his or her welfare benefits under Title IV are terminated. Courts, it seemed, offered citizens the greatest protection of their rights in cases of suspension or revocation, but even then, that protection extended mainly to a consideration of whether or not the legal *process* had been observed. The right to a standard of living that was "adequate" on the basis of any objective criteria had not been made a constitutional issue or even a matter to be formalized in public law. After all, it is worth remembering that the minimum benefits promised by the s.s.i. program still fall below the government's own official "poverty line."

I have purposely focused on the rights of the low-income elderly and welfare recipients to Social Security. This is because the extent to which the judicial and legislative branches were concerned about the disadvantaged helps us to understand the nature and scope of rights under various programs of Social Security during a period in which the system's growth was so dynamic. But it would distort the historical record to suggest that a concern for welfare beneficiaries or a commitment to accentuating the redistributive features of social insurance explained why Social Security had become a central feature of American life.

The major reason that the social-insurance program was so enormously popular in the 1950s and 1960s was that it worked so well for middle-class Americans. For more than three decades, Social Security had been self-sustaining. Contributory tax rates and benefit schedules were periodically adjusted, but such adjustments resulted mainly from a desire to safeguard the system's financial integrity or to expand its effectiveness in ways consistent with the program's internal dynamics. Not only was little additional government intervention required, but the administrative expenses required to operate such a far-flung program were remarkably low. In the words of that eminent economist Paul Samuelson: "Often, government is one of the 'cheapest' ways of providing insurance against important risks."[50]

Indeed, the very stability and efficiency of Social Security operations were contributing to the well-being of American society at large without appearing to jeopardize the nation's adherence to time-tested principles. At the same time, Social Security was contributing to overall prosperity. "A high level of economic security is essential for maximum production," observed John Kenneth Galbraith in his seminal *Affluent Society* (1958).[51] More importantly, according to its supporters, Social Security bolstered individual self-reliance while fostering a sense of mutual responsibility. Because "Social Security was a social mechanism for the preservation of individual dignity,"[52] it was viewed as a conservative institution that strengthened individualistic values. Workers were willing to make contributions for present beneficiaries, because they assumed that when they became disabled, superannuated, or died, that the then current generation of workers would honor their obligation to support them and their survivors. Social Security "worked" because individuals benefitted from participating in a system of mutual responsibility. That operating a system in this way made sense was rarely questioned—mainly because it *did* work and seemed to conform to quintessential American values.

J. Douglas Brown, from the very beginning one of Social Security's most thoughtful and eloquent defenders, realized that the notion of "mutual responsibility" being applied to the principle of social insurance had thus far eluded systematic examination. Yet he thought the system was supported by a venerable, covenantal tradition:

> The strongest support for the indefinite continuance of the transfer of funds . . . is the sense of mutual responsibility deep in the minds of people. The tradition of mutual responsibility has long been a cohesive force among industrial workers. It was exemplified in the first mutual aid societies, which later evolved into governmentally established contributory social insurance systems. Such systems embodied a covenant between the young and old, the gainfully employed and the dependents of those who die, and the strong and disabled. The covenant is not a legal entity but it has a subtle and powerful force in a democracy, in which the government must reflect a general consensus of its citizens. . . . History is on the side of those who believe that the covenant between those who contribute and those who need help will continue.[53]

To Brown, the soundness of Social Security was not really a question of demographic ratios or the proper ratio between contributions and disbursements. Ultimately, he believed, the only issue that truly mattered was whether or not government had the capacity to fulfill the promises of its intergenerational covenant. If it could, its ability to honor basic commitments made in the name of all citizens corroborated continued faith in the American system. If Social Security were to become vulnerable in the long run, its bankruptcy would then have to be addressed in moral as well as financial terms. Such a haunting prospect grew into more than idle speculation during the past decade, as Social Security became the subject of more controversy than at any other time since its formative years.

During the past decade the nature and scope of risks covered under Social Security have changed very little. The program continues to offer a floor of financial protection against several of the major hazards of modern life that threaten the well-being of most Americans. "In a democratic society, it is a judgment of Congress, tested from time to time against experience and response," notes J. Douglas Brown, to determine the extent to which the protection against hardships is adequate. "The goal is a fair and reasonable balancing of the extent to which the social insurance system should and can obviate hardship among persons and families of different levels of normal earnings, given the limited funds available for the purpose."[54] Currently dispensing roughly $11 billion in benefits each month to more than 36 million Americans, Social Security has become Washington's largest domestic social program. The meaning of the risks adopted under the federal system, however, has not been static. As more and more people have become eligible for benefits on the basis of their prior and current contributions, there has been an anxious and fractious—not to mention confused and confusing—debate over the ultimate purposes and unexpected liabilities of having government underwrite such an expansive (and expensive) social insurance program.

The cumulative impact of expanding Social Security coverage and increasing benefits has encouraged the American people to demand less risk and greater protection from their public and private institutions. For more than three decades, Americans have responded to the problem of economic insecurity as if it were some disease that could be cured and possibly even conquered if only the right combination of medications were prescribed and conscientiously administered. Besides concerning ourselves with the potential risks of old-age dependency and unemployment, over time we have become involved in sharing the burden of risk in more and more spheres of our daily life. Through an increasing welter of government programs, we have attempted to insure ourselves against an extraordinary variety of likely natural and man-made disasters, ranging from guarantees to federal assistance in the wake of earthquakes and floods to quality-control standards in the marketplace and intricate safety regulations in the workplace. "The welfare state has been turned into an insurance state, as all individuals are protected against a whole array of risks by shifting the burden of their consequences to a larger group or the whole community or simply by eliminating them," Yair Aharoni declared in *The No-Risk Society* (1981). "The movement is away from a reliance on the rational individual as a decision maker and a bearer of the consequences of his choice to a socially determined allocation and distribution of resources, much of which is designed to shift the responsibility for both new and existing risks from individual to society."[55] Large private institutions, in response to public pressure and their own internal requirements, have also allocated greater portions of their capital and resources in order to complement and expand the coverage against "risk" that their employees were gaining from the elaboration of the federal "insurance state." Thus most corporations now offer their workers supplemental unemployment, health care, and retirement benefits that enable them to maintain their standard of living during temporary layoffs, long-term illness, and in their later years. It is not by accident that many of these corporate and union policies were designed to dovetail with existing governmental programs.

The expansion of the social insurance programs, especially in the public sector, led some to believe that full protection against the hazards of contemporary life was genuinely possible. Paradoxically, however, heightened expectations about the degree to which a risk-free society could be achieved inexorably fueled unrealistic demands on our socioeconomic and political institutions. It quickly proved difficult to sustain the momentum of translating greater expectations into better protection. Skepticism about the efficacy of such initiatives mounted amid new economic uncertainties. "Today's new insecurities exist along with a gut appreciation that the urge for absolute security may be futile and, more than that, responsible for some of the present predicament," political analyst Robert J. Samuelson argued. "The attempt to satisfy everyone's desire for job security and rising living standards led to inflationary policies and, in particular, to inflationary money growth. . . . What emerges is a pervasive confusion with everyone professing allegiance to yesterday's ideals while trying to cope with today's realities. . . . All this marks a continuing eclipse of Depression-era psychology and politics."[56] Public opinion polls revealed a sharply declining confidence in public officials. In this context, the parameters of the debate over the responsibility and capacity of government to protect citizens against risks became more partisan.

At one end of the political spectrum, conservatives bemoaned the dire consequences and emphasized the hidden (and wasteful) costs of pursuing the chimera of a risk-free society: "The riskless society, with all its misallocation of resources, regimentation, and erosion of individual freedom, is evolving rapidly. . . . Unless its nature is recognized and appreciated, there is little reason to believe that this trend will be reversed."[57] Writers emphasized that government must regulate itself and correct its own excesses by

cutting back and eliminating those programs that squander valuable resources and fuel cynicism by promising far more than they
can possibly deliver. Elaborating on this viewpoint, conservative
reformers recommended that it was reasonable to shift some of the
burden for underwriting protection against major risks back to individuals, for as more and more people acknowledged that there is
no such thing as a free lunch, it followed that individuals would
behave in a more prudent manner in order to eliminate unnecessary expenses and keep costs down.

Thus far, the liberal camp's response to such arguments has
been to suggest that the remedies proposed are more pernicious
than the problem that an image of a risk-free society poses. In
terms of Social Security, for instance, defenders of the system
could (rightly) note that the individual and family have always
been expected to make provisions against the vicissitudes of everyday life. No one could maintain an adequate standard of living
supported exclusively through publicly funded provisions. The costs
of *not* attempting to address the risks of old-age dependency,
broken homes, unemployment, and disability through social insurance, they argue, far exceed the net outlays of helping individuals
help themselves.

Nevertheless, at this point in the debate, even the most earnest
supporter of the social-insurance concept is willing to acknowledge
the illusory qualities embedded in the notion of a risk-free society.
Yet because they are reluctant to abandon the idea of economic
security for everybody, many liberals try to preserve as much of it
as they can for the aged. More than filio-piety influences this choice
of the elderly for special consideration. Many policymakers and the
public at large still believe that the aged are different from the rest
of us, and thus deserve and need categorical assistance. And they
remain certain that administering programs on the basis of age
entails less invidious criteria than a means-tested index would require. Furthermore, they are convinced that events along the life
course have become so uniform that chronological age per se can
roughly predict when risks covered by Social Security normally
affect most Americans.

Unfortunately, the best available data and scholarly studies do
not sustain this position. In recent years, it has become increasingly
apparent that age-based criteria do not meet the needs of large segments of the population: "A case can be made that at the same time
that age itself is becoming less relevant in the society, legislators
and administrators have been proliferating laws and regulations

that are age-based."[58] Age-specific assistance and protection may have the ironic effect of denying services to those older persons who need the most help. For instance, feminists since the 1960s have been arguing that older women are penalized by the ways in which Social Security benefits are calculated. Those women least likely to qualify for benefits—very old heads of households (whose husbands died prematurely) with limited work experience outside of the home—are typically those who have limited personal assets and little access to other sources of income.[59] Similarly, blacks complain that as a group they do not live long enough to qualify for the whole range of old-age benefits because of racial differences in life expectancy. (Those who wish to challenge this argument point out that life expectancy at age sixty-five among blacks is greater than it is among whites.) Are these complaints unwarranted, or is there a larger issue involved here?

It could be argued that protecting old-age entitlements as other programs are cut back and eliminated discriminates in favor of the elderly at the expense of the young and middle-aged. It is possible, moreover, that age has become a less valid predictor than gender, race, income, education, or employment status in determining need. Those over sixty-five as a group, after all, are healthier, wealthier, and better educated than any comparable cohort in American history. The men and women in this age group who need the most help typically suffer from some long-term disadvantage, often exacerbated by sexism, nativism, or racism. What strategy, then, best addresses the fact that most poor older Americans are women—making the problem a "women's issue" or dealing with it as a special feature of the economics of late life? Might it not make more sense to tackle the racism that is endemic in our culture than to focus on the specific woes of elderly minorities?

The trouble with posing questions in this manner has been that it lulls policy analysts and the American people into missing a critical point about the interconnections among risks, rights, and mutual responsibility under Social Security. Rather than trying to isolate the effects of age and need in choosing how to proceed, it might be wiser to remind ourselves that the purpose of social insurance was to protect a majority of *citizens* against well-known risks. In putting the matter this way, we quickly realize that in analyzing the nature of risks, we must reconsider *who* is at risk and *who* deserves some measure of protection through social insurance. Discussing risks from this perspective leads us at once into the equally problematic question of rights.

In a series of cases involving eligibility for Social Security benefits, the Supreme Court often placed itself during the 1970s in the position of having to decide whether rights should be differentiated on the basis of gender, need, or some other criterion. A review of recent decisions leads us to two conclusions. On the one hand, the court succeeded in drawing finer lines in determining the constitutional basis for entitlements under Social Security. On the other hand, it hardly resolved the question of what rights were at stake. Thus in *Weinberger* v. *Wiesenfeld* (1975) the court overturned a gender-based distinction between widows' and widowers' benefits by declaring that whatever was provided for a surviving mother must also be granted to an eligible surviving father. In order to ensure equal protection under the due process clause of the Fifth Amendment, the court ordered that a father with children be paid a benefit of 75 percent of his deceased wife's benefit in addition to the benefits his children received: "Given the purpose of enabling the surviving parent to remain at home to care for a child, the gender-based discrimination . . . is entirely irrational. The classification discriminates among surviving children solely on the basis of the sex of the surviving parent."[60] Feminists and supporters of children's rights hailed the decision. Yet two years later in *Mathews* v. *DeCastro*, the court ruled against a divorcée with a minor to support (who had been married for more than twenty years to a retired contributor) who claimed to have the same right to benefits as did the wife of a retired or disabled worker who had a child to support.[61] The court did not believe that due process was being violated in this case, because divorced persons typically choose to live lives independent from their previous spouses. Such reasoning, however, leaves moot the question of whether divorced parents have also severed their family responsibilities. Insofar as promoting the welfare of children was a major rationale for social insurance provisions, then it indeed is quite pertinent that child-support payments tend to be low and irregularly paid. So did the decision rendered in *Mathews* v. *DeCastro* advance rights or subject them to further adjudication? Grappling with such questions ensured that the issue of women's rights under Social Security would continue to be a lively topic of debate.

Similarly, the court continued to be sensitive to the *procedural* contexts in which rights to benefits are determined and terminated. Here too, distinctions were drawn on very precise grounds. In *Goldberg* v. *Kelly* (1970), it will be recalled, a welfare recipient's AFDC benefits could not be terminated without a prior hearing. In

Mathews v. *Eldridge* (1976) the court ruled that an "evidentiary hearing" was not required prior to terminating disability benefits as long as the beneficiary was notified beforehand of the proposed action and had the right to review his or her file and supply additional evidence. In this verdict, more than procedural issues were at stake. The court relied heavily on the fact that Social Security disability benefits under Title II, unlike AFDC payments, were not based on need: "The private interest that will be adversely affected by an erroneous termination of benefits is likely to be less in the case of a disabled worker than in the case of a welfare recipient."[62] Thus the question of need *did*, under certain circumstances, influence the Supreme Court's thinking about due process. No wonder defining rights under the law was so perplexing. Besides such familiar categories as privileges and claims, legal scholars had to distinguish among procedural, administrative, statutory, and contractual rights, and even then they had not exhausted the possible ways to define the basis of entitlements to Social Security benefits.[63]

Perhaps the most important effort to redefine the basis of rights in modern America during the 1970s, however, took place in halls of philosophy rather than in courts of justice. The study of public ethics, which had languished in recent years, was reinvigorated by the publication of several brilliant monographs and the exchange of ideas disseminated in prestigious magazines and journals such as *The Public Interest*, *The New York Review*, and *Philosophy and Public Affairs*. Determining the nature of rights under Social Security was not the primary issue preoccupying public philosophers, of course, but much that was written about justice, liberalism, and equality had a direct bearing on this subject.

John Rawls's seminal *A Theory of Justice* (1971) elevated the debate over individual rights and entitlements to a new level, and remained the work most regularly cited and attacked for the rest of the decade. If a society truly wishes to be *just*, in Rawls's view, it must protect the fundamental rights of the least fortunate members of society. A rational agent "situated behind a veil of ignorance" must take steps to guarantee that everybody has an equal right to satisfy his or her basic needs: "All social primary goods— liberty and opportunity, income and wealth, and the bases of self-respect—are to be distributed equally unless an unequal distribution of any or all of these goods is to the advantage of the least favored."[64]

How would adopting Rawls's concept of justice affect the allocation of rights under Social Security? A plausible application, and one that Rawls comes close to endorsing, would be to emphasize the redistributive features of the program's benefit structure. Under the present situation, the Title II benefits (based on their prior covered earnings) that retired low-income workers can expect to receive do represent a proportionately greater return than is the case for those who pay the maximum rate. Such a feature has been defended historically in terms of "social adequacy." It has never been a primary objective of Social Security, however, to redistribute income through social insurance, though policymakers do acknowledge that a modest redistributive effect does take place. The reason for *not* making redistribution of income an explicit priority is that such a policy change might go beyond the range of powers accorded the central government of a liberal democracy. "It is all too easy to make the mistake of regarding redistribution as a logical extension of—or even simply a way of rationalizing—the welfare spending of the liberal state," an editor of *The Public Interest* noted. "This is an error to which economists are particularly prone, given their penchant for focusing on economic effects (i.e., how much is being transferred to whom) rather than political principles (i.e., on what grounds the money is being transferred)."[65] According to most theorists, there is a vital distinction between the "welfare state" and the "redistributive" state that must be preserved. For this reason, it might be wiser for policymakers to talk about the "insurance" rights, that people can claim under Social Security than to make claims based on presumed rights to income transfers that will help citizens safeguard their well-being, and enable them to satisfy their basic needs.[66]

Rawls's Harvard colleague, Robert Nozick, presented quite a different philosophical basis for promoting individual rights in *Anarchy, State and Utopia* (1974). Nozick premised his views on the idea that property should be distributed in terms of entitlements, rather than concerning himself with whether or not structural inequalities in society were intolerable and unjust: "The holdings of a person are just if he is entitled to them by the principles of justice in acquisition and transfer, or by the principle of rectification of injustice (as specified by the first two principles)."[67] Thus, in a Nozickian world, a person is "justly" entitled to Social Security benefits to the extent that he or she "owns" them as property—that is, through legitimate acquisition or earning them as a right. As long as a beneficiary can claim proper title to those benefits, no one can legitimately take them away.

The positions taken by Rawls and by Nozick diverge markedly. Rawls opts for an activist, interventionist polity; Nozick prefers a state with minimal duties and powers. They build their conceptual frameworks with different materials: "Rawls makes primary what is in effect a principle of equality with respect to needs. . . . Nozick makes primary what is a principle of equality with respect to entitlement."[68] While Rawls presumes that conforming to the principles of just distribution limits the possible extent of legitimate acquisition and entitlement, Nozick holds that sanctioning acquisition and protecting entitlement constrains governmental action in the area of redistributive justice. Thus, in philosophical discourse no less than judicial decisions, the basis and significance of rights under Social Security remains a matter of broad speculation and intense debate.

For all their differences, however, it is worth noting that both Rawls and Nozick share at least two assumptions about how to define individual rights. First, both have adopted the economist's view of modern man. This tack facilitates their efforts to discuss ways that people can maximize and preserve the attainment of desired and desirable goals. Still, viewing human nature in this way imposes certain political and moral blinders: "The questions about which both of them are most passionately concerned is the distribution of income and wealth, and while this is, to be sure, an important issue, it has but little relation to the decline in legitimacy that has befallen all our leading social and political institutions. About this crisis, game theory, decision theory, and economic analysis can tell us next to nothing."[69] And why are such concerns about the state of the polity—as differentiated from an interest in the state of human nature—not given much consideration? Asking this question leads us at once into a second similarity in these two scholars' books. The *Homo oeconomicus* that both Rawls and Nozick describe has been largely ripped out of nature and society. The identification of individual interests in both *A Theory of Justice* and *Anarchy, State and Utopia* is made primary in—sometimes even independent of—the social fabric that gives contextual grounding to the individual rights in question.

Both Rawls and Nozick have taken individual rights so seriously that they have tended to ignore or at least to minimize the extent to which unpredictable historical factors and dysfunctional societal norms and structures confound personal options even as they shape individuals' choices. Society is best seen as a utopia in both men's books. Rawls takes for granted that a "well-ordered" society is stable, homogeneous, and smoothly functioning, and regulated by a clear sense of "justice."[70] It is doubtful that such arrangements are possible anywhere save in a utopia; none has yet been discovered by historians. Nozick's "minimal state" similarly has no life independent of what it can do for individuals: "Treating us with respect by respecting our rights, it allows us, individually or with whom we choose, to choose our life and to realize our ends and our conception of ourselves, insofar as we can. . . . How *dare* any state or group of individuals do more. Or less."[71] Can we really analyze individual rights in such an analytic framework? I think not.

Political commentators and public philosophers have long emphasized the extent to which societal values and structures influence our thinking about individual rights: "What marks . . . a community is not merely a spirit of benevolence, or the prevalence of communitarian values, or even certain 'shared final ends' alone, but a common vocabulary of discourse and a background of implicit practices and understandings within which the opacity of the participants is reduced if never finally dissolved."[72] Neither risks nor rights, in my opinion, can be understood outside of the distinctive sociohistorical milieu that produced them. The current meaning of "mutual responsibility," accordingly, must be probed in terms of recent national experiences.

Just as recent events and scholarly inquiry have exposed illusions in our understanding of risks and contrarieties in our definition and application of rights, so too it has become increasingly apparent that our prevailing notion of mutual responsibility rests on shaky grounds. Prior to the 1970s, people who wrote about Social Security typically characterized the system of intergenerational transfers as a major component of the larger covenant that bound the American nation together. In recent years such assumptions have been subjected to critical scrutiny. Not surprisingly, a new—and not terribly comforting—perspective on the meaning of responsibility is being formulated in analyses of the contemporary American polity.

For openers, students of American civilization have demonstrated that puncturing myths about the republic's "covenant" with nature and nature's God has been a central motif in the writing of American history since at least the 1830s. Successive generations of social commentators, essayists, historians, and philosophers have wrestled with the presumably distinctive features of the American experience, only to (re)discover that as a nation we have been unable to transcend the limits of history and human nature any more successfully than any other country.[73] Indeed, insofar as America was conceived having a millennial role, its ability to fulfill Enlightenment principles was called into question almost at once. As Robert Bellah, a Berkeley professor of religion writing in 1975, put the matter: "The covenant . . . was broken almost as soon as it was made. For a long time Americans were able to hide from that fact, to deny the brokenness. Today the broken covenant is visible to all."[74] Such a grand and grandiose term as "covenant" does not accurately describe the pact between generations that is manifest in Social Security's operations.

If we cannot reasonably draw analogies between Social Security and some American covenant, is it fair to emphasize the system's intergenerational features? Most commentators apparently think so. During the debate since the late 1970s over ways to shore up the system, we heard a lot about the problems of the so-called "gypped generation." According to some critics, the baby boom generation probably would get less back in lifetime benefits than they would have to contribute, while the current beneficiaries, who had made comparatively small contributions (due to lower tax rates then in force), were already roughly ahead fourteen months after "normal" retirement and could expect to reap even greater "windfalls," thanks to the indexation of benefits. Defenders of the status quo, on the other hand, challenge the assumptions embedded in such arguments. The young and their dependents, they point out, also benefit from Social Security in the event of premature death or disability. Families of middle-aged workers are in better financial shape because the elderly have an alternative source of support in times of need. Furthermore, supporters attack the critics' claim that social insurance operates like an annuity, preferring instead to stress its intergenerational qualities: "While the intergenerational transfer model emphasizes immediate costs and benefits . . . the willingness of each cohort of workers to bear the costs of a collective income transfer program is based, in part, on the expectation that they will in turn be provided a 'floor of protection' by their children's generation."[75] While they disagree about how Social Security functions, note that neither critics nor supporters define "generation" with any precision.

Little wonder: after even a moment's reflection, one must concede that the meaning of "generation" is both fuzzy and arbitrary. Less clear-cut than the distinction between parent and child, the term might refer with equal plausibility to all people between certain ages, to progenitors of any age (as opposed to their progeny), and/or to people who lived through a monumental experience (such as the Great Depression). The very ambiguity of meaning makes it hard to know who is precisely included or excluded in such a definition. Worse, referring to people as being of a certain generation attributes to them characteristics that they may or may not possess. Who, after all, is a member of the "gypped generation"? Where and how does one draw the line: on the basis of age? birth order? income? expectations?[76]

Even if the exact meaning of "generation" in the Social Security context were perfectly clear, some commentators question the legitimacy of claiming that the system's intergenerational income transfer is based on the moral responsibilities that children owe their parents *as* parents. Peter Laslett, an eminent British social historian and political philosopher, frames the issue this way:

> Hence it is possible to pronounce that duties go forward in time, but rights go backwards. Duties of parents to children reciprocate rights of parents: rights of children in parents are reciprocated by duties of these children towards their children (i.e. the grandchildren of their own parents). . . . A crude metaphor would be that of a chain made out of hooks and eyes, where hooks have all to lie one way, and at the point where the chain stops a hook without an eye is always hanging forward.[77]

In this passage Laslett offers an interpretation of familial obligations that differs in thrust from scriptural injunctions or the presumption embedded in many state laws. Laslett does not mean to say that children have no responsibilities to their parents. Natural affection, historical precedent, and common law do combine to reinforce reciprocal care and concern. Nevertheless, in Laslett's view, "the duties of children towards parents, in later life at least, must be looked on as predominantly social or even political in character—as instances in fact of the universal obligation we all have towards contemporaries in need—rather than as generational."[78] The younger (working) generation's responsibilities to their (retired) elders is similarly based on a contract that is political, not demographic, in nature.

Justifying Social Security's modus operandi in political terms, alas, offers no firmer basis for confidence than does invoking the image of a covenant or taking refuge in the murkiness of the idea of generation. Paradoxically, as we have become more and more

concerned with our individual rights and the possibilities of distributive justice, we have been less inclined to talk about what we
owe one another as members of a democracy: "Our sense of citizenship, of social warmth and a shared fate, has become thin
gruel."[79] In part, this reflects the loss of a common vocabulary with
which to discuss the nature and meaning of such basic elements
of a polity as rights, justice, virtue, and responsibility. The incom-
mensurability of the terms we use, in turn, results from the multi-
fariousness of meanings that we have inherited from western civilization—fragments of thoughts, cliches, and epigrams that have
lost some of their richness because they have been divorced from
the milieu in which they once imposed a sense of collective purpose. Now they must vie for support in the faddish marketplace of
ideas, in a culture that lacks both the inclination to nurture among
its citizens an appreciation for the noblest of political principles and
an ability to teach the body politic how to make discriminating
choices about where the republic is headed: "In any society where
government does not express or represent the moral community
of the citizens, but is instead a set of institutional arrangements for
imposing a bureaucratised unity on a society which lacks genuine
moral consensus, the nature of political obligation becomes systematically unclear."[80] If we truly lack a clear sense of mutual responsibility, then we can debate but never really quite know what
guidance we can derive from the ethical foundations that presumably are embedded in our country's political fabric.

It appears, then, that we the elders of the twenty-first century
must hang our hopes for getting Social Security when we reach
sixty-five (or sixty-seven or whatever the "normal" retirement age
is then) on one of two hooks, to use Laslett's metaphor. We can
assume that the dynamics of bureaucratic inertia will continue to
fuel the pay-as-you-go system of contributions and benefits indefinitely. Or we can pin our confidence on faith in the American
system. Is it possible that I have painted too grim a picture? Does
a third option exist?

By way of conclusion, let me address this last question by re-
casting the evidence presented in this essay in a different manner.
Consider, for the moment, simply the definitions of risk, rights,
and responsibility used by the architects of Social Security and by
those charged with monitoring its operations and ensuring that it
can meet its future obligations and objectives. It becomes quickly
apparent that there has been very little change in the basic stance

taken by Social Security policymakers over time. Social Security's creators and protectors have consistently defined risk in narrow terms. Furthermore, they have continually reiterated that the rights beneficiaries could claim under Social Security were not contractual. This meant, among other things, that current benefits could be altered in light of changing economic conditions, Congressional votes, and judicial wisdom. And this, from the policymaker's view, was how the system *should* operate, because social insurance embodied a commitment to responsibility that demonstrably could advance the well-being of society as a whole.

Yet when we put the bureaucrats' definitions of risks, rights, and responsibility into a broader perspective—that is, when we consider how changes in American society and culture have affected the meanings of these three terms—a different picture emerges. When times were good, when the economy was booming and public confidence in government was high, there was less concern about the limits to broadening rights and expanding benefits, and little critical attention was paid to the meaning of mutual responsibility. Now, after a decade of serious economic dislocation, political upheaval, and social unrest, despair and dubiety are rampant. We are less confident than before about where we stand and where we are headed.

We can learn two lessons from our past experiences that might influence present choices and future options. First, we should take the bureaucrats' definitions as the basis for our future discussions: they constitute a reasonable and consistent starting point for discussions. The 1983 amendments to the Social Security Act, after all, basically reaffirmed the status quo. Indeed, policymakers took special pains to emphasize the soundness of the structural and normative foundations that had long girded the system. Thus in presenting its findings to the President and Congress on January 20, 1983, the National Commission on Social Security Reform declared as its first recommendation:

> The members of the National Commission believe that the Congress, in its deliberations on financing proposals, should not alter the fundamental structure of the Social Security program or undermine its fundamental principles. The National Commission considered, but rejected, proposals to make the Social Security program a voluntary one, or to transform it into a program under which benefits are a product exclusively of the contributions paid, or to change it to a program under

which benefits are conditioned on the showing of financial need.[81]

That such a recommendation was unanimously endorsed, at a time when various experts and critics were urging that Social Security be converted into a strict annuity program or welfare scheme, underscores the depth of support for maintaining Social Security in its present form as far as practicable. This theme was reiterated in both House and Senate debates. Hence it would not be too far-fetched, once the "crisis mentality" that made the eleventh-hour compromise over the financing problems of Old Age Survivors Insurance such great theater has abated, to see these reforms as yet another development in the larger process of the politics of incrementalism. Whatever the system becomes, it will be no less than it already is. But this realization quickly leads us to a second point.

Even if we believe that the rationale articulated by the first generation of Social Security's policymakers should remain the cornerstone of all future initiatives, we must acknowledge that major changes nonetheless are inevitable. Social Security turned fifty in 1985. The society that has sustained its evolution continues to undergo profound transformations. Consequently, we must be ready to amend the normative underpinnings of America's social insurance program if it is to meet the challenges and opportunities of an aging population. In this regard, the words of Thomas Jefferson, invoked during congressional debate over the 1983 Social Security amendments, are illuminating:

Some men look at constitutions with sanctimonious reverence, and deem them like the ark of the covenant, too sacred to be touched. They ascribe to the men of the preceding age a wisdom more than human, and suppose what they did to be beyond amendment. I knew that age well. . . . It was very like the present; and forty years of experience in government is worth a century of bookreading; and this they would say themselves, were they to rise from the dead. . . . Laws and institutions must go hand in hand with the progress of the human mind. As that becomes more developed, more enlightened, as new discoveries are made, new truths disclosed, and manners and opinions change with the change of circumstances, institutions must advance also, and keep pace with the times.[82]

Hence we should reconsider with "civility"[83] what we *want* to mean today by individual rights and mutual responsibility under Social Security, and how we intend to go about achieving that end. A continuing and constructive debate over the meanings of simple words that form the basis of economic well-being in aging America is not only essential; it is unavoidable.

Robert A. Burt

Legal Reform and Aging:
Current Issues, Troubling Trends

Editor's Introduction. With the same moral and psychological
acuity that distinguishes his *Taking Care of Strangers* (1979),
Robert Burt presses us to reconsider the meanings embedded in
recent laws designed to uproot age discrimination. Advocates for
legal rights of the elderly commonly invoke a civil rights paradigm, assuming that the status of the elderly resembles that of a
vulnerable minority. Yet this assumption is of dubious validity
and, as Achenbaum (in the previous chapter) and Cole (in the
next) demonstrate, it redounds largely to the benefit of vigorous,
middle-class old people while masking the needs of the poor and
frail aged.

The civil rights paradigm rests on the seemingly unassailable
American belief that employment decisions based on individual
merit are always and everywhere more just than decisions based
on arbitrary rules for classifying individuals. Discussing the implications of recent age discrimination legislation for academic
institutions, Burt shows that considerable harm and suffering may
result from this belief. He points out that while opponents of mandatory retirement argue that it arbitrarily reflects a preference for
youth, their insistence that the elderly be allowed to demonstrate
their continuing productivity reflects the same preference.

This poses the issue of the cultural meanings attached to
frailty and dependency, a central theme of Cole's chapter. The
widespread devaluation—or de-meaning—of frailty and helpless-

ness infuses even the apparently beneficent right-to-die movement. Hence the right to die may be subtly transformed into an
obligation to die before lapsing into an embarrassing and expensive senility. Again and again, Burt forces us to confront the
darker side of our drive to overcome debilitating disease and to
ensure individual autonomy.

T. C.

Our legal system has only recently discovered the problem of aging. This is not to say that age has previously been irrelevant under the law. State and federal statute books are honeycombed with age-based qualifications and restrictions. The Founding Fathers enshrined the practice in the Constitution itself, setting out minimum age qualifications for election to Congress and to the Presidency. This use of age, however, seemingly honors the elderly: the Constitution denotes that a candidate must be old enough to be President; it does not say that a candidate can be too old to be President. And one might suppose that respect for elderly people has reached its highest peak in our time with the election of Ronald Reagan, the oldest man ever to serve as President.

This supposition would be wrong, however, if laws recently enacted and lawsuits recently filed about the status of elderly people are any guide in this matter. To read these laws and lawsuits is to conclude that the elderly suffer serious discriminations that require uprooting by legal force. Thus in 1967 Congress enacted the Age Discrimination in Employment Act which prohibited age-based involuntary retirement prior to sixty-five in most public and private employment; a decade later, Congress increased the minimum age for mandatory retirement to seventy, and at the same time forbade imposition of any involuntary retirement age on most employees of the federal government.[1] Employment discrimination, moreover, has not been the only target of congressional action; in

1975 Congress enacted legislation which proscribed discrimination on the basis of age by any recipient of federal financial assistance.[2] This enactment essentially followed the pattern of earlier civil rights legislation prohibiting discrimination against blacks and women.

Advocates for legal rights of the elderly have repeatedly invoked this civil rights paradigm as the proper way to think about the status of the elderly in American society—to think of them, like blacks, as a vulnerable minority who have repeatedly suffered mistreatment at the hands of a prejudiced majority.[3] These advocates have not been satisfied with the legislative victories in Congress and have brought lawsuits with the object of persuading courts that the elderly should be seen in the same constitutional category as blacks, in order to invalidate various exceptions in the congressional acts I've mentioned which permit age-based discriminations in some circumstances and generally to ban all age-based discriminations in our social life. Thus far the courts have rejected this constitutional claim; but the argument has not yet been definitively rejected and these advocates press on.[4]

These advocates and their clients obviously believe that there is a serious problem of age discrimination in American society. The passage of the congressional acts I've mentioned is even more compelling testimony to the existence of a widespread belief that a problem exists. To say that many people believe a problem exists is not the same thing as saying that a problem does in fact exist. I am not prepared, however, to discount this widespread belief. If so many elderly citizens feel what they regard as the bite of wrongful discrimination—so many that they have successfully mobilized their political resources to demand congressional protection—then I am prepared to take their claims at face value.

I am, nonetheless, troubled. It seems likely to me that the problem of discrimination against the elderly is in fact composed of several different kinds of problems, and that solving one kind of problem may in fact make it more difficult and perhaps even impossible to solve another kind.

I want to begin exploring this proposition by posing a question that I draw from an excellent recent article by Professor Thomas Cole.[5] (See the following chapter.) Professor Cole asks, in effect, "Who *are* the elderly in our society?" Are they vigorous activists who are being excluded from socially constructive pursuits because of prejudicial stereotypes? Or are they frail and vulnerable people who are being excluded from social resources necessary to sustain them in their adversity?

This may seem to pose a false dichotomy. It may seem obvious that some elderly people are vigorous while some are frail, and that an adequate social policy must first of all properly differentiate between the two categories. This indeed is the proclaimed goal of the congressional statutes I've mentioned. The Age Discrimination in Employment Act, for example, does not forbid mandatory retirement of anyone under seventy; it permits forced retirement but only on the basis of a specific showing that the particular individual is no longer fit for the job. The premise of the act therefore is that the question of "who are the elderly" cannot properly be answered on the basis of stereotypes that characterize them all, even presumptively, as vigorous or as frail.

This is a seemingly sensible position. But unfortunately it is not so easy to escape stereotypic thinking. This is the essential point that I draw from Professor Cole's article: that the current reform-minded view of the rights of the elderly—what he calls "the 'enlightened' view of aging"—depends on a social vision of elderly people as predominantly vigorous and active and, moreover, that this upbeat vision tends to cloud the reformers' capacity to see *any* elderly person as in fact frail and needy.

I don't claim—and I don't think Professor Cole claims—that reformist advocates assert that there are no frail elderly people or that there are no problems of social policy for such people regarding provision of financial resources, medical services, residential facilities, nursing home care. The point is more subtle than this; it is a question of emphasis. Of course frail elderly people exist, but the fact of their existence and the further fact that there are no adequate social resources currently available to care for them—these facts tend to be ignored because many reform-minded advocates have concluded that it is more important to focus social attention on the problems of the vigorous elderly who are wrongly labelled as frail. These reformers admit that frail elderly people exist and that social policies should be adopted to meet their needs; but this admission is more an afterthought with the implicit understanding that there are conflicting interests between the frail and the vigorous elderly, and that in such conflicts the interests of the vigorous should prevail.

In making this suggestion, I don't mean to point an accusing finger at any contemporary advocate for the rights of the elderly;

nor do I yet see any clear-cut indication that these conflicts between the two classes of elderly people have become sharply drawn.
I am quite prepared to believe that both the vigorous and the frail
are wrongfully harmed (though obviously in different ways) by
current social practices and that legal redress is required. Indeed,
all of the evidence that I now see suggests that contemporary advocates for the rights of elderly people are outraged at the different
harms being worked on both groups of elderly; these advocates
are strenuously arguing for redress of all these harms. But there
is an unacknowledged potential for conflict between the interests
of these two groups so that, even in the not-so-distant future,
choices must be made to favor some elderly over others. In the
face of this conflict, I also see trends that could readily lead this
society toward preferring the interests of one group (the vigorous
elderly) over the other (the frail elderly) without any explicit admission (and perhaps even without much awareness) that such a
preference was being indulged.

Consider the retirement age issue. When Congress first acted
in 1967 essentially prohibiting mandatory retirement before age
sixty-five, this enactment did not require any obvious or dramatic
shift in the employment practices of most private or public employers. But the 1978 amendment increasing the permissible age
for mandatory retirement to seventy did demand a significant
change. And this change has highlighted the ways in which this
apparent legal protection may not in fact serve the interests of
some elderly people. The amendment clearly does protect the
vigorous elderly—those whose work capacities are undiminished
despite their age and who would be forced to retire by the imposition of an obviously arbitrary age limit of sixty-five. But there is
another group of elderly people who might also be affected, and
adversely affected, by this change. Though it would be an over-
statement to call these people the frail elderly, let me call them the
less-than-vigorous elderly.

The problem created for these people is particularly apparent
(or perhaps it is simply particularly visible to me) in academic institutions. The congressional act does not forbid involuntary retirement before age seventy; it permits such retirements but only on
the basis of an individualized finding that the employee is no longer
adequately fit to perform his or her job. University tenure policies
have generally avoided this kind of late-career review for fitness.
But the new congressional act puts considerable pressure on this
basic tenure principle. If age-based mandatory retirement is, how-

ever, no longer available as a graceful and gradual but guaranteed route for the transition from one generation of scholars to the next, then merit review of older scholars will become mandatory. Under such a regime, for every elderly scholar of great distinction, vitality, and undiminished productivity, there will be some number of scholars whose important work now seems dated, whose bibliography no longer grows at the same pace and quality, and who will thus cap their distinguished careers with a final insult—a "bum's rush," if you will—from their colleagues. The scheme of mandatory age-based retirement protected these less than fully vigorous scholars from this experience.

Moreover, the new prospect of this kind of final parting may infect all tenure deliberations in a particularly insidious way. When I participate in hiring decisions or tenure deliberations about younger faculty, my own objectivity is in some degree protected by the fact that I have no direct personal stake in the outcome. But if I know that these younger colleagues will one day judge my fitness to continue, then this knowledge puts considerable pressure on the objectivity of my own judgment about their merits. In particular, I am likely to worry about their sympathy for my kind of work, about whether they subscribe to the same conceptions of scholarship as I do, in order to defend myself against the prospect that in ten or twenty years they will judge me to be unfashionable and expendable. The practical effect of the congressional prohibition against mandatory retirement thus does not simply protect the vigorous elderly scholar at the expense of the not-so-vigorous. The new policy in effect presses even middle-aged scholars like me to worry about whether and how I should protect myself against the prospect of declining vigor. And it tempts me and my older colleagues to protect ourselves at the obvious and direct expense of younger faculty. The congressional act thus at least raises the prospect of considerable exacerbation of intergenerational conflicts.

I am certainly not the first to see the possibility of these pervasively adverse effects in university settings from this congressional act. Many university representatives foresaw these problems when Congress deliberated the 1978 amendments; they testified against raising the mandatory retirement age and requested, at the least, an exemption for university scholars. This position was of course rejected in the final act. Of the many possible reasons for this rejection, let me speculate about one which seems likely to have played some role at least in influencing members of Congress.

In our society it has become virtually an article of faith that an individualized judgment on the merits is more fair, more consonant with basic principles of justice, than the application of an admittedly arbitrary rule for classifying groups of individuals. When university representatives argued that by undermining the tenure system a regime of individualized judgments regarding retirement might have adverse effects, they were standing against the tide of this powerful social ideal. The universities, that is, seemed to be asking for permission to act unfairly, to judge individuals on the basis of arbitrary categories rather than on their merits.

There is, moreover, a corollary to this idea, and this is what I want to focus on specifically. The corollary is that because judgments on the basis of individual merits are the fairest means of judgment, then no individual can properly protest the application of such an individualized judgment in his or her case. No one, that is, has a *good* reason to fear this kind of judgment, though people of lesser merit obviously have reasons—*bad* reasons, of course—to be fearful. And thus it seems to follow that the good people in academic institutions are prepared to accept the regime of late-career merit judgments and that the bad cling to tenure and arbitrary enforcement of retirement age. The good, that is, are prepared to think of themselves as vigorous, or to aspire to this status and to accept the imposition of negative consequences on themselves and others from declining vitality. Indeed, from this perspective, the rigor of one's willingness to embrace this regime for oneself and others itself becomes a measure of one's vigor, of the degree to which an individual conceives him- or herself in the socially approved mode—as fully vigorous, or likely to be fully vigorous, in old age.

I stress these propositions because they seem to me to illuminate a pervasive characteristic of public policy debate generally about the status of the elderly. The opponents of mandatory retirement age have argued that such arbitrary impositions reflect a prejudiced view of elderly people, a prejudice derived from the excessive "youth worship" of our society. But in their insistence that the elderly be permitted to demonstrate their continuing vitality, the opponents in effect endorse the value premise, the high approbation of youthfulness that—so they charge—had led in the first place to the imposition of negative stereotypes on elderly people. This position has two results: it permits some elderly people to free themselves from the perceived social stigma of having stereotypically elderly characteristics; but at the same time this position accepts and amplifies the negative implications of those stereotypes.

This amplification has several consequences. I suggested earlier that abolition of mandatory retirement age in universities would produce a regime of forced retirement for lack of merit, and that this would impose negative slurs on many people as the culminating mark of their careers. This strikes me as unfortunate for these people at least; and it leads me to ask what important social value is served that requires this imposition of humiliation and suffering on some people and whether this value might be served by some other means that avoids this imposition. This question leads me to wonder about how many vigorous elderly scholars might find adequate protection even in a continued regime of mandatory age retirement because they would continue to publish, their reputations would be known, and a few academic institutions at least would find it in their own interests to hire these scholars who have been retired by their former employers. This happy result would not follow for all truly vigorous scholars; some would undoubtedly find their careers and their finances sadly diminished. But though these people would be hurt by the continuation of the regime of mandatory age-based retirement, other elderly people— the less than vigorous elderly—would be helped.

The central task for this kind of public policy analysis is to calculate and to compare the magnitudes of these conflicting interests. It is certainly not easy to make this comparative calculation and to arrive at some satisfactory resolution. But it seems to me that policy debate today about the legal status of the elderly tends simply to ignore this question of comparative burdens and benefits. The question is ignored because the burdens imposed on one group—the burdens of forced age-based retirement for the vigorous elderly—are defined as wrongful while the burdens of forced retirement for the frail, or the less than vigorous elderly, are defined as a deserved infliction—unfortunate perhaps, but deserved nonetheless. In accepting this pejorative view of frailty in old age, the protectors of the vigorous ignore the possibility that the vigorous elderly are in fact better able to protect themselves than their less vigorous age cohorts, and that the added burdens inflicted on these less vigorous elderly are therefore essentially gratuitous insults, a mirror reflection of general prejudice in this society of the young against the old.

There is another way—an even more troubling way—that

unacknowledged but implicit prejudice against the less than vigorous elderly has unfortunate consequences. The prejudice not only distorts the attitudes of would-be advocates for the elderly; it can also distort the attitudes of elderly people toward themselves, leading them to inflict added suffering on themselves because they implicitly accept the youth-exalting norms and are accordingly prepared to punish themselves for their real and imagined shortcomings in embodying those norms.

I am most concerned about the harmful effects of this paradoxical attitude in an analogous area of legal reform activity—the so-called "right-to-die" or "death-with-dignity" movement. The underlying value premise of this movement is the norm of self-determination. Advocates of the "right to die" quite accurately see that past and current socially sanctioned medical practices deprive patients of the capacity to choose their own fate—to choose, for example, a shorter but pain-free life in familiar surroundings in preference to a prolonged but painful life in a hospital setting. This wrongful medical paternalism treats all patients (whether young or old) as incompetent children, necessarily frail in mind as well as body. The reformers' answer to this problem was to write the principle of "informed consent" into the law and to draw the "right to choose death" as a corollary from this principle.[6]

I agree with the underlying principle and with its corollary. In practice, however, there is an ominous implication in this correlative right to die, an implication that follows from its implicit high valuation of self-determination. The reformers rejected the model of social incompetency that had led others to assume that all patients were too frail to make decisions for themselves (just as, in the context of legal policy toward mandatory age-based retirements, the reformers rejected the assumption that all people older than sixty-five or seventy were too frail for regular employment). But in both contexts the reformers did not simply reject the incompetency model because it was factually inaccurate; they rejected it because they viewed it as insulting. The reformers thus implicitly accepted the general social attitude that gave higher value to self-determining acts than to choiceless passivity, to people capable of vigorous action than to helpless, frail people.

In the right-to-die context, the endorsement of this social attitude implicitly puts a higher valuation on people who "choose to die" than on people who supposedly "wait passively for death to overtake them." The right, that is, is not simply conceived as a neutral construct, as available for anyone who wants to take ad-

vantage of it. A moralistic overtone accompanies the right, implying that it is better to exercise it than to let it go by default, better
to face death as an active, vigorous, self-determining person than
as a frail, passive victim clinging to life and to the doctors' prescriptions. From this perspective, the legal reform movement for
the right to die does more than free patients from the previous
coercions of physicians; the new right carries its own coercive implication that people are morally obliged to exercise it.[7]

As a matter of formal logic, of course, the right to die need
not imply an obligation to die. But there are a considerable array
of social practices and attitudes that press sick people, and elderly
sick people in particular, toward this conclusion. Consider, for
example, this observation by a physician writing in a recent issue
of the *New England Journal of Medicine:*

> The old, chronically ill, debilitated, or mentally impaired do
> not receive the same level of aggressive medical evaluation
> and treatment as do the young, acutely ill, and mentally nor-
> mal. . . . Many patients are allowed to die by the withhold-
> ing of "all available care." There seems to be, however, a
> general denial of this reality. . . . In medical schools, in
> medical literature, even in conversations between physicians
> it is assumed that all patients (with the possible exception of
> the "terminally ill" who have requested no heroics) receive
> the maximal possible care. [But] . . . the reality is . . .
> grossly different. . . .[8]

Some physicians may be able to obscure this reality in polite
conversation among themselves or with the general public. But
considerable numbers of elderly patients are not fooled; they are
on the receiving end (or, one might say, on the accurately perceiving end) of this reality. Yet rather than protesting this reality
many elderly patients will paradoxically accept it and even actively collaborate with medical personnel in their own mistreatment because these patients share the underlying social norm that
their worth is diminished since they are old and frail. For such
elderly patients, demanding the right to die can serve as a final
affirmation of their allegiance to the social ideal of youthful vigorous activity both by actively choosing to die and by lifting the
burden of their dependency from others who seem (like them)
intolerant of their dependency.

The burdens of adequately caring for frail elderly people extend, of course, beyond directly participating medical personnel.

The headline of a recent news article in the *New York Times* makes the point with trenchant economy; the headline reads "Longer Lives Seen as Threat to Nation's Budget."[9] The article quotes officials of the federal Office of Management and Budget as "warning" that the recent "historically unprecedented" decline in mortality rates among older Americans "will increase the 'already ominous' growth potential in costly programs for the aged." This financial reality points to one of the many sources of intergenerational conflict in our society. An elderly person who shares (or who aspires to share) the social devaluation of the elderly has at least one socially valued route for joining forces with the young in ending the threat to the nation's budget portrayed in the *New York Times* headline, the threat posed by "longer lives."

This is the route by which the right to die becomes transformed into the obligation to die, by which elderly people are persuaded to join as agents in their own social devaluation and, consequently, in their own physical destruction. The irony is that this route is first of all marked out by advocates who claim and believe that their proposed legal reforms will serve the best interests of elderly people and will save them from the harmful effects of social prejudice.

In pointing to this irony, I do not mean to impugn the good faith of these advocates; nor do I mean to oppose the idea that people should have a right of choice regarding death. I mean only to identify ways in which this right readily slides into something more (and more ominously) coercive, and to suggest that this transformation may occur without adequate acknowledgment and without adequate efforts to design countervailing safeguards. This can occur, I believe, because the advocates of the right to die may share (however unwittingly) pejorative social attitudes toward the frail elderly and may accordingly be prepared to legislate as if all elderly people are or should be vigorous, activist, youthful.

This same trend can also be seen regarding the retirement-age question. The congressional act that I discussed earlier purported to provide elderly people with a right to remain employed. But tandem social forces are also pressing to transform this right into an obligation. The primary pressures are financial and intergenerational. Until recently political advocates for the elderly fiercely resisted pressures to raise the minimum retirement age in the federal Social Security program. But that resistance masked the existence of a potential conflict of interest among elderly people themselves.

The lines of conflict here extend beyond the different perspectives of the vigorous and the frail elderly. Class differences also exist that lead higher-status workers to value their continued employment more than their lower status age cohorts for whom work is more like drudgery, more like time reluctantly served until retirement leisure has been earned. There is no necessary logic which will transform the right to resist age-based retirement into the obligation to resist it. But there is a social, a political logic that makes this a likely future outcome because it favors the more socially prized elderly at the expense of other elderly people who are already considerably devalued. Whatever principles may favor this outcome, it would certainly not reflect a public commitment to protect the most vulnerable elderly people from harmful inflictions based on social prejudice against them.

(I should note that this same transformation of a right into an obligation in a way that protects middle-class against lower-class interests has already occurred in an analogous context. Proponents of women's rights successfully pressed in the late 1960s and early '70s for federally subsidized child day care facilities that would permit mothers to enter the work force if they chose. This "right to day care" was promptly transformed for welfare recipient mothers into an obligation to place their children in day care facilities and enter the work force, or else lose their welfare payments.[10])

There is one final issue on the current law reform agenda for the elderly that I find weighted with particularly poignant irony. This issue does not embody any specific substantive question affecting elderly people; it is an issue of process rather than substance. As a general matter, law reform advocates have looked increasingly to judges and to the judicial process for protecting elderly people. This is especially notable in the right-to-die context where law reform advocates are promoting the use of judges and courtroom procedures to decide whether medical treatment should be withheld from incompetent sick people. Judicial process is also held out as the model for protecting the rights of elderly people against age-based termination of employment. And at the highest level of constitutional law generality, advocates for the elderly are asking judges to rule that all age-based discriminations should be forbidden, just as the Warren court proclaimed regarding race discrimination.

In all of these contexts the central claim of law reform advocates is that judges can be better trusted than others—such as physicians, family members, or elected representatives—to protect the interests of elderly people. This was the claim of those who looked to courts to protect the interests of other vulnerable minorities against popular prejudice. But the special irony here is that judges in our society are virtually all elderly people. Indeed, the role of judge is perhaps the clearest expression of an honorific status for elderly people in our society.

Does this fact support the belief that judges are best suited to address problems of "low-status" elderly? Does this mean that elderly judges can be specially trusted to protect their vulnerable cohorts? Or should we expect to find the same conflict among judges that we can see elsewhere among the elderly and in our society generally—the conflict between the vigorous and the frail elderly?

Surely judges are as much caught in this conflict as anyone else. Indeed, I would speculate that federal judges in particular are more caught in this conflict than most people because their clearly extraordinary power and their life tenure stand in such stark contrast to the inevitable prospects for all of us—declining vitality and ultimate death. If this speculation is correct, then how would a judge's special involvement in this question affect his or her judgment?

I can offer no clear-cut answer to this question. But I can offer at least one troubled speculation: that because the rest of society sees judges as the quintessential embodiment of power and vigor in old age, the society implicitly expects judges to speak on behalf of the conventional norm that vigor is good and frailty is bad in old age, and accordingly to reward the vigorous elderly and punish the frail. Judges are not obliged to serve this norm, and I do not think it inevitable as a matter of law or psychology that they will do so. But unless the expectation and the temptation are identified, and unless judges and the rest of us are adequately skeptical of anyone's capacity to step away from this conventional devaluation of frailty in old age, then there is no hope for avoiding increased infliction of suffering on an already much-afflicted group.

For any individual—whether responding to an elderly person as judge, as fellow-citizen, or as family member—avoiding hurtful inflictions ultimately depends on a capacity to accept one's own frailty and acknowledge empathic identifications with the frail elderly. It is easy to describe this imperative but dauntingly difficult to act on it in private or public capacities. I have described these difficulties elsewhere regarding litigation on behalf of retarded people; in that context, recent Supreme Court decisions offer little assurance that a current majority of the justices understand either the social importance of, or the proper judicial role in, cultivating a sense of communal identification with and obligation toward specially vulnerable people among us.[11] It remains to be seen whether this court in other cases, or other public officials in other settings, or citizens in their various communal and individual roles—whether any of us will find adequate empathy for the frail elderly among us and within us.

Thomas R. Cole

The "Enlightened" View of Aging:
Victorian Morality in a New Key

Editor's Introduction. Thomas R. Cole's essay blends history and cultural criticism in an effort to illuminate what he calls the "enlightened" view of aging. This view, seemingly born in the recent attack on ageism and the attempt to emphasize positive aspects of aging, is actually rooted in an historical dynamic whose enduring influence Cole emphasizes. Today, however, the "enlightened" view has become a new ideological orthodoxy—which prompts Cole to "call attention to its conceptual limitations, its existential evasions, and its moral and political dangers."

Along with Sally Gadow, Kathleen Woodward, and David Plath in the second half of this book, Cole believes that mainstream gerontology's empiricist debunking of "myths" of aging is partly misplaced. The problem is not only that negative myths and stereotypes may be false. Literal truth and falsity do not satisfy the human need for meaning, which requires culturally compelling symbolism and mythology. The question is, why are the cultural meanings of old age so unsatisfying today?

According to Cole, the answer lies in the history of bourgeois morality, the dominant value system in the United States since the early nineteenth century. This morality, that of a class committed to limitless accumulation of wealth and health, demands relentless control over one's body and physical energy and views physical decline and disease essentially as failure or sin. Arguing

that the recent attack on ageism retains the essential value commitments of its Victorian forebears, Cole implies that the search
for new meaning in old age will have to grapple more directly with
the limits of bourgeois values.

T.C.

Over the last decade, America has witnessed a formidable effort to eliminate negative stereotypes of and prejudice toward older people. Academic gerontologists, humanists, health professionals, social workers, organized elders, and others have attempted to debunk "myths" of old age and to substitute positive images of aging for negative ones. This movement, which attempts both to redress the social conditions of old age and to reform cultural sensibilities toward aging, has relied heavily on the loose notion of "ageism"—conceived as the systematic stereotyping of and discrimination against older people, analogous to racism and sexism.

In some academic, professional, and government circles, the attack on ageism has so quickly achieved the status of an enlightened prejudice that its limitations have gone unnoticed. Not the least of these limitations is that we know very little about ageism itself—its origins, historical development, social, and cultural functions. Rather than continue to settle for the orthodox critique of ageism, uncritically invoked at the first hint of a negative feeling or idea about old age, it is time to refine our understanding of ageism—to decide whether it is a useful concept at all.

I believe that the contemporary attack on ageism originates historically in the same chorus of cultural values that gave rise to ageism in the first place. Ageism and its critics represent the alternating, dominant voices of an American fugue on the theme of growing old—a fugue in which successive singers have performed virtually the same parts for roughly a hundred and fifty years. As a result, ageism and its critics have much more in common than is generally realized.[1] By placing the contemporary attack on ageism in this historical perspective, I wish to call attention to its conceptual limitations, its existential evasions, its moral and political dangers.

The term "ageism" was originally coined in 1968 by the psychiatrist Robert Butler, who has since emerged as the most influential and prolific opponent of prejudice and age discrimination against the elderly.[2] Butler directed the National Institute on Aging from its inception in 1974 until 1982, when he moved to Mount Sinai Hospital in New York to head a department of geriatrics and adult development. Butler's Pulitzer Prize-winning *Why Survive?* (1975), probably the most widely read exposé of aging in the United States, did much to popularize the notion of ageism.[3] According to Butler, ageism is a "deep and profound prejudice against the elderly," manifested in "stereotypes and myths, outright disdain and dislike, or simply subtle avoidance of contact; discriminatory practices in housing, employment and services of all kinds; epithets, cartoons and jokes."[4] Systematic stereotyping of and discrimination against people simply because they are old, Butler argues, allows society to ignore the condition of those who are old and poor, even as it allows individuals to distance themselves from frightening thoughts of their own aging and death.

Critics of ageism aim their fire primarily at the negativity, futility, fear, and hostility that have pervaded the culture of aging in modern America. Social researchers have documented amply the widespread acceptance of negative stereotypes while striving to demolish them.[5] According to Butler, the very idea of chronological aging itself is a myth, since advancing years bring more individuality and diversity than uniformity. Other discredited myths typify the old person as conservative, unproductive, disengaged, inflexible, senile, serene, poor, sick, or in a nursing home.[6]

The term ageism obviously derives its cultural resonance from recent movements for racial and sexual equality. Unfortunately, we do not yet have the careful, critical scholarship that might justify or illuminate its analogies to racism and sexism.[7] They may be deeply flawed and misleading. At a minimum, however, we must be skeptical of the liberal assumption underlying these analogies— that age is irrelevant, that old people differ from young people only in their chronological age. In age, as in race and sex, the Scylla of prejudice is not far from the Charybdis of denial of human differences—differences that ought to be acknowledged, respected, and cherished.

As a conceptual tool, ageism suffers from the same intellectual parochialism that plagues social gerontology generally. It is neither informed by broader social or psychological theory nor grounded in historical specificity. On the one hand, myths and stereotypes are often treated as if they were scientific hypotheses to be falsified. "Facts" and "reality" are invoked against "myths" and "fancy."[8] This naive empiricism, however, cannot explain why people continue to believe such obviously false stereotypes; nor can it explain why until quite recently so much biomedical and social science research served to reinforce and legitimate negative stereotypes.

On the other hand, many who emphasize the social and cultural "construction" of old age[9] have yet to acknowledge their own participation in an alternative mythology—a mythology that appears to be new but has functioned historically as a bracing counterpoint to the lugubrious melody in the American fugue on growing old. An emerging consensus among health professionals, social workers, and researchers insists on a view that is the mirror opposite of ageism: old people are (or should be) healthy, sexually active, engaged, productive, and self-reliant.[10] At a popular level, the most apt slogan for this mythology, whose spokespersons include Alex Comfort, Hugh Downs, and Maggie Kuhn, might be: "Down With Ageism! Up With Activism!"

In contrast to mainstream gerontology, I do not use the words "myth" and "mythology" to refer to empirically false beliefs. In this essay, "myth" refers to a controlling image and "mythology" to a more or less articulated body of controlling images that a society uses to infuse experience with shared meaning and coherence.[11] (Similarly, stereotypes also express such images, constellations of which are embedded in larger archetypes.) Mythologies (or archetypes or existential paradigms) of aging, therefore, attempt to make sense out of growing old; the key to understanding any particular mythology lies in figuring out why it satisfies (or fails to satisfy) the human quest for meaning in a specific context.

From this perspective, the empiricist debunking of myths of aging is another sign of the widely perceived impoverishment of social meaning in old age. Ironically, mainstream gerontology's reified conception of aging (as a process whose "meaning" amounts to the sum of its empirical parts) intensifies this impoverishment.

And, for reasons I will explore, the currently fashionable activist mythology of aging perpetuates the same failure of meaning.

Ageism and its critics, then, need to be understood in relationship to each other, in light of their common social and cultural history. This history begins with the transition to a middle-class system of values in the northern United States.[12] Before 1800, when most men and women lived in families and communities regulated by religious and social principles of hierarchy, dependency, and reciprocal obligation, acknowledgment of the intractable sorrows and infirmities of age remained culturally acceptable. New England Puritans, for example, constructed a dialectical view of old age— emphasizing *both* the inevitable losses and decline of aging *and* hope for life and redemption. According to the Calvinist view (which persisted in some areas down to the middle of the nineteenth century), old age normally entailed physical, mental, and moral deterioration.[13] Pain and chronic disease were considered part of man's punishment for the sin of Adam. Prolongation of health and usefulness into old age constituted a "distinguishing favor"—a rare exemption from the ills of unrenewed human nature granted by an inscrutable God.[14]

Today this view would be attacked as ageist, negative, or hopeless; but for the orthodox believer it offered an alternative to despair. Physical decay underscored human dependence on God— the real source of hope. Listen to Nathaniel Emmons (1745– 1840) exhorting his parishioners at the turn of the nineteenth century:

> You will soon be old and feel the infirmities, burdens, and accumulated evils of old age, which without piety, may sink you in gloom, despondency, and wretchedness. Can you bear the thought of losing your health, strength, and activity, and becoming blind, or decrepit, or helpless without the supports and consolations of piety?[15]

For Emmons, the last of the great Puritan divines, the pious old were "visible monuments of sovereign grace," revealing the Lord's righteousness, his faithful support and comfort of friends. God's grace did not alter the signs of physical decay; it transformed their meaning. With the tested and refined piety of old age came the strength and courage to face one's condition openly and to fulfill final obligations. At the close of life, suggested one old Massachusetts minister, the aged Christian could "take pleasure in his infirmities, regarding them as kind intimations that 'now is his salvation nearer, than when he believed.' "[16]

Before the late eighteenth century, Anglo-American culture generally prescribed "veneration" as the proper attitude of youth toward age.[17] The ideal of veneration, however, was observed mainly in the breach and did not ensure economic security or respect for the aged per se. (In virtually all societies, economic security and respect depend as much on control over resources and the perceived contributions of old people as on cultural prescriptions.[18]) Yet the prescription of veneration, in a society that believed that the soul developed gradually over time and that generally pictured God as an old man, contained nourishment for the preservation of vital meaning in old age. Veneration and the widespread ideological preference for age and seniority also provided support for the maintenance of patriarchal power and hierarchical social relations.[19]

The ensuing revolt against patriarchy and communalism, therefore, struck hard at old age, a convenient symbol of hierarchical authority. If old age in America had only suffered the usual misfortune of being identified with an old order, the impact might have been short-lived. But old age not only symbolized the old order, it represented a blind spot in the new morality of self-control. The primary virtues of Victorian morality—independence, health, success—required constant control over one's body and physical energies. The decaying body in old age, a constant reminder of the limits of physical self-control, came to signify precisely what bourgeois culture hoped to avoid: dependence, disease, failure, and sin.

The historical key to understanding ageism and its contemporary critics lies here—in the emergence of a society committed to the limitless accumulation of individual health and wealth. The problems currently attributed to ageism originate *not* in negative stereotypes of aging in themselves (these exist in every culture and perform important social functions), but in their new cultural significance and in the ideological and psychological splitting apart of negative and positive aspects of growing old.

To understand these problems, we must look to the emergence of bourgeois values, here referred to as "civilized" or Victorian morality. This system of values arose in the first quarter of the nineteenth century—ushered in by health, sex, and temperance reformers, revivalists, ministers, and educators who espoused

an especially rigid form of moral self-government amidst the decline of hierarchical and communal authority. Coinciding with the
decline of household production, the growth of a market economy,
the cult of "true" womanhood, and a new emphasis on domesticity,
civilized morality relied heavily on female childrearing and voluntary church organizations to instill its ideals of conduct in young
people, especially males, who would soon face the dangers and opportunities of the marketplace.

Civilized morality was the secular value system of the modern bourgeois male, free to pursue the main chance unfettered by
tradition. This ideal required tight inner control over the "passions"
in order to harness the body for work and restrain the excesses of
individual competition. To discipline his desire for material wealth,
calm the persistent anxieties of his lonely struggle for advancement, and anchor his identity, the would-be self-made man was to
follow a strict regimen of industry, self-denial, and restraint.

Observers have long associated rigid sex roles and a repres-
sive style of sexuality with Victorian morality. And scholars have
recently revealed this morality's intimate relationship with the rise
of liberal capitalism.[20] It has not been generally realized, however,
that highly restrictive norms of aging and rigid stereotypes (both
positive and negative) of old age derive from the same cultural
matrix.

The rise of liberal individualism and of a moral code relying
heavily on physical self-control marked the end of early American
culture's ability to hold opposites in creative tension, to accept the
ambiguity, contingency, intractability, and unmanageability of
human life. Initiated by antebellum revivalists,[21] Northern Protestantism's overwhelming commitment to civilized morality deeply
compromised its existential integrity and consequently its approach to aging and death. For nineteenth-century evangelicals, the
purpose of religion was not to glorify God, but to develop virtu-
ous citizens. Post-Calvinist piety elevated the bourgeois virtues of
honesty, sobriety, industry, faithfulness, and thrift (which Jona-
than Edwards had described as secondary or instrumental virtues)
to the status of primary virtues. Transforming piety into moralism,
these evangelicals gradually suppressed the inherent tragedy of
human life by abandoning a central element of Calvinist realism:
respect for what Edwards called "Being in general" and for human
connection with and dependence on a world often indifferent to
personal welfare.[22]

Buoyed by faith and the vision of life as a spiritual journey, early American believers had sought strength and personal growth by *accepting* frailty and decay in old age. Hope and triumph were linked dialectically to tragedy and death. This existential integrity was virtually lost in a liberal culture that found it necessary to separate strength and frailty, growth and decay, hope and death. A society overwhelmingly committed to material progress and the conquest of death abandoned many of the spiritual resources needed to redeem human finitude.

If evangelicals fashioned the spiritual dimension of civilized morality, popular health reformers constructed its physiological rationale and technique. Between 1830 and 1870, the leaders of physiological societies, sexual reform, dietary reform, preventive medicine, hydropathy, phrenology, and the initiation of hygiene and physical education in the schools generated an unprecedented enthusiasm for individual health and medical self-help. Health reform offered a method of anchoring identity and authority in the autonomous individual; self-government could be accomplished through a regimen of ascetic bodily hygiene. As William Alcott summarized a career in religious health reform: "Credulous as everybody is and will be in this matter of health and disease, till they can daily be taught the laws of hygiene, they will lean upon somebody."[23]

Impelled by their perfectionism in physical and spiritual matters, and by their belief in the power of individual will, Victorian moralists dichotomized and rationalized experience in order to control it. Ideological and psychological pressures to master rather than accept old age generated a dualistic vision that retains much of its cultural power (in altered form) today. Rather than acknowledge ambiguity and contingency in aging, Victorians split old age into: sin, decay, and dependence on the one hand; virtue, self-reliance, and health on the other. According to the consensus constructed by revivalists, romantic evangelicals, and popular health reformers between 1830 and 1870, anyone who lived a life of hard work, faith, and self-discipline could preserve health and independence into a ripe old age; only the shiftless, faithless, and promiscuous were doomed to premature death or a miserable old age.

The marriage of health reform and evangelicalism helped replace the view of life as God's mysterious gift with the notion of life as individual property, to be indefinitely defended and extended. While Calvinists had left longevity and death in God's hands, the apostles of civilized morality linked them to individual conduct. Just as salvation became a matter of personal volition, length of life and quality of old age came to hinge on bourgeois self-discipline.[24] Health reformers' most common metaphor referred to the body and its energy as "physical capital." Like other forms of capital, the body needed as much protection as possible from capitalism's boom-bust cycle. Individuals who lived too fast, or squandered their fixed supply of "physical capital," would quickly fall into sickness or bankruptcy. On the other hand, for those who carefully hoarded their energies, the accumulated capital would yield dividends of longevity—the culmination of perfect health.

Health reformers insisted that disease and suffering owed their existence not to God's will but to human transgression. Sin alone—understood as ignorance of or disobedience to God's natural laws—caused physical pain, disease, and infirmity. "Old age, whenever it is wretched, is made so by sin," argued Alcott. "If Methuselah suffered from . . . the infirmities of age, it was his own fault. God, his Creator, never intended it. The very common belief, that old age necessarily brings with it bodily infirmities, besides being a great mistake, reflects dishonor on God."[25]

Throughout much of the nineteenth century the positive pole of this dualism, the myth of healthy self-reliance, remained culturally dominant. Existing levels of poverty in old age did not (as happened in the early twentieth century) cause reformers to question the habit of blaming the poor; nor did chronic disease overwhelm the capacity of sentimentalism to obscure the illusions of civilized old age: that obedience to God's natural laws of health and hygiene would guarantee longevity, healthy old age, and a painless, natural death. By promising to abolish pain and disease, however, civilized morality essentially repressed fear of decay and dependency, thereby assuring their return.

Developments in the late nineteenth century made it clear that these promises could not be kept and unleashed previously repressed fear of hostility toward old age—the negative pole of the dualism. Although this self-made view of health and longevity had always owed more to middle-class wishes than to social and biological reality, the gap between these widened irrevocably after 1870. An emerging scrap heap of older industrial workers (often immigrants), the medical recognition of old age as a clinically distinct period of life, and the early stages of an epidemiologic transition from infectious to degenerative diseases, all drew attention to decay, dependency, and pathology in old age.[26]

No longer a comfortably distant goal, elusively wrapped in

the hazy sentimentality of a Currier and Ives print, old age emerged as the most poignant—and most loathsome—symbol of the decline of bourgeois self-reliance. The image of isolated, dependent, and deteriorating old age haunts popular writing at the turn of the century: old age had come to epitomize the previously unacknowledged though always inexorable barriers to the American dream of limitless accumulation of health and wealth.

Moreover, by the 1870s civilized morality itself was aging. Its original social base—a society composed largely of Anglo-Saxon family farmers, shopkeepers, self-employed artisans, and small businessmen—was giving way to an increasingly complex world of urban immigrant workers, industrial and financial corporations, and a "new" middle class of professionals and white-collar workers.[27] In this context new visions of order and authority, invoking the virtues of interdependence, social cooperation, scientific expertise, and professionalism, reduced the emphasis on individual potency.

Of course, advocates of civilized morality did not surrender without a struggle. At midcentury, Ralph Waldo Emerson was already protesting the depreciation of old age amidst the competitive bustle of urban life: "Seen from the streets and markets and the haunts of pleasure and gain, the estimate of age is low, melancholy and skeptical. Youth is everywhere in place. . . . In short, the [view] in the street is, Old Age is not disgraceful, but immensely disadvantageous." Attacking this "cynical creed . . . of the market," fifty-seven-year-old Emerson replied: "We know the value of experience. Life and art are cumulative."[28]

As late as 1901, Frederick L. Hoffman of Prudential Life Insurance, for whom the relationship between longevity and dividends was more than a metaphor, reiterated the increasingly unrealistic argument that temperance, frugality, and industry were the sole requirements for a comfortable, healthy old age. Hoffman, soon to become embroiled in the struggle against state pensions, claimed that life insurance statistics substantiated the "Art of Living a Hundred Years." "Proof is not wanting," he wrote, "that the man who works has allotted to him a longer share of life than the man who does not work, an idle aristocrat or vagabond and tramp."[29] Twenty years later, G. Stanley Hall summed up the Victorian view of old age at the moment when it no longer commanded popular favor: "A rich old age is . . . the supreme reward of virtue," he wrote in his last monograph, *Senescence*. "Only [for] those [in] whom asceticism and sublimation have

done their perfect work will there come an Indian Summer of
calentures for the higher ideals of life and mind, while those who
fail can never know the true joy of old age."[30]

The defense of civilized morality, however, was no match for
the combined power of scientific professionalism and corporate
capitalism, which perfected the "cynical creed of the market" by
reducing human value to measurable productivity. Beginning with
the neurologist George Miller Beard (known primarily for his
American Nervousness), the scientific study of aging invariably
reinforced the negative pole in the dualism of old age.

Throughout the 1870s, Beard repudiated virtually all the popular health reform ideas about longevity and old age. The "law of
the relation of age to work," he said, revealed a sharp and continuous decline after the age of forty, accompanied by physical,
mental, and moral deterioration. Scientific investigation now described old age as an inevitable casualty in the "great race of life";
medical expertise would provide the appropriate diagnoses and
standards of care.[31] Beard's work foreshadows the progressive
alliance between American medicine and industrial capitalist efficiency. Although his ideas about old age offended contemporaries,
by the turn of the century they would be commonplace (though
not uncontested).

In 1905 William Osler echoed Beard as he gave his valedictory
address to the Johns Hopkins University Medical School. Osler
argued that the great work of the world was accomplished between the ages of twenty-five and forty; and that men above sixty
ought to stop work because they were useless. When Osler jok-
ingly referred to Anthony Trollope's novel about chloroforming
people over age sixty-seven, he could not have anticipated the
public uproar and rash of suicides that followed.[32]

Yet Osler's address correctly registered the drift of corporate
capitalism: an economy and culture committed to wealth and productivity in increasingly large, bureaucratic organizations found
it only rational to exclude the aged. By 1900 scientific assessment
of efficiency and productivity had begun to dominate public evaluation of old age. The demise of the old Protestant vision of life
as a spiritual voyage meant that no one came forward any longer
to defend old age on the grounds that old people had more important business to attend to—for example, meeting final obligations
to God, family, community, and self.[33]

While decline in old age had been ideologically repugnant to
the emerging bourgeoisie of the early nineteenth century, the

reconstructed professional and corporate middle class of the late nineteenth and twentieth centuries found ample reason to acknowledge, if not to exaggerate, the degenerative qualities of age. Often with the best of intentions, academic and helping professionals reinforced and legitimated age discrimination and the separation of older workers from the increasingly rationalized workplace of advanced capitalism. In order to win support for new programs of social insurance, reformers had to break the power of the old Victorian consensus by showing that many old people were truly sick and in need, through no fault of their own. Between 1909 and 1935, social reformers, academics, and helping professionals often stereotyped old people as sick, poor, and unable to support themselves.[34] The myth of healthy self-reliance was replaced by its opposite.

Abraham Epstein, perhaps the most vigorous and persistent advocate of old age security before 1935, epitomized this tendency. In *The Challenge of the Aged* (1928), he attacked the wishful thinking of those "moralists" who argued that modern industry should find a place for the aged. This argument, he claimed, would

> prove as effective as the famous order of King Canute to the tides. . . . Older workers undermine the whole morale of an industrial establishment. Aged and incapacitated employees are considered "drags" upon production. For not only can they not maintain the pace required by modern machines, but with advancing age disabilities multiply and once impairment sets in, the superannuated workers must be eliminated for the good of the business.[35]

Until the late 1960s most gerontological research and practice reinforced this negative pole in the dualism of old age. Unlike the nineteenth-century version, however, this view did not hold old people responsible for their failings. Modern science amply documented the inevitable declines in physiological capacity, mental ability, and overall health that accompanied aging. While civilized morality had insisted that all properly disciplined individuals could attain health and self-reliance in old age, professional science presented a secularized version of Calvinism's view of aging as unrelieved deterioration. In place of piety and divine grace, gerontology offered scientific knowledge and professional expertise as the path to salvation.

The view of aging as a series of problems (whose "solutions" lay in the intervention of trained professionals) dovetailed neatly with social gerontology's explanation of the plight of old age in modern society. According to a vague and sweeping modernization theory,[36] in preindustrial society the extended family assured the security and status of the aged. With the collapse of the extended family and the coming of modern industry, the position of old age deteriorated into what Ernest Burgess called a "roleless role." Although this theory represented little more than scientized nostalgia, it helped legitimate the growth of a professional aging industry by focusing on the isolation and dependency of the aged.

During the middle third of the twentieth century, the aging industry initiated what might be called the "scientific management of old age." In the name of scientific knowledge and professional expertise, it helped ease the old out of the workplace and socialize them to a marginal position by channeling their needs into the consumption of goods and services. The dangers to individual autonomy and existential integrity posed by the growth of the aging industry can be glimpsed in psychologist George Lawton's lecture to a class of old age professionals in 1941: "Best for old people would be real jobs, real family relationships, real functioning in society. But if they cannot be given real lives, they must have proxy ones. Nine million old people today . . . need schools, recreation centers, arts and crafts centers, sheltered work shops, adult playgrounds, marriage brokers. . . ."[37]

This vision of old people as dependent, in need of services, and incapable of leading "real" lives, was enshrined in national policy by the Older Americans Act (1965). Rather than provide direct income maintenance that would allow older people to make independent choices, federal policy followed a strategy of subsidizing service providers. Although this legislation emphasized the need for dignity, social integration, and independence, its implementation fostered the reverse.[38]

In the atmosphere of the Vietnam war and movements for social justice, a new consciousness began crystallizing among organized elders, who were gaining considerable political clout. The movement to reform popular views of old age began among these older people, and their allies in gerontology, advertising, the media, labor, and business.[39] The campaign against ageism, a central part of this movement, has enjoyed considerable success in the last decade. Its accomplishments, which have been important and impressive, need not be recounted here. Rather, by placing it in the perspective of cultural history, we can see its limitations and dangers more clearly.

In my view, the same drive for accumulation of individual health and wealth, the same preoccupation with control of the body that gave rise to ageism in the nineteenth century, now informs the attack on ageism. In repudiating the myths of dependence, decay, and disease, contemporary critics have not transcended the dualism (or the matrix of cultural values that supports it) but essentially have rehabilitated its positive pole. The new form of the old American dualism of aging finds its clearest expression in the current distinction between the "young-old" and the "old-old."[40] The young-old, it is argued, are breaking down negative stereotypes of old age because they are relatively healthy, often well educated and well off, free from responsibilities of work and family, and politically active. Today's champions of the "new" old, in other words, remain bound to the false dichotomies and coercive standards of health that have plagued middle-class views of aging for a hundred and fifty years. Contrary to the hopes of those who foresee the fluidity of "age-irrelevant society," we are witnessing the adjustment of long-established values and myths to new realities without fundamental cultural change.

The revitalization of the positive pole in the dualism of old age has generated a new mythology of older people as healthy, sexually active, engaged, productive, self-reliant. This mythology is politically and ethically dangerous, since it tends to reduce public support for sick and needy old people by masking their existence. In fact, there are two highly unequal classes of older people in America today: the aged poor, who have generally been poor all their lives yet receive a small proportion of government benefits for the elderly; and the middle-class elderly, who receive the bulk of the tremendous increases in social welfare expenditures for old people.[41]

Apart from its class bias and its empirical deficiencies, the attack on ageism perpetuates the existential evasiveness of its Victorian forebears. The currently fashionable positive mythology of old age shows no more tolerance or respect for the intractable vicissitudes of aging than the old negative mythology. While health and self-control were seen previously as virtues reserved for the young and middle-aged, they are now demanded of the old as well. Unable to infuse decay, dependency, and death with moral and spiritual significance, our culture dreams of abolishing biological aging.

At the same time, there is a growing awareness that aging is more than a "problem" which requires a scientific "solution." A broad search for new meaning in old age[42] has begun to pose important questions: What does it mean to be old? What are the virtues of old age? How ought we to behave as we grow older? What are the responsibilities of older people to themselves, their families, their communities, their Gods? Unless we grapple more openly with the profound failure of meaning that currently surrounds the end of life, our most enlightened view of old age will amount to perpetual middle age.

Part Two

Subjectivity: Literature, Imagination, and Frailty

Introduction. Historical, legal, and economic interpretations mark aging as an objective phenomenon, open to general, cultural understanding. But aging is only in part a public phenomenon. It is at heart subjective. It has, like all experience, an objective overlay of social meaning, including scientific theory, economic policy, and political/religious ideology. Beyond these, however—in keeping with them, in spite of them, or indifferent to them—the central meaning of aging is individual, subjective.

The subjective meaning of aging cannot be located by the methods used to understand phenomena objectively. Those methods uncover only evidence of aging. The paradigm is the clinical investigation of an elderly patient, described thus by Prior and Silberstein: "The physician . . . is hunting for his criminal, the disease that makes the patient ill. After the witness (the patient) has told his story in his own way, the medical detective will ask many searching questions. . . . This may include interrogation of family and friends if the patient will not or cannot give a straight story."[1] The medical detective is concerned with the experience of aging as little as the criminal investigator is concerned with understanding the experience of being assaulted. Indeed, in both cases subjectivity is an impediment to the search, a morass of distortions from which few worthwhile clues can be extracted.

In contrast to clinical investigation, understanding the experience of aging requires an approach that is—in a culture com-

mitted to the literal on one hand and to generality on the other—
much more difficult to achieve. It is an approach that invites answers eliptical rather than literal, individual rather than general.
Oliver Sacks says, "The fundamental questions—'How are you?'
and 'What is it *like?*'—can only be answered analogically, allu-
sively, in terms of 'as if' and likeness, by images, similitudes,
models, metaphors, that is, by *evocations.*"[2] This does not require
that the literal, categorical approach be abandoned; it requires
that categories be augmented by allegories, that the question "How
old are you?" be joined with the questions "What is it like for
you?" and "What does it mean to you?" Nor does answering these
questions require the creation of new terminology, taking age in
one hand "and a lump of pure sound in the other . . . so to crush
them together that a brand new word in the end drops out," as
Virginia Woolf said.[3] What is needed is not more precise literal
language but a willingness to ply existing language in evocative
ways. It is, after all, the attempt to find exact means for reducing
experience to terminology that drives us toward the categorical,
even to the numerical. In the spirit of devising more exact terms,
age obviously can be expressed most precisely in numbers, a designation no more void of subjectivity than words so precise that they
lack evocative power. The language needed is not that which will
capture an experience conclusively and efficiently—with a single
word, as a diver spears a fish on the first throw. The terms needed,
says Sacks, are metaphysical—"the terms we use for infinite
things. They are common to colloquial, poetic and philosophical
discourse. . . . 'How are you?', 'How are things?', are metaphysical questions, infinitely simple and infinitely complex."[4] "What is
the meaning of aging?" is such a question when addressed to individuals, for individuals are infinite things. As objects they of
course are not infinite, able to transcend space or time; theirs is
the infinity of the subject, the self, that which transcends fixed
categories to recreate reality and meanings.

Within the categorical perspective that governs gerontology,
the objectivity of science is preferable to the infinity of the subjective. This is due in part to the contemporary view of science as
a categorical (rather than hermeneutical) inquiry, in which subjective meanings are not only irrelevant but subversive. The failure of
gerontology to attend to the subjectivity of aging is thus in part a
function of the way objectivity is construed. But the neglect is due
as well to the prevailing view of subjectivity as the realm of the
incommunicable, the inarticulate, where we can launch only futile

raids "with shabby equipment always deteriorating / In the general mess of imprecision of feeling," in T. S. Eliot's words.[5] The error lies in approaching the subjective with the tools of objectivity, attempting to apprehend it in the nets of prepared formulations. Then indeed it remains elusive, ineffable. It must be allowed to manifest its own forms, though they be—like aging itself—at first unfamiliar and uncanny.

Those forms of expression are especially compelling in literature, where subjectivity is elaborated with greater detail and force than is often evident in "real" life. Characters in fiction can manifest more reality, in effect, than actual persons—more variousness and complexity and thus greater subjectivity. For readers in a culture where objectivity reigns and who therefore have few examples of metaphor in which words clarify experience, literary characters become those examples, the readers' "means of translating what they know into thoughts which they can think," the means of enhancing their own subjectivity.[6] Two authors in the following section, Kathleen Woodward and David Plath, are concerned with literary characters. Woodward and Plath make clear that aging is not only an objective reality but an act of the imagination, its meaning a crafted dialectic of "fact" and "fiction."

Often the most immediate meaning of aging is frailty. Three writers in Part II address this dimension. Christine Cassel analyzes the health professional's view of aging and frailty in relation to the older person's own meaning and to society's general view. From a different perspective, that of neighborhood, Natalie Rosel portrays intersubjectivity as a means of guarding subjectivity against the encroaching finitude. Finally, my essay contrasts alternative ways in which individuals experience and interpret their frailty, whether as tragic and alienating or as opportunity for intensity.

The frailty of age addressed by these authors is a potential loss of freedom at two levels, the personal and the social. At the personal level, the body becomes an object in opposition to the self when a person experiences physical limitations. When those are extreme, a part of the body may lose all connection with subjectivity, Oliver Sacks says, ". . . it was like watching someone else's leg, or a piece of furniture, being moved. My own leg, in this moment, was no longer my own, and no longer part of my body or my self."[7] Frailty at the physical level extends to the social when the body as object becomes the person as object. The experience of medical patients, once again, elucidates this phenomenon: the parallel, as Sacks says, "between the way I regarded the leg, and the way the surgeon regarded me. I regarded the leg as 'a thing', and he, apparently, regarded me as 'a thing.' Thus I was doubly 'thinged.' "[8]

The aged, like the disabled, are doubly "thinged," objects in both a physical and a social sense. The effect on the individual of the body's objectification can be kept within bounds, since the body is only part of a person's reality. But a social identity such as being "old" is an encompassing designation of the individual's entire being. A characterization meant to refer to the whole can be escaped only by the most severe measures: an ageless, timeless self must be posited beside (outside, inside) the old one in order to preserve subjective reality against the force of external meaning. The inexorable logic of total categories, like the power of total institutions, obliterates the individual's freedom of self-definition, negating thereby the essential difference between persons and objects.

The crucial means of opposing the reduction of persons to objects is through an emphasis upon individuality. In different ways the three authors concerned with frailty illustrate that emphasis: Cassel, in relation to medical care; Rosel, in the form of life-structures and friendship; and my essay in interpreting physical limitation. These are only three among the many contexts in which subjectivity can be affirmed, individuality recovered. But from these it is clear that overcoming the objectification of aging entails a reorientation toward both objective and subjective reality—a reorientation requiring a new hermeneutic in which a designation like "old" is rendered eliptical enough to evoke rather than suppress subjective meanings of aging. That hermeneutic will approach aging as an infinite, alive and changing text susceptible of interpretation—an approach not unknown in earlier traditions. According to D. H. Lawrence, "Once a book is fathomed, once it is known, and its meaning is fixed or established, it is dead. A book only lives while it has power to move us, and move us *differently;* so long as we find it *different* every time we read it."[9] The new hermeneutic, then, will be as much an act of the imagination as the text it interprets; it will be as much an expression of subjectivity as the aging whose meaning it seeks.

Sally Gadow

Kathleen Woodward

Reminiscence and the Life Review: Prospects and Retrospects

Editor's Introduction. In the first chapter of this section, Kathleen Woodward examines the crucial element of subjectivity, the individual's relationship to the self. Because much of that relationship already has developed as aging advances, the meaning of aging involves the meaning of the past, of time and memory: she examines portrayals of dementia (Inoue, Roach), life review (Cary, James), and the tape-recorded past (Beckett). Behind each of her analyses looms the question central to the issue of meaning in aging: Is the act of imagination that creates, for example, literary works, the same process whereby the individual makes meaning and sense of aging?

In composing a novel and in reminiscing, the same tension exists between the given and the created, between meanings that are uncovered (by orthodox psychoanalysis, science, tape playback) and meanings that are created through reinterpretation of the given. Moreover, in both fiction and life review the dichotomy between the two types of meaning is dialectical; neither can exist apart from the other, though when the tension between them becomes great, the temptation arises to discount one or the other. Woodward points out that Inoue, confronted with the dark side of his mother's frailty, retreats from his tendency to understand his mother's aging through metaphors offered by the imagination. If metaphor is discounted as a form of meaning, then of course in a conflict between a "fact of life" and a "fact of the imagination," the latter will be defeated. And defeated it must be to avoid madness, as long as the two are considered irreconcilable—as they seem to be in both science and madness. But literature maintains the dialectic. If Inoue's metaphors of buoyant, airy frailty are defeated by the fact of defecation, more complex metaphors can be created. Just as meaning is never merely clinical, so too is it never merely lyrical. The latter may be more pleasing, but both are too narrow to express more than a fragment of the human condition. The solution offered by literature is not to quiet the imagination when confronted with events seemingly intractable to sense, but to create still more elaborate interpretations, wide enough to encompass contradiction yet complex enough to preserve ambiguity. Inoue, after all, like each of the writers Woodward considers, composed an intricate narrative of aging when a simple image would not suffice.

S.G.

These old P.M.'s *are gruesome, but I often find them—*
(Krapp switches off, broods, switches on)—*a help*
before embarking on a new . . . (hesitates) *retro-*
spect.—Samuel Beckett, Krapp's Last Tape[1]

1

How are we to make sense out of the deterioration of a life by
the mysterious, virulent, and relentless attacks of Alzheimer's disease? Or does the very way in which I have framed this question
cancel the desire to invest such an end to life with meaning? Would
it not seem more reasonable to say that the ravages of Alzheimer's
disease testify to the absurdity of the human condition? I suspect
most of us in the twentieth-century industrial West would agree
with the latter formulation. But as the recently published English
translation of Yashusi Inoue's *Chronicle of My Mother* suggests,
our answer is a culture-bound response.

Although the well-known Japanese novelist Inoue does acknowledge that a disease such as Alzheimer's can "make one pessimistic about the purpose of existence," the author's account of his
mother's fifteen years with senile dementia is arresting precisely
because he does *not* dwell on the clinical nature of the disease.[2] In
fact, while he does refer in passing to his mother as "senile," at no
time does he *name* the disease itself. Nor throughout the entire
memoir does he relate any visits to doctors or detail any hospitali-
zations (indeed we are given to understand that there were none).
His story takes place entirely within the intersecting circles of the
Japanese family, and within that protective and intimate social
sphere we witness the son's desire to lend psychological meaning

to the symptoms of her disease and thereby to dignify the end of her life.

From our point of view in the West, the tone of *Chronicle of My Mother* is understated, almost detached, discreetly delicate, yet apparently so straightforward as to be often coolly matter-of-fact. But this disarming quality is accompanied by speculation, by the work of the son's literary imagination. Inoue writes of his mother's life as being under erasure, as if the pencil that had drawn the line of her life from left to right has now reversed itself and is subtracting decade after decade. As his mother's memory falters, she virtually forgets the dominant role her husband had played in her life (and for what reasons the Japanese narrator daringly ponders, wondering if she had not been a victim to his father's demands and thus her forgetting an act of retrospective resistance). His mother's mind comes to rest with her first love, a cousin whom she had grown fond of—tenaciously so, it now appears—at the early age of seven or eight. As she speaks of him, as her mind returns to her childhood, she is transformed, almost miraculously so, her son implies, for at such moments he adopts a stance of hushed respect for her experience:

> As I watched, I could not help being moved. How that young girl must have loved that boy! I thought. For in her worn words and her worn expression was a pathos quite apart from anything attributable to mere age. And in the light laughter that is unique to the aged and the serenity that I saw on these occasions, there was something that told me I should stand back and watch silently. . . . if an emotional love—even just a tiny fragment—has endured throughout a person's life, then one cannot say that life has been entirely wasted.[3]

This passage points to a major theme of the book—the often strange shuttlings in old age between the worlds of childhood and maturity, the unpredictable surfacing of the visage and voice of Inoue's mother as a young girl in her old body. The son—in fashioning for himself a memory of his mother's past, a past he could not have known—sees into the past, not the future, and is comforted by it. At the same time, through emphasizing the continuity of "even just a tiny fragment" of meaning throughout her life, he is retracing the pencil-line of her life which her illness had effaced. He is thus offering himself the consolations of imagined permanence. The narrative is also, of course, an offering to her, his way of affirming that her long life has not been useless, empty, meaningless, "wasted."

Elsewhere in his *Chronicle*, Inoue offers metaphors—for us, rather conventional metaphors—to capture the irritating repetitive quality of his mother's conversation as well as the disturbing discontinuity of her behavior and thus the fragmentation of her self. "The scratched record in Mother's head," he writes, "rarely played the same words for any length of time. For some reason the resident who had inhabited her mind and occupied her complete attention would suddenly depart and a new resident would appear."[4] This repetition is rote, mechanical, lifeless, hence lacking in meaning for him, just as her identity is itinerant and her character shifting. But on the whole Inoue's impulse to make meaning, rather than deduct it, dominates. On balance, he concludes that his mother's life has not been in vain if love has bestowed emotional constancy upon it. Interestingly enough, in her son's eyes, a small "fragment" from her past—her young love for her cousin—has the power to repair his mother, now broken by illness, to restore her to a certain wholeness.

I do not mean to suggest that Inoue is blinded by sentiment to the pathos of his mother's condition. On the contrary he is self-conscious about the limitations of metaphor, as the following passage suggests. Thinking of his mother's flesh shrinking with age, he is reminded of "the other place to go than to its ultimate end."[5] This sober reflection is reinforced by a frightening dream in which he imagines his mother terrified that the wind will carry her away, so weightless is her body. But the language of Inoue's account of the dream harbors more positive meanings of her frail condition. He writes of her body's "strangely buoyant and airy quality," of its "fragile lightness,"[6] phrases that suggest loveliness and liberty. But when he mentions his dream-thoughts to his sister who is responsible for taking care of their mother day in and day out, she bluntly returns him to the reality of everyday life: "Try living with Granny for three days," she retorts. "Then you wouldn't have the luxury of thinking about her frailty."[7] In this way the author qualifies his tendency to grant his mother's life meaning within the metaphors he has constructed for himself, whether based on the recurring cycle of nature or on the psychological continuity of the self.

Even so, the emphasis in Inoue's *Chronicle* is on a literary rendering or interpretation of the disease rather than on clinical description of it as is so often found today in the West. I am thinking of a similar chronicle by an adult child of her mother, also a widow who suffers from Alzheimer's disease. Published in the *New York Times Magazine* in early 1983, the essay, a competent example of the journalistic genre of the feature story, is by the Alzheimer patient's daughter Marion Roach.[8] Unlike Inoue's *Chronicle*, which we may conclude was written primarily for personal reasons, the purpose of Roach's essay is to bring Alzheimer's disease to the attention of the public. The essay is not so much about her mother—or about herself—as it is about the disease, which in the course of the essay is reified. The figure of the mother is the vehicle for the subject of the essay—Alzheimer's disease as an inhuman and inhumane entity.

The writer relates the history of the discovery of the disease, its statistical incidence, and the current state of research on it. She discusses what sort of medical care is available under our national health policy for victims of Alzheimer's and reports on a meeting of an association of the families of the disease. She mentions how her mother's friends, as well as her own, have withdrawn from their lives. She sketches her mother's background and the course her mother's disease took. And she details at some length instances of her mother's forgetfulness and disorientation, from which I quote just two:

> She would forget, for example, that we had a burglar alarm and would set it off regularly. One night she came into my room with a fistful of colored, mangled wires. She had set off the alarm and, not knowing how to shut it off, she had ripped the wires from their connections in the control box.[9]

> Today, my mother can no longer drive a car. She cannot be left alone. Until my sister locked the phone several months ago, she called the operator or friends many times each morning to ask what day it was.[10]

I might pause to observe that both of these incidents are concerned with her mother's relation to technological objects—the burglar alarm, the car, the telephone—that serve to mediate her relationship to the world "outside" which is portrayed as predominantly dangerous, public, institutional, scientific, impersonal. Fittingly, then, Roach's essay is entitled "Another Name for Madness," not a "Chronicle of My Mother." By contrast, Inoue's world in Japan is characterized by the natural landscape, the overlapping private circles of families, and the traditional rituals that enable one to meet death with dignity.

It is abundantly clear that this American daughter has suffered from her mother's ordeal (oddly, perhaps, we do not feel the same sense of anguish and outrage in Inoue's account, a difference I do not think can be explained by the fact that Marion and her sister are the only two family members responsible for their mother's care while Inoue's sisters, not he, took care of his mother on a daily basis). Yet Marion Roach's mind is not oriented toward overtly presenting her mother's experience, or her own, for that matter, in psychological terms. The only place in her essay where she does comment on her relation to her mother is rendered in a short parenthesis: "(I realize now that, despite her actions, I still clung to my parental image of my mother. There were certain things that I thought she would always be able to do)."[11] How different this is from Inoue's account of his experience one evening when his elderly mother disappeared from his home "explaining" that she had lost her infant son:

> I felt a sudden chill. In my mind I saw the road leading to Nagano reflected in the piercing white light of the moon. On one side were paddy fields a level higher than the road, and on the other side were more paddy fields, but that side was terraced and the terraces ended in a ravine. Bathed in the white light of the moon, Mother was walking along this road. She was looking for me, the infant. . . .
>
> An overwhelming urge to go somewhere came over me. In a sense, if Mother was out looking for me, then I, too, must find Mother. I was born in Asahikawa in Hokkaido, lived there for only three months, then was taken by Mother to her family home. If her actions now were based on hallucinations about that period, then I was one, and if I was a year old Mother was twenty-three.
>
> In my mind's eye I conjured up a picture of myself as an infant with my twenty-three-year-old mother on the same road. One picture was permeated by a chilling quality, the other by a certain awesomeness. These two images, however, immediately became juxtaposed and merged. There was I as an infant and there was my twenty-three-year-old mother; there was my sixty-three-year-old self and there was my eighty-five-year-old mother with her aged face. The years

1907 and 1969 came together and the sixty years converged, then diffused in the light of the moon. The chill and the awe also fused and were penetrated by the piercing light of the moon.[12]

These moments, narrated simply, provide us with a remarkable example of what Carolyn Smith has termed "generational time," by which she means the vivid understanding of the interpenetration of the cycles of generation (an Eriksonian formulation, although she does not say so), the ability to imagine those changes we—and others—will undergo as we grow older and then old. "It is in this largest perspective of generational time," Smith believes, "that life comes to have positive meaning," if not a purpose.[13] In his *Chronicle* Inoue sees into the heart of generational time. His description of his experience of simultaneity, of the heartrending fusion of two moments of time into one, suggests what it was for him to be a son to a mother over the long arc of his life. The instant in which he accepts the fact that the roles between the two of them have reversed is truly magical, illuminating and haunting, dark and light, a moment of both dread and wonder. It is also an eloquent rendering of Erikson's poignant theory that each earlier stage of our lives is present in all the later ones.

But we cannot rest easy with this basically reassuring, although assuredly painful, vision of generational time. If Inoue's narrative concludes on a poignant note, Roach's unflinching story gives us another version of generational time. While the former grants a positive meaning to the old woman's last years by an act of the imagination, the latter protests the disease which robs a mother's life of dignity. And if generational time is the ability to imagine ourselves as we grow older, to see ourselves in the image of our parents whom in a sense we are all destined to become (the genetic code is one of the powerful writers of generational time), then Roach must imagine that tragic fate for herself. For this daughter no metaphor—no tiny fragment of emotional constancy—can rescue her mother from the nightmare her life has become. Nor can it rescue herself from her own all too imaginable old age.

Both of these narratives offer us truths in different voices, and I do not want to say that they complement one another or balance one another, providing us with a full picture of how one might figure an old age compromised by a crippling disease. I most certainly do not want to say that Inoue's work with metaphor can redeem his mother's experience with a devastating illness. However, I do want to observe that both this son and this daughter give us interpretations of an old age that is not yet, or may never be, theirs, and that both are working within well-defined genres—the personal diary and the feature story—that circumscribe what they might see or say. Both writers are still in what we might call the middle of their lives—their relative youth still somewhat protected by their still living mothers. Both are necessarily concerned with their own possible futures, and both are unable to inhabit the bodies or minds of their disabled mothers. They are "reporting" what they see and feel, of course, but what they see and feel is in part determined by what they either wish to project onto an incapacitated old age or what they would wish to deny for themselves.

2

I offer this contrast between two recent nonfiction accounts of women suffering from senile dementia to make two points in particular: that meaning is always produced within a specific cultural tradition and historical context, and that we must always be especially heedful of accounts of the *experience* of the elderly produced by a younger generation. I also offer this contrast as prologue to some observations on Robert Butler's "interpretation" (the word is his) of reminiscence in the elderly, which has, as we shall see, some affinities with a literary mode of thought. Theory about psychological development in old age, as well as literature, exists in history. Theory, like literature, is produced at a certain time and in a certain place in response to both external conditions as well as internal desires. Erik Erikson takes care to make this same point in an essay originally presented at a symposium on the biography of innovating ideas organized by *Daedalus* in 1969. He rightly observes that "mental disturbances of epidemiological significance or special fascination highlight a specific aspect of man's nature in conflict with 'the times' and are met with by innovative insights."[14] The classic example is of course Freud's encounter in the late nineteenth century with female hysteria—the symptom of repression of sexuality characteristic of his Victorian era—which led to the discovery of the unconscious. Similarly Erikson points to the development of his theory of the identity crisis from the perspective of his historical moment, a period in American society characterized by aggravated identity confusion, "by all the neurotic or near psychotic symptoms to which a young person is prone on the basis of constitution, early fate, and malignant circumstance."[15] Likewise, Robert Butler's now celebrated formulation of the life review—developed when he was in his mid-thirties and based largely on his clinical experience with severely disturbed elderly patients who refused to acknowledge consciously the fact of their aging and their coming death—was an innovative response to the repression of the idea of aging in the United States and thus the oppression, or suppression, of the elderly themselves. Butler understood that the aged, like blacks and women in the 1960s, constituted the political unconscious of the United States, to borrow the title of Fredric Jameson's book on literature and Marxist social theory.[16]

Butler's theory of the life review, which was published in 1963 in an essay entitled "The Life Review: An Interpretation of Reminiscence in the Aged," is briefly this: impending death triggers an appraisal of the life-long unconscious conflicts that have marked one's life, which may bring about a new and more accurate understanding of those conflicts, allowing one to face death resolutely; the outcome, however, may be one of increased depression rather than serenity or wisdom.[17] He wrote that the life review is "a naturally occurring, universal mental process characterized by the progressive return to consciousness of past experiences, and, particularly, the resurgence of unresolved conflicts; simultaneously, and normally, these revived experiences and conflicts can be surveyed and integrated. Presumably this process is prompted by the realization of approaching dissolution and death, and the inability to maintain one's sense of personal invulnerability."[18]

Within the broad tradition of psychoanalysis, Butler is heir in general to the American tradition of ego psychology and in particular to Erikson's emphasis on human life as a series of psychosocial identity crises as well as Erikson's basically optimistic social conscience. It is thus no mere coincidence that Butler closes his essay with a reference to Erikson's theory of the development of identity as corroboration for his own theory. And if in 1963 Butler was himself working within an Eriksonian framework, he also perceived the role of his theory as a step in the direction of rescuing the elderly from contempt by American society at large. Psychological theory was to play an important role in social reform, and indeed his work has had just this effect.

Over the last twenty years the notion of the life review has attained the status of a myth which passes for reality. Within our historical moment the concept itself has been a necessary fiction that has achieved its mission of rescuing reminiscence from disdain. Butler honored reminiscence by placing it within the framework of normative psychological development. The life review has in great part created the ethical climate of our time in relation to the elderly and has since been absorbed into it. But its optimistic thrust has dominated, as we see, for example, in a recent article in *Nursing*.[19] Here the life review is cleansed of its potentially disturbing outcomes, which Butler was always quick to acknowledge. "This therapy," explains the author, who is a nurse, "helps the patient maintain his self esteem, reaffirm his sense of identity, reduce his feelings of loss and isolation, and emphasize the positive aspects of his life."[20] She is not talking of "analytic interpretation," she insists, rather, about "listening supportively and promoting the patient's own self-expression."[21] The endings are to be only happy ones.

Yet we should also realize that at bottom Butler's emphasis is ultimately positive rather than negative, and by this I do not mean only that he invokes attributes of wisdom (candor, serenity, resolution) in his characterization of a possible outcome of the life review. He stresses the meaning of *life*, not *death*, even as he hypothesizes that death is the trigger of the life review.

If we locate Butler's theory within the broad framework of the psychoanalytic tradition and point to its genuinely innovative role in our historic moment, we can also point to some of its ties to the Western literary tradition. In the twentieth century in particular, Western literary culture has been given shape by the consciousness of death, if I may be permitted a generalization of sweeping proportions. Indeed death has been understood as the source of all narration. Like Butler, the distinguished twentieth-century literary critic Walter Benjamin claims much—perhaps even more ideally than Butler—for those final years or days when one is threatened by death. Benjamin wrote in an essay on the storyteller which foreshadows Butler's own essay on the life review that the "unforgettable emerges" in the imminence of death: "not only a man's knowledge or wisdom, but above all his real life—and this is the stuff that stories are made of—first assume transmissible form at the moment of his death."[22] Like Benjamin, Butler argues that a person's knowledge of his "real life," or his rejection of that wisdom, issues at precisely that time when personal death is near. And although Butler does not go so far as to say that one's story is only then given shape or "transmissible form," clearly his very sensibility could be described as "narrative," as the following quotation from "The Life Review" reveals: "The nature of the forces shaping life, the effects of life events, the fate of neuroses and character disorders, the denouement of character itself may be studied in the older person."[23] For Butler, the life review takes the shape of a narrative whose denouement is the final unraveling of the plot and the explanation of the secrets involved in the events of one's life. His notion of plot is Aristotelian; that is, it is the initiation of an action, which for Butler necessarily possesses "wholeness" (it has a beginning, middle, and end), and thus unity.

Butler is sensitive to literature's role in making meanings, and his own literary world is richly eclectic. His essay on the life review is replete with allusions to the Western literary tradition, twentieth-century work in particular. He opens his essay with epigraphs from Aristotle, Cowper, and Maugham. He alludes to novels by Joyce Cary, Henry James, and Georges Simenon, to work by the poet Adah I. Menken and the memoirs of Supreme Court Justice Felix Frankfurter, to Ingmar Bergman's film *Wild Strawberries* and Samuel Beckett's one-act play, *Krapp's Last Tape*. He also alludes to the Biblical tradition (the story of Lot), and to Greek mythology (the myths of Orpheus and Narcissus) as well as to such relatively modern fairy tales as *Snow White* and *The Arabian Nights*. Yet Butler does not trouble himself with the vexing question of the relationship of works of the imagination—let us call them fictions also—to the laws of human behavior. Although his notion of the life review is fundamentally psychoanalytic, he does not subscribe to a Freudian theory of narrative. Rather literature serves him unambiguously as evidence for the very existence of the life review. Like Benjamin in his essay on the storyteller, Butler elevates literature to the status of truth in the scientific sense. I of course cannot agree, but rather than pursuing this point here it seems to me more useful to look closely at what the stories of a few of the authors mentioned in Butler's essay tell us about aging.[24] Some twenty years after the publication of "The Life Review" the very literature he invoked can help us examine critically his assumptions and conclusions. What questions about reminiscence and aging can these stories help us raise? What do they suggest to us now about the psychological theory of the life review? In what follows I devote most of my attention to Joyce Cary's novel *To Be a Pilgrim* and then turn briefly to James's "The Beast in the Jungle" and Beckett's *Krapp's Last Tape*.

3

Footfalls echo in the memory
Down the passage which we did not take
Towards the door we never opened
Into the rose-garden.
—T.S. Eliot, Four Quartets

Of these three works, Joyce Cary's *To Be a Pilgrim*, first published in 1942 when Cary was fifty-four, most faithfully dramatizes in fictional form Butler's notion of the life review. At the same time it also departs in a significant way from Butler's description of the life review. Butler refers to Cary's novel as an example of a constructive life review, in which "reconsideration of previous experiences and their meanings occurs, often with concomitant revised or expanded understanding. Such reorganization of past experience may provide a more valid picture, giving new and significant meanings to one's life; it may also prepare one for death, mitigating one's fears."[25] But in the fictional world of *To Be a Pilgrim*, it is not only the psychological process of the life review that allows the main character to accept death with grace but also the events, which the elderly character brings about, that provide his life with resolution, with an appropriate and meaningful conclusion. The plot, we might say, fulfills the wish of the character's lifelong dreams, and thus the literary world of Joyce Cary with its satisfying denouement may have served more as a *model* for Butler's notion of the life review than as evidence of it.

The protagonist of *To Be a Pilgrim*, which is the second novel in a trilogy, is an irritable, often irascible seventy-one-year-old lawyer who suffers from heart trouble and unfulfilled desires (he is laboring under the delusion that he wants to marry his former housekeeper). He is brought back under ostensible duress to the family manor, Tolbrook, where is he cared for by one of his nieces, a doctor. Near the beginning of the novel a marvelous, almost magical scene confirms that the protagonist, Thomas Wilcher, does indeed know that he is very near death. Yet he refuses to acknowledge this fact to the younger generation. He is, we can conclude, not yet ready to relinquish a measure of control over his life.

One winter day his niece Ann remarks thoughtfully, "To-day is like the picture in the back passage, isn't it—with the old squire and the little girl."[26] She is referring to the quality of the weather. For her the glinted, snowy landscape outside mirrors the landscape of the steel engraving, and life is for that instant lovely, like the work of art. But for her uncle, who even as a child believed it is rather *art* that should be faithful to *reality,* the hard truth revealed by the engraving is his coming death. He first thinks:

> It was a January afternoon, with a sprinkle of snow, and the grey fields, the silver sky, the cottages seen at a distance through the fine lines of the branches, certainly made a scene just like the engraving. And for a moment, as often at such unexpected strokes of imagination, I did feel like the old man in the picture, whose hat and cape coat, wellingtons and stick, I had often examined as a child, climbing upon a chair to discover, with my short-sighted eyes, whether the stick made real holes in the snow, and whether the artist had put in all the footprints.[27]

He cannot bear, however, the reality of this mirror image of his aging self, contained all the while in his childhood but never foreseen, and therefore he rejects the truth of what he has unquestionably understood, preferring willfully to misinterpret his niece's motivations, thinking maliciously to himself that she is trying to deprive him of life. "I don't think this afternoon is at all like a picture," he retorts brusquely.[28] By denying that he belongs to the past, he symbolically refuses to yield his capacity to act, and as we shall see, this will work to his advantage. At the same time, however, by flatly contradicting his niece, even when in his heart he agrees with her, Wilcher dismisses her warm invitation to enter into an intimate conversation, into agreement rather than opposition. It is this double denial that moves the plot of *To Be a Pilgrim* toward its resolution.

Taking Butler's cue, we ask: what conflict has characterized the life of this man who refers to himself in the course of his narrative as a "life-battered gnome"? What past experiences does he reconsider, perceiving them now in a new light? Of many, I will mention here only two, both of which have to do with the deaths of close relatives. Significantly, the difference between the ways he reflects on these two deaths is the difference between those statements about the human condition which we might call "wise" and those which yield knowledge specific to the life of an individual, allowing the reorganization of experience in a meaningful way. The first episode involves the death of Wilcher's father after his third stroke. Remembering the final hours of his father's life with the new pain brought on by his own advanced years, the son thinks:

I tried to soothe the old man, but I could not do so. His excitement grew worse, and I had to send for the doctor, who gave him an injection. I looked upon that operation with calmness. But now, when I remember my father's eyes, as he watched the syringe brought towards his helpless body, I feel such a pang of grief that my own heart knows the pain of death. For I know what he was saying to himself, "Now they are putting me to sleep, because I want to tell them this thing, which only I can tell. Only a dying man, upon his death bed, can know it. And because they do not know it, they don't know its importance, they don't want to hear it. And they will keep me asleep till I die."

At the first prick of the needle my father struggled again. Or rather, not he struggled, but something within him violently strove to overcome the weight and barriers of his dead flesh. Then quickly the morphia took effect. And during the night he died. Without knowledge of the agonies which life can bring, and of this last-long agony in the presence of death, I could not understand the look on his face, and in his eyes. Only the old know enough to console the old; and then all their friends are dead.[29]

Just as we speak of anticipatory grief, we may speak of retrospective empathy, as this fine passage from *To Be A Pilgrim* suggests. In the presence of his father's death, Wilcher could not recognize the meaning of death. As T. S. Eliot wrote in "The Dry Salvages," "We had the experience but missed the meaning." Such meaning as Cary speaks to in this passage about the death of the father occurs only in absence, as Eliot so well understood:

. . . the past experience revived in the meaning.
It is not the experience of one life only
But of many generations. . . .[30]

What was Wilcher's father trying to say? His son did not know then, and he does not know now. But what he believed to be the mark of his father's success is a key to understanding his *own* desires. The son says to the father, who cannot speak: "But you have pulled the property together. Tolbrook is saved for the family."[31] Pulling the property together emerges as a major theme in the son's life except that his gift to posterity—and to himself— is the converse: he will save the family for Tolbrook. The resolution will be not of one life only but of many generations.

I want here to distinguish between the character's distressing

insight into the awful solitariness of the aged, an understanding
that comes only when he himself is old and *only as a result of his
being old* (and near death), and his insight into his treatment of
another major figure in his life which issues from deeper, if unconscious, psychological work. In the first case, we learn these
general truths about life and death. In the latter, we learn about the
character himself, what motivated his life. Thinking back on his
family's insensitive behavior toward Amy, the sister-in-law whom
he and the rest of the family belittled yet depended on, Wilcher
only now realizes, he says, the extent of the family's cruelty to her,
and he asks her forgiveness, though she has been long dead. Such
acute remorse in retrospect is of course quite common, and we are
not surprised by his silent and belated confession. But we may very
well be surprised to learn that later that night Wilcher dozily
dreams of the young, exuberant, and plumply succulent Amy only
to recall that sometime before she married his brother he had once
thought to himself that he should like to marry her. We see that
concealed beneath his deathbed atonement for his callous disregard is an assertion of unfulfilled desire. This important memory,
which we may assume has long lain hidden, reveals a basic pattern
to his life. It has been Wilcher's temperament to resist what he
desires rather than actively to pursue it. He has always denied
himself what he desired, and he has not yet found a way to work
creatively within the terms of his resistances. He has structured his
life so that the objects of his erotic desire are essentially forbidden
to him. Whom did he love most passionately? His strong-willed
sister Lucy. He also loved his sister-in-law Amy and was attracted
to his other brother's mistress, whom he in fact refused to marry
when it was possible for him to do so. He has also harbored the
delusion that he wished to marry his former housekeeper who, his
family is quick to point out, is not only a petty thief but also much
younger than he and of a lower social class.

We may go further and generalize that Wilcher has consistently pulled back from the experience of any strong feelings,
whether erotic, religious, sentimental, or aesthetic, as the following recollection suggests. As a child he adored the landscape of
Tolbrook, and in particular the great lime whose "delicate branches
. . . had stood before my bedroom window and the nursery win-
dows on the same floor, for all my life."[32] This tree, one of his
earliest companions, was an enduring and stabilizing presence
throughout his life. But he felt he had to resist the powerful feelings it awakened in him. "Only to stand beneath the lime was such

a delight to me that often I turned aside to avoid that strong feeling," he admits to himself. "Especially in summer, when the tree was in flower, pouring out that sweet scent which seemed to float on the falling light like pollen dust on the moor waterfalls, and every crevice was full of sailing bees; I shrank from an excitement so overwhelming to my senses."[33]

If his thoughts about Amy reveal the persistent lack in his life—he could never bring himself to marry—Wilcher's reflections on the last time he saw his beloved sister yield the recognition that he should have led his life differently. "And now I think," he muses, "How did Lucy know at twenty-one, even in her whims, what I don't know till now from all my books, that the way to a satisfying life, a good life, is through an act of faith and courage."[34] Given what we now understand about Wilcher, this insight is no mere proverb, no bare banality or maxim, but rather a resolution grounded in his meditation on his past inadequacies.

I say resolution because Wilcher is allowed by his author Joyce Cary to act on that recognition. In this fictional world, in other words, the life review is not merely a frank assessment of whether or not he sees things correctly, that is to say, fairly (in the notebooks Wilcher keeps he draws up what he calls a "balance sheet" about his past and present behavior, but this has virtually nothing to do with the life review). In *To Be a Pilgrim* the life review is concerned with desire. Recognition allows Wilcher to appraise his life from a new perspective, to provide himself with "a more valid picture," to echo Butler's words. But this understanding does not mitigate his fears about death, as Butler implicitly suggests. Instead, his understanding, which I think is at first unconscious and only later conscious, propels him to meaningful action. Only as a result of these *actions*—not just his reminiscences, not just his review of his life—does resolution occur. The creative act at the conclusion of this character's life is the discovery of a way to embrace the life he desired within the terms of his denials. The man who all his life had refused to affirm life finds a way to do so in a way commensurate with his temperament. This resolution lends the novel something of the quality of a fairy tale, and we must not forget that what occurs so easily in this fictional world— a romance—seldom occurs in our everyday lives. It need hardly be added that this is one of the reasons we are drawn to such fictional narratives: they offer fulfillment of our wish that our lives end with a certain poise and balance.

What did Wilcher find especially meaningful to him and how

did he—or rather, how did the novelist—move the plot so as to grant him the satisfactions of meaning? What Wilcher needs in order to feel alive, and thus, paradoxically, to die in peace, are the storms of "family weather," as he puts it.[35] Wilcher treasured his painful struggles with his hot-tempered sister, quarrels that took place for the most part at Tolbrook, the family home. Indeed the family home is the key to meaning for Wilcher. "Family" and "home"—the two needed to be united with him as master of both.

How this union is accomplished in the world of the novel raises an interesting question about the process of the life review that Butler does not address. As we know from Cary's notebooks, he intended *To Be a Pilgrim* to be Proustian, that is, to be concerned with how chance occurrences evoke memories of meaningful experiences in one's life, with the unaccountable surfacing of the ever-elusive past in the present. Among many such examples from Proust's *Remembrance of Things Past* is a brief scene from the final volume *The Past Recaptured*. The middle-aged Marcel, slipping on the flagstones in the courtyard of the Guermantes, experiences precisely the same feeling of happiness he had felt years before in the baptistry of St. Mark in Venice. That moment is for Marcel magical, time suspended in a space in which he feels "indifferent to death."[36] But if in *The Past Recaptured* a past emotion presents itself for no apparent reason, like grace, in *To Be a Pilgrim* we find instead a kind of circular logic within the locus of the family home itself, a kind of reverberation between the structure of past and present events that calls forth meaningful memories. In other words, the structure of relationships and events in the present echoes, or repeats, the structure of relationships and events in the past. Moreover, the very place where meaningful events occurred becomes as important as the events themselves. The family home both contains the memories and is in retrospect their source and substance. One of the most striking aspects of the novel is the way in which the main character literally returns to various spots in the house—to this corridor, that room, this chair—to recapture his past in palpable fashion. But the more interesting question is: does his remembrance of things past allow him insight into the present? Or do present events, which resonate with the past, cause and compel him to reinterpret the past? In the novel, a crisis in the younger generation often repeats a past crisis in his life. Does the present crisis beckon the memory? Or does the memory provide him with the means of understanding the crisis? I think it is a matter of the interpenetration of the past and the present, each acting upon the other. But the critical point is that Wilcher lives still in the thick of things and must confront problems other than the fact of his impending death, however much that may be a catalyst for insight.

As Wilcher walks through the rooms of Tolbrook, he makes his way through the course of his life. Early in the novel, which Cary casts as the notebooks the old Wilcher has begun to keep, he concludes, "Ten years ago I would have told you that my childhood was peaceful and happy. . . . But an old man's memories, like his bones, grow sharp with age and show their true shapes. The peace of the nursery, like all my peace, dissolves like the illusions of my flesh."[37] While this may at first strike us as a wise remark, we would do well to call again upon the caution of T. S. Eliot which will permit us to raise yet another question about Butler's formulation of the life review. Here is Eliot, again from "The Dry Salvages":

> There is, it seems to us,
> At best, only a limited value
> In the knowledge derived from experience.
> The knowledge imposes a pattern, and falsifies,
> For the pattern is new in every moment
> And every moment is a new and shocking
> Valuation of all we have been.[38]

If, to alter somewhat Eliot's phrase, the pattern is new in every *significant* moment (I think it is—we reevaluate our lives constantly), then how can we be sure that we do have "a more valid picture"? Perhaps the final picture is only more valid by virtue of being last. How do we know when and if the life review is ever completed? Perhaps like psychoanalysis itself, it never really is; one does the best one can armed with provisional understanding. Thus perhaps it is only in the fictional world of narrative that we bestow final meaning on our ends. In *To Be a Pilgrim* we find that Wilcher himself revised his late opinion of his childhood: "I saw again," he writes, "the richness that had been given to us; the fortune of those who have had a lively childhood and who have never lost their homes."[39]

Tolbrook, his single possession, has served Wilcher as if it were his child. The very dependence of the estate upon him, the ongoing care it necessitates, has not only called forth his strength but consoled him as well. Thus Cary vividly suggests one way in which meaning can inhere in objects. Wilcher remembers: "In these savage family quarrels of 1913 [his childhood], I would clap on my hat and go out to walk under the trees. And gradually I would feel their presence. I would even stop to touch their bark, as I had seen Amy, after some quarrel with Lucy, take Francie upon her lap. She, too, was unresponsive, but Amy had consolation in her. All the Tolbrook trees . . . were like children to me."[40] But moving as this passage is, Cary believed that meaning ultimately inheres in relations between people, and that the difficult Wilcher who never married and whose parents and two brothers and one sister are all now dead, the Wilcher who continually revises his will, must forge new relationships with his family to bring his life to a meaningful conclusion.

As Cary constructs the novel, it is the elderly Wilcher who brings the daughter of his brother and the son of his sister back to Tolbrook. In a short time they marry, grow attached to the manor, and produce a son. But we must not be misled. Their relationships to each other are difficult and combative, not sentimental. Wilcher is suspicious and resists their care. Yet he treasures their child whom he insists should carry the name of the mother's father. By this action in the plot, we are given to understand that Wilcher can only embrace life at two generations removed. And as we see a repetition in the present of a past crisis, we find the crisis resolved for the better.

Precisely at the moment when the marriage between his niece and nephew is threatened with collapse, with Ann and her son leaving Tolbrook, Wilcher's mind turns to the deathly emptiness of the house after the death of his sister Lucy. "I felt for the first time in its quiet corridors, what I feel now," he confides in his notebooks, "the weight of a deserted and childless home,"[41] and he further reflects: "When living and dead inhabit the same house, then the dead live, and life is increased to that house. In Ann's eyes I saw her father and sometimes in her voice there was the tone of Lucy's courage. In the child's step [his great-nephew], how many children ran along the upper corridor. But when the living go from a house, then the dead are cut off in their death. And death stands in every room, silent and unmeaning."[42]

Having repressed passion all his years, having never extended himself to another generation, Wilcher finally refuses his living death. Dreaming that the family manor has become a coffin—"The wall closed in; the roof came down upon me. . . . The undertakers were screwing down the lid"—he flees the house. "And what was most terrible; all my body, quite apart from me, seemed full of bitterness against me. As if every cell were complaining," he writes.[43] What is his body telling him? He has denied himself extension in a child, and it is the child he misses ("I miss the boy's voice, his bare feet running in the passage, from the bathroom to the nursery"), he says, referring to his little great-nephew Edward who also represents of course the child he once was.[44] He laments the loss of his childhood and wishes it restored.

How does the plot work so as to fulfill his wishes? What is the denouement of *To Be a Pilgrim*? In response to his act of faith and courage in leaving the house, in giving up what he thought he most desired, his niece Ann and nephew Robert "rescue" him and bring him back home. Significantly, the author does not feel it necessary to explain how or why these characters become reconciled. In this fictional world we need no psychological explanation. We need only know that this is what Wilcher desires. He saves himself and the family for Tolbrook, just as they save him. At Tolbrook, he is at once master of a family *and* in the care of a family. Tolbrook, as he had once realized, "fulfills a purpose. It is necessary. It is a complete thing. It is living history." He also concludes that "to be a master of a house, with children; that is high dignity."[45] The narrative closes, then, with an affirmation of the meaning of generational time.

A final observation. It is only when Wilcher has succeeded in achieving—or receiving—what he desires that he faces death with true equanimity. *To Be a Pilgrim*, in other words, concludes as a romance (albeit a bizarre romance for reasons I have not the space to discuss here) rather than as a realistic novel.

Interestingly enough, Henry James's short story "The Beast in the Jungle," the only literary work to which Robert Butler devotes more than passing reference, also concerns a male character whose life is marked by a lack of passion. But if Cary's narrative concludes as romance (it ends with the word "yes"), this short story by James takes the form of a tragedy and is, in Butler's view, an "illustration" of "the terrifying nature of some of the insights accompanying aging."[46] With the latter I agree, but I do not read the story as an example of the life review, as Butler defines it. The narrative structure of the story has more in common with Sophocles' *Oedipus Rex* than with Proust's *Remembrance of Things Past*. Published in 1903, "The Beast in the Jungle" tells us more about those who live out their lives in *prospective* time, in anticipation of things to come that will invest their lives with meaning, than about those now old whose sense of time is *retrospective*, who reminisce about the past and meditate on the meaning their lives have held.

In "The Beast in the Jungle," the life of the main character, John Marcher, is ruled by his secret conviction (shared by only one other person, May Bartram) that "something rare and strange, possibly prodigious and terrible" was sooner or later going to happen to him.[47] Brilliantly structured as a series of scenes of failed understanding that culminate in a final recognition of the catastrophe, the story suggests the profound extent to which a sense of one's future, one's end, may—in this case, cruelly—determine it. Marcher is so blinded by his belief that an apocalyptically meaningful event will occur to him in the future that he is blind to the opportunities, the plenitude—however mundane—of the present. His mode of being is deferral. He is not capable, until too late, of seeing what there is to see—that to love May Bartram deeply would permit him to live his life fully—and thus the moment when it is still not too late is lost forever. Marcher cannot imagine his end, which only May Bartram, who ages into "the picture of a serene and exquisite but impenetrable sphinx, whose head, or indeed all whose person, might have been powdered with silver,"[48] clearly understands: that he is "the man of his time, *the* man, to whom nothing on earth was to have happened."[49]

How does this knowledge come to Marcher? The scene of recognition, set in a cemetery, is prompted not by Marcher's intuition of his impending death (he is now old, but not *that* old), but rather by his vision of what he *could have been in his old age*. He meets his double—a man of middle age haunting the grave of someone he had fiercely loved, just as Marcher visits the grave of May Bartram, the woman he never loved—and recognizes with a shock what was his fate: to have lived without passion, without the desire to possess, to have spent his life passively, in want:

> This face, one grey afternoon when the leaves were thick in the alleys, looked into Marcher's own, at the cemetery, with an expression like the cut of a blade. . . . What had the man *had*, to make him by the loss of it so bleed and yet live?
>
> Something—and this reached him with a pang—that *he*, John Marcher, hadn't; the proof of which was precisely John Marcher's arid end. No passion had ever touched him, for this is what passion meant; he had survived and maundered and pined, but where had been *his* deep ravage?[50]

Thus does James's story remind us that meaning—or meaninglessness—in old age is not conferred upon one's life retrospectively but is created throughout the course of one's life by acts of the mind as well as by the facts of life. The self-fulfilling prophecy of Marcher's vacuous imagination deprives him of life in old age—"The wasting of life is the implication of death," James wrote elsewhere[51]—just as the wish-fulfilling narrative of Cary's novel grants his character Thomas Wilcher life on his deathbed.

Butler sees Samuel Beckett's one-act play, *Krapp's Last Tape*, which was first performed in 1958, also as an illustration of the life review that ends in "the horrible insight just as one is about to die of feeling that one has never lived, or of seeing oneself realistically as in some sense inadequate."[52] One can of course read the drama this way but one can read it further as a critique of ego psychology, even as it retains the reflexes of the old humanism. Given the title of the play and given the age of its sole character (the play takes place on the evening of his sixty-ninth birthday), we may assume that this is the beginning of his end. Krapp has adopted the habit of recording his thoughts and impressions of the past year on the day of his birth. Thus the play is a kind of one-sided confrontation between Krapp at thirty-nine (he plays portions of the tape from that year and from that year only) and Krapp as he is now. In this way *Krapp's Last Tape* affords us the opportunity of making a distinction between calling up the past by turning to a recording of it and returning to the past in the present by way of reminiscence. In addition, Beckett's portrayal of the workings of memory contradict both Proust's notion of involuntary memory as the path to a lost paradise in the past (there is nothing involuntary about memory in *Krapp's Last Tape*) and Freud's theory of repression of significant events (Krapp does not seem to be repressing anything).

On Krapp's thirty-ninth birthday, he related two stories about two lost loves—the death of his mother and his declaration that he and his lover would soon separate—and a third story about his vision into the meaning of his life on the stormy evening of the March equinox. But at age sixty-nine as he rummages through his tapes trying to decide which one to play, reading their notations of what is contained within, most of his jottings convey nothing to him. His mind is a blank. So assured at thirty-nine that he would never forget the meaning of the black ball (an important object intimately associated with his mother's death), thirty years later he is puzzled by just what those words "black ball" refer to. Similarly, the phrase "memorable equinox" means nothing to him; upon reading those words, he shrugs and *"stares blankly front,"* as the stage directions specify.[53] He literally, and figuratively, does not remember these past events. Or, we might better say, he does not possess a past, although he does have recorded versions of it. There is no continuity of the self, only fragments of stories, virtually empty words. "It is an illusion that we were ever alive," as Wallace Stevens wrote at age seventy in his splendid poem "The Rock," "Lived in the houses of mothers, arranged ourselves / By our own motions in a freedom of air."[54] But Krapp is not only perplexed by his lack of relation to his past self; he is also contemptuous of the person he was at thirty-nine, just as at thirty-nine he scorned the person he was in his late twenties. In sum, his life is a disconnected series of repudiations of his former selves. Theoretically, then, "reintegration" or "reorganization" of the personality, to use Butler's terms, are impossible. The only words from his thirty-ninth year that Krapp desires to hear again and again, he also disdains. Three times he returns to the narrative he entitled "Farewell to love," but the return is one of simple repetition. The past is not re-membered in the present. It exists only as a mechanical duplication of words once spoken, and as such the past cannot be redeemed. Thus, to quote again from "The Rock," that meeting appears to resemble:

> An invention, an embrace between one desperate clod
> And another in a fantastic consciousness
> In a queer assertion of humanity.[55]

Unlike the narrative world of *To Be a Pilgrim,* in *Krapp's Last Tape* the past does not seem to be new at every moment. The form Beckett's narrative takes is not that of romance. The play ends with spool five from box three running on in silence.

Yet Krapp is ambivalent about his losses. What does the "rusty" Krapp record this year? The speech is rich, and I can only abbreviate here, but his accounting is bleak. He admits that perhaps all meaning was contained in the lost stories of box three, spool five. During the last year seventeen copies of his book were sold. He wished himself dead. He screwed Fanny, a "bony old ghost of a whore," a couple of times. Yet he does refer to the past once or twice as if with pleasure: "Went to Vespers once, like when I was in short trousers." "Scalded the eyes out of me reading *Effie* again, a page a day, with tears again." These are reminders, references in a minor key, to the religious and cultural traditions of the West. But the happiest moment of the year is his satisfaction in speaking the word *spool*—"Spooool!"[56]

This calls to mind Freud's celebrated anecdote about his little grandson who, throwing out a spool with strings attached, utters *"fort"* (gone) and reels it back with the word *"da"* (here). For Freud this action illustrates the process of adapting to loss, a phenomenon that punctuates and permeates our entire lives. The little boy attempts to master loss of the mother in another medium, to control her presence and absence through the language and physical action of apparent play, to compel her return in the form of a surrogate, a substitute. For every psychic loss, we seek restitution. And although Krapp has not resigned himself entirely to his losses, he has not sought to rebuild his life in their wake. Moreover, what he can retrieve, what he can reel back in, is by and large now meaningless to him. Freud's grandson said *"da"* with gratification; what is "here" for Krapp—that is to say, what is present—is no longer his past. Nothing is present. Absence characterizes his life, and his dismal end. What is lacking is the listener to whom he would relate his story.

With the end of *Krapp's Last Tape*, with Krapp staring motionless before him, alienated from his past self, we are returned to the opening of this essay. The Japanese Inoue affirmed the psychological continuity of the self even in the face of the partial loss of memory, while the American Roach denied it. Beckett's vision of old age, so emblematic of the Western mid-twentieth-century literary imagination, also refuses it. Is it a mere coincidence that three of the examples Butler chose from twentieth-century Western literature portray men who lead dry, passionless lives? These images of aging have permeated this century's cultural consciousness. In a sense they reveal, in another medium, precisely what Butler sensed in our society's treatment of the aged—a shameful relegation of our elderly to the margins of society.

4

"The End," the literary critic Frank Kermode has written, "is a fact of life and a fact of the imagination, working out from the middle, the human crisis."[57] Although I am uncomfortable with his apocalyptic capitalization of the word "end" (more about this in a moment), I do agree that the end of a life—and here this also means an understanding, perhaps even assessment, of a life as a whole—is given shape and value and tone by both the facts of life and the imagination (cultural, historical, personal) by which those facts are perceived and interpreted. How could it be otherwise? The vastly different accounts of Inoue, a Japanese son, and Marion Roach, an American daughter, demonstrate this clearly. So does Butler's use of Western literature—embodiments of our cultural imagination—as an interpretive frame for his clinical work. The literature itself, as we have seen, can in turn help us raise questions about Butler's conclusions even as his conclusions help us to read these works.

Butler, for example, believes that the course of a life can be compared to an Aristotelian plot, that it is characterized by wholeness, a wholeness that may either be embraced or denied at the end of one's life. But much twentieth-century literature, including the work discussed in this essay, suggests that locating the end of a life can itself be problematic. In Cary's *To Be a Pilgrim* the main character reaches different conclusions, as an elderly man, about his life at different points throughout the course of the novel. In "The Beast in the Jungle," the end, we could say, is situated in the middle of Marcher's life. And *Krapp's Last Tape* confirms that not all plots are Aristotelian. Like much postmodern literature, this short play merely comes to an end; it by no means concludes with a denouement. Furthermore, for Butler "integration" of "revived experiences and conflicts" is accomplished by reminiscence. To this, Cary's novel helps us pose an objection. In *To Be a Pilgrim* Wilcher achieves his desires through action in the world as well as through the psychic work of reminiscence; and, significantly, the novel informs us that this integration is attained only through the magical agency of the author's power. Finally, *Krapp's Last Tape* suggests two even more radical questions that can be put to Butler's notion of the life review. Why should integration and reconciliation necessarily be valued or prized? And are our memories necessarily available to us, or to put it differently, is the continuity of the self itself a fiction?

The second part of Kermode's statement—his emphasis on the middle of one's life—also requires pause. Butler's interpretation of reminiscence focusses solely on remembrance of things past in the elderly, reminiscence impelled by the crisis of imminent death. But as I have mentioned already, Butler was a young middle-aged man when he published that essay and was as passionately concerned with the *prospects* of the young and middle-aged who were destined to become old in America as he was with the *retrospects* of the elderly, to use Beckett's perfect word from a passage in *Krapp's Last Tape*. The two stories about older women with which I open this essay are not by the women themselves and are not so much about reminiscence in the elderly as they are, indirectly, stories about the relationship between the late middle-aged son and his elderly mother, the middle-aged daughter and her older mother. In those two stories the emphasis to be sure is on the review of a life, but it is the review of a mother's life by her child seen from twin points of crisis—the end and the middle. Both children are trying to understand the experience of their mothers—for the latter's sake as well as for their own. For the imagination is of course prospective as well as retrospective, as the extraordinary story by James illustrates. And we must remember too that Thomas Wilcher in Cary's novel, Marcher in "The Beast in the Jungle," and Krapp in Beckett's play are all characters given voice—if not voices—by their authors. Wilcher is not telling us his story. Rather Cary is narrating a story in which his character named Wilcher tells us—readers who bring other perspectives—a story. The story is not a single story. It is doubled (if not tripled). It is both prospective and retrospective, prophecy and remembrance. Reminiscence, then, is not just a prerogative of the elderly. And we in the crisis of middle age project our own interests onto our evaluation of the lives of others, onto our review of *their* lives, as children inevitably do with their parents and as readers do with literary characters, thereby constructing another kind of life review and thus certain prospects for ourselves. "p.m.'s," post mortems, may be "gruesome," as Krapp would maintain in his grimly solitary way, but they are, he admits, "a help before embarking on a new . . . (*hesitates*) . . . retrospect."[58] To this we could also add that post mortems—and I include the reading of fiction and drama here—are also helpful before embarking on a new . . . (*hesitates*) . . . prospect.

David W. Plath

The Wizard of Pilgrimage, or What Color Is Our Brick Road?

Editor's Introduction. Imaginative literature is important to an exploration of subjectivity in aging for two reasons. The first, addressed by Kathleen Woodward in the preceding chapter, is the correspondence between the act of imagination involved in the creation of metaphor and the act of sense-giving involved in the creation of personal meaning. The second reason, explored in the following chapter by David Plath, is that literature provides a vast phenomenology of the sometimes startling forms that aging can take. Unlike the nets of objectivity cast over aging to contain its meaning—interviews, surveys, questionnaires—literature enhances rather than reduces the variousness of human experience. It reminds us, if we have forgotten, that no phenomenon as profound as aging can be compressed into categories.

Plath, examining the coming-of-age of Dorothy in *The Wizard of Oz*, defies the very category most closely associated with aging, that of chronological time: the meaning of Dorothy's aging is related not to temporal advance but to moral development. If we object that her "aging" then is only metaphorical (she is after all still a child at the end of the story), Plath like Woodward reminds us that meanings are not mere facts but works of the imagination created in order to make sense of facts. The vitality of Dorothy as a literary image of aging arises not from a disdain for fact and an infatuation with freedom. The vitality derives instead from the dynamic balance between freedom and finitude, subjectivity and its objects, the self and its others. As Plath demonstrates, the pilgrimage of Dorothy through Oz accomplishes her development into a morally complicated, more advanced self precisely through her moments of impasse, her encounters with the baffling others—tin man, lion, wizard, witch. Not the least important of those moments is the encounter with her own, now older self—a self so much older that it is new to her.

S.G.

Wonderland is what we Are.
Oz is what we would hope and like to be.
The distance between raw animal and improved human
can be measured by pegging a line between
Alice's Rabbit Hole and Dorothy's Yellow Brick Road.
—Ray Bradbury[1]

Lyman lived in the midst of a city by the great Illinois prairie, with his wife and their four sons. Their house was small, for even after twenty years of struggle as an author he had won no fame. To support his family and his literary ambitions Lyman was working as editor of a monthly magazine called *Show Window.* This man named Fibber was producing a journal for those who construct window displays: the craftsmen of commercial illusion.

One day the mischief-loving Lyman was carried away by a tornado of inspiration. It changed not only his life, but the lives of millions of people ever since. In the year 1900, L. (for Lyman) Frank Baum went off to become the first Ozmonaut, exploring a new country in the mind. And his first little extraterritorial step that year rivals John Glenn's first little extraterrestrial step sixty years later as a force shaping popular consciousness not only in the United States but in many other parts of the known world today.

The moon, after all, has turned out to be only rocks and grey dust, with no soil fertile enough to grow images of human life. We even talk about using the place as a dump for environmental pollutants; nobody wants to live there. In Oz, by contrast, industrialism has been scaled down to appropriate technology; the cities not only have had a greening but have gone all the way beyond green to emerald. And—according to later reports—in Oz nobody has to grow old.

Lyman was not in the business of drafting a theory of life span development. Ever the clever illusionist, he says that his sole purpose is to provide pleasure; and so he will gladly leave it to the schools to teach people how to live. "Modern education includes morality," he writes in his introduction to *The Wonderful Wizard of Oz;* "therefore the modern child seeks only entertainment in its wonder-tales."[2] Consequently his book only "aspires to be a modernized fairy-tale."

But for all the giddy fantasy that takes place in the land of Oz, Dorothy is propelled there the first time by a very sobering problem: why should anyone want to grow old in dusty, grey Kansas? In order to work her way back home again she has to struggle like a Sartrean character with existential concerns, with issues of being born of human flesh, with the "problem of evil," with a curious array of little people and big people and the meaning that may lie in and behind all of these different states of being.

Eight decades after Baum created them we continue to retell the stories of Dorothy and the Wizard and the other Ozmians. As totemic figurines are for nonliterate tribes, so presumably our film and print figures of Oz are, for us, "good to think." They help us express some of the mystery in human cultivation, in the transformations of the ungrown into the grownup, the making over of raw animal into improved human. Dorothy's journey through Oz has become one of the master *bildungsroman* in our twentieth-century library of popular narratives of growth.

The Wonderful Wizard of Oz was an overnight bestseller, and it continues to be one of the most widely sold and reprinted children's books in the United States. Within months after the book first appeared, a musical comedy based on it had reached the popular stage, there to run for another nine years. The show is said to have set a fashion for other extravaganzas about childhood, such as *Babes in Toyland.*

Some Ozmologists, perhaps having *Gulliver's Travels* in mind, claim that Baum wrote *Wizard* as a disguised satire on the Populist movement of the 1890s.[3] There is a touch of the plausible in this; Baum may have let his left hand have private fun while his right hand was doing the main work on the story. Some of his later Oz books definitely contain episodes mocking suffragettes and other features of the political scene at the time. But it was as "modernized fairy tale," not as satire, that the *Wizard of Oz* ballooned into popularity and remains there.

Whatever Baum's initial motives, he soon found—as do, for example, creators of comic strips or soap operas—that though he had authored the concept he no longer could claim sole authority to define it. Audience demand began to take hold. Baum was able to resist public appeals for another Oz volume for four years while he tried, instead, to peddle other books he was writing. After responding with several more Oz books, he grew so weary of the whole venture that he announced in 1910 (in *Emerald City of Oz*) that earth no longer was in communication with the place. By 1913, however, he was back again with *Patchwork Girl of Oz*, explaining that the Barrier of Silence now could be leaped by the miracle of radio telegraphy. He delivered a fresh Oz volume in time for the Christmas gift-buying season every year from then until he died in 1919.

Oz productions have been a growth industry ever since. Other writers picked up and continued the book series for nearly forty volumes. *The Wonderful Wizard of Oz* has been translated into all Western European languages and several Slavic ones as well as into Chinese, Japanese, and Turkish. Since 1939 the MGM technicolor musical film probably has been the chief vehicle for retelling Dorothy's journey to successive generations of children and their guardians around the globe. Dorothy and Toto very likely are as familiar to people everywhere today as Santa Claus and his reindeer—an earlier American contribution to the modern redefinition of childhood (or to rephrase this: the modern imagery of little people and what must happen in order for them to become big people).

Not surprisingly, then, Oz is a major export nation in the worldwide trade in vernacular symbols for apprehending human events in our era. Recall, by the way of recent example, the brouhaha in August 1983 when a spokesman for the United States Department of Justice told reporters that a certain female staff member was, after all, only a "low-level Munchkin." Or on a more upbeat note, you may remember that the first large-scale search, launched some years ago, for signs of intelligent life elsewhere in the cosmos carried the official title Project Ozma.

Oz has come to be modern mythwork, a great cathedral of symbols that model features of the world and our purposes in it. As often happens, later generations have altered its very architecture as they have used the structure. The life course dimension has been radically redefined. Oz has been assimilated into the heritage of visions of a land where the genetic clocks of aging do not operate; time has slowed almost to a steady state.

Aging is not depicted consistently across the forty-volume sweep of the Oz books. But according to Ozmologist John C. Tower, who combed the entire corpus for ideas about aging, the general view is along these lines: The Wizard grows older at a more or less normal rate but Dorothy remains the ingenue we first met. The indigenous population of Oz, the reader of later volumes is told, is frozen in time, each at the age attained at the moment when the Wizard first arrived. It is hinted that a person could choose to get older, or even appeal to the Wizard to be made younger. But once the Wizard cast the Enchantment over the land, biological *angst* was banished. From then on, according to *The Tin Woodman of Oz*,

> No one in Oz ever died. Those who were old, remained old; those who were young and strong did not change as the years passed by; the children remained children always, and played and romped to their heart's content, while all the babies lived in their cradles and were tenderly cared for and never grew up. So people of Oz stopped counting how old they were in years, for years made no difference in their appearance and could not alter their station.[4]

In this later Oz, then, the sting of meaning has been pulled from aging, and with it the sting of morality. Since years make no difference in one's appearance or station, nobody need feel responsible for them. There is no new station that one must adjust to—or can strive for. In post-Enchantment Oz there is no "problem of biography." Life there has become a perpetual fish-fry, another edition of the implausible Green Pastures.

In contrast, the first Oz book is firmly addressed to dilemmas of plausible human growth. Dorothy's manifest journey takes her through an outland full of off-scale critters, but we can readily interpret her adventures as expressions of an inner pilgrimage. Readers of a Levi-Straussian persuasion could easily reduce the structure of the tale to a set of binary oppositions: logical contraries such as innocence/experience, play/responsibility, death/life, country/city, and so on. Dorothy's task is to mediate each of these contraries, or else accept them as paradoxes, in order to come to terms with the grand enigma posed in the opening scene: Why should anyone want to grow bigger and older if that will mean being like Aunt Em and Uncle Henry—grim victims of developmental burnout, living on a great burnt treeless prairie, who never smiled and "did not know what joy was."[5]

Already Dorothy herself is at risk of becoming as dead-to-life as the people around her. All that holds her back is the incarnate spirit of animal play, her dog Toto. When Toto runs off and Dorothy dashes to retrieve him—chooses life, shall we say?—the two are whisked by tornado to technicolor land. We never learn Dorothy's prehistory, but her life history has begun.

On arrival in Oz, Dorothy finds that the logical contraries have not disappeared but have duplicated. Now she is surrounded by Munchkins, people no bigger in size than she is, "although they were, so far as looks go, many years older,"[6] indeed "about as old as Uncle Henry."[7] The Munchkins thank her for having freed them from the Wicked Witch of the East, who was crushed to death when Dorothy's house fell from the sky. Dorothy is terrified by this attribution of grownup responsibility. She is "an innocent, harmless girl . . . and she had never killed anything in her life."[8]

All Dorothy wants is to go home to Kansas. Un-Edenic as it may be, Kansas is civilized, that is, liberated from the power of witches. The Munchkins, however, know nothing about Kansas; Dorothy will have to find her own way there. All they can suggest is to try the Yellow Brick Road, which will take her to the Great Wizard, who may know something about world geography. The Munchkins also present her with the silver shoes from the feet of the dead witch, shoes that they know to be charmed although the nature of that charm-power is unclear.

In less than a day's walk down the road Dorothy is shedding her innocence and gaining adult-like experience in nurturing others. In rapid succession she extends help to Scarecrow, Tin Man, and Cowardly Lion, offering to take them in train to the Wizard. This curious trio looks very much like aspects of self that Dorothy must bring under more conscious control.

Scarecrow, for example, wears the clothing of a person but is filled with straw. "It must be inconvenient to be made of flesh," he tells Dorothy, "for you must sleep, and eat and drink. However, you have brains, and it is worth a lot of bother to be able to think properly."[9] By contrast he stumbles like a klutz and cannot do his job properly, for even crows have brains enough to see through his humanoid pretense. Scarecrow also suggests that only people with brains are capable of living in a place like Kansas. Woodman and Lion teach her other lessons in psycho-biology. From Woodman she learns the need for heart as well as brains, because "brains do not make one happy."[10] From the Cowardly Lion she learns the need to be king of one's beastly inner ragings; or to be less Freudian about it, the need for regal confidence in one's native talent.

Helping one another, Dorothy and her entourage begin to out-grow their smallnesses. When danger threatens, Scarecrow is able to think out an escape plan; Lion growls boldly at predators; Woodman shows compassion for a trapped field mouse. Woodman and Scarecrow team up to rescue Dorothy when she is overcome by opium fumes in a poppy field. Before long Dorothy is boldly knock-ing on doors and demanding room and board for self and crew, evidencing an assertiveness that would do credit to the Avon Lady.

Dorothy is just as bold when she is admitted to the throne room of the Great Oz, and she answers his thundering questions without flinching. But now the stakes are higher. From ordinary Oz folk she could ask the favor of food and rest that ordinary courtesy extends to the wayfarer. From the Wizard she wants much more: passage back to Kansas. Colorful as the land of Oz may be, she doesn't like it, she tells him. And, she adds in a grownup note of empathy, "I am sure Aunt Em will be worried over my being away so long."[11]

Why should I help you? snorts the Great Oz. Dorothy appeals to adult role-duty: "Because you are strong and I am weak; be-cause you are a Great Wizard and I am only a helpless little girl."[12] Helpless? says Oz; you were strong enough to slay the Witch of the East. Oh, but I didn't mean to kill her, Dorothy replies, it just hap-pened.

The Wizard rejects her claim for protection as an innocent. He evokes, in no uncertain terms, the first law of adult reciprocity: "Help me and I will help you. . . . You have no right to expect me to send you back to Kansas unless you do something for me in return. In this country everyone must pay for everything he gets. If you wish me to use my magic power to send you home again you must do something for me first."[13] Or to translate this into an-other master idiom of nurturance, the Wizard will not play Santa Claus, lavishing his powers on the innocent. The Wizard's motto—to use a vernacular phrase—is that nothing buys you nothing; Santa Claus is dead.

When she hears what she must do, Dorothy weeps. Her part of the bargain is to become a hit-woman; she must kill the wicked

Witch of the West. She must acknowledge her strength, and she must use that strength to slay, must deliberately do what is wrong even though her action may be for the sake of a greater good.

The Wizard imposes the same terms upon her three friends: a favor for a favor. So the team of four sets out from the city, this time without even a road to guide them. There is no road, the Guardian of the Gates tells them, because "no one ever wishes to go that way."[14] One has to overcome innocence in one's own way.

Dorothy and her guileless squad are no match for the wily Witch, however, and soon are made captive. When the Witch sees Dorothy's silver shoes she trembles. She knows (though we and Dorothy still do not) what power they convey: "She happened to look into the child's eyes and saw how simple the soul behind them was. . . . I can still make her my slave, for she does not know how to use her power."[15] Dorothy remains deficient in self-awareness. Or to borrow a phrase from James Agee, she still is successfully disguised to herself as a child.

But not for long. Soon Dorothy is tearing at her self-disguise, making a complex moral choice and carrying out her decision with deviousness. The Witch has been attempting to starve the Lion into submission. In order to save him from this fate, Dorothy waits until the Witch is asleep, steals food from her cupboard, and takes it to him under cover of darkness.

Her altruistic deceit is followed by an incident of selfish deceit. The Witch trips the girl, snatches one of the silver shoes for herself, and then compounds the offense by laughing at Dorothy's anger. In righteous rage Dorothy dumps a pail of water on the Witch, and this causes her to melt into nothingness. Dorothy apologizes at once; she did not know that water will trigger meltdown in witches. She did not intend to kill; her crime is only the lesser one of negligent witchslaughter in self-defense. She had, nevertheless, done wrong. She had left Emerald City with a contract on the Witch, and her actions resulted in the woman's death. And with this self-admission Dorothy moves to a new level of self-assertion.

She displays the command presence of a dowager empress. She barks orders to the Winkies to repair her injured teammates, and musters in the winged monkeys to transport the four of them back to the city. She manipulates social networks like an old pro, calling in a favor from the field mice her team once had rescued. And when the Wizard stalls, refusing to meet her again, Dorothy stands up to him as an equal, threatening to set the simian air corps on him if he goes back on his part of the bargain.

Toto playfully tugs on a curtain, and suddenly the Great Oz is exposed as a petty illusionary. What had appeared to be a fearsome father figure, booming like an angry Jehovah, turns out to be only a little old man with bald head and wrinkled face, begging not to be punished. I am only a circus ventriloquist from Omaha, he says, blown into Oz by chance. The people here believe that I have great powers of enchantment, and that makes them happy. What would be the virtue in exposing my little deceptions?

To win the team's understanding the Wizard gives them a seminar on the tricks of his trade. Oz actually is as grey as Kansas, for example, but he ordered all the Ozmians to wear green eyeglasses, and now they are convinced that their country is emerald all over. Dorothy struggles to remain an ingenue. She reacts with the wounded feelings of any child who has just learned that grownups are not, after all, pure little Boy Scouts. "I think you are a very bad man," she snaps at the Wizard. But he corrects her gently. "Oh, no, my dear; I'm really a very good man; but I'm a very bad wizard, I must admit."[16]

A good man will return a favor, and Dorothy's companions demand their due. The Wizard tries to persuade each of the three that he already has the wished-for quality within him and needs only to act with awareness of it. You don't lack for brains, the Wizard tells Scarecrow: "You are learning something every day. A baby has brains, but it doesn't know much. Experience is the only thing that brings knowledge, and the longer you are on earth the more experience you are sure to get."[17]

But Scarecrow, Woodman, and Lion are Ozmians and do not have Dorothy's potential for living without self-illusion. So the Wizard must fall back upon sideshow routines. To Lion he offers a placebo drink of "courage," to Woodman a stuffed-silk heart. Then, resurrecting puns that must have been dead by the time of Shakespeare, he fills Scarecrow's head with pins and needles (to show that the mind is sharp) and with bran (so it will be brannew).

Dorothy, however, wants no phony reward; she wants a genuine return-trip ticket to Kansas. Oz announces that he has grown tired of the job demands of being Great Wizard and would rather go back to his old line of work with the circus. The two of them set about building a hot-air balloon for the journey home. But before Dorothy can climb aboard, once again she races after the wayward Toto—and the balloon lifts off with the Wizard as its sole passenger. (And that was the last ever seen of him, or so we are told in this first Oz book.)

Now Dorothy has to find a way home by herself, relying on her own experience without even the illusions of paternal guidance. Her research in Emerald City turns up a suggestion that she consult Glinda, the Good Witch of the South, a woman who may know how to safely cross the desert that separates Oz from Kansas.

On the road for the third time, Dorothy and her crew enter a land of living china dolls. These are beautiful creatures but they are small and fragile. They can be mended when harmed, but the cracks of experience are visible ever after. Dorothy would like to take some of them home as souvenirs for Aunt Em. But she is told that when they are removed from their natural habitat they freeze into immobility and can only stand stiffly and look pretty. Able to control her greed—"I would not make you unhappy for all the world!"[18]—she respects the integrity of weaker beings who have to rely upon the self-control of those who are larger and stronger.

With Glinda the team of four, now veterans at the business, easily negotiate an exchange of favors. Glinda arranges for Scarecrow, Woodman, and Lion each to become ruler of a domain in Oz; they encourage Dorothy to stay on, too. But Dorothy's habitat is Kansas, and this time her reasons for returning are other-centered and concrete, not just whimperings of dislike for Oz: "Aunt Em will surely think that something dreadful has happened to me, and that will make her put on mourning; and unless the crops are better this year than they were last year I am sure Uncle Henry cannot afford it."[19]

Glinda reveals to Dorothy the capstone lesson of her pilgrimage, the need to know one's own strengths and to guide them by experience. Your silver shoes have the power to take you wherever you want to go, she tells Dorothy. They will take you home now. They would have taken you home the moment you arrived in Oz—had you but known how to use them.

Now, perhaps, Dorothy can cope with the enigmas of Kansas. Even without souvenir dolls in hand, she can face once more her humorless aunt. For Dorothy has found a female role-model. We are told of Glinda—and it is all we ever know about her—that she is "kind to everyone . . . a beautiful woman, who knows how to keep young in spite of the many years she has lived."[20]

The Oz books are scorned by some critics and banned from some public libraries. They are charged with failing in literary grace and social significance, with offering nothing to edify the minds of children. The official indictment is exemplified in these lines by C. Warren Hollister: "Baum's *Wizard of Oz* doesn't measure up. It appears to have no underlying theme—no unity of conception. Its characterizations seem shallow. Dorothy has no inner problems, doesn't develop, doesn't grow. Oz never really changes. As for plot, it rambles. . . . The style, which has been described, unfairly, as 'sentimental' is, in fact, straightforward, but undistinguished."[21] The charge may hold for some of the later hackwork volumes in the series. But readers who are not literary Hammerheads see no fatal flaws in the early Oz books, and certainly not in the first one. Hearn's recent collection of essays on Oz includes chapters of applause from such twentieth-century masters of fantasy and whimsy as Ray Bradbury, Paul Gallico, James Thurber, and Gore Vidal.

Even a shallow and rambling tale of wizardry might capture attention for a faddish moment. But the story of Dorothy's journey has sustained transmission to several new generations of readers, translation into several foreign languages, and transposition into the idioms of stage and screen. (A new feature film of *The Wizard of Oz* is in production as I write.) So it seems reasonable to assume that Baum's narrative has tapped a pool of widely held popular ideas about the brick road of human life. Just what ideas are in that pool we can only guess from the appeal of the story itself. An analysis of the pool in any empirical detail would require the energies of an international battalion of investigators. I am only suggesting that if the story makes sense—has a unity of conception that is more than a string of emeralds of fantasy—it may be because Dorothy is a believable figure who is struggling to prepare herself for a plausible future.

Baum's introduction to the contrary, *The Wizard of Oz*, as many critics point out, is not even a "fairy tale" at all. Though Oz has diminutive critters in its population none of them is able to cross the great desert and influence *our* world, as do the wee people of European tradition. The story is much more in the heritage of fantastic voyages; Lyman himself remarked later that he had been particularly inspired by *Alice in Wonderland*. Oz is not wonderland but it has a wonderful Wizard, and Dorothy looks a lot like an Americanized Alice, stripped of her dainty dress and upper-class accent. At the same time, Dorothy is not just another stranger in a strange land: she is on her way to the even stranger land of adulthood and is busy assembling a survival kit.

Dorothy's is not a psychological narrative of *personality* development in the usual sense of resolving complexes imposed by infantile traumata. She is not coiled in an identity crisis over who she is or was—we never learn anything about her parentage. She is not riddled with guilt over the sins of her past, but is trying to come to terms with the sins of deception and destruction that she too may have to commit as an adult. The animal vitality she struggles to retain is not that of a Freudian id-beast but of a bouncing terrier who is her All.

Dorothy is on a pilgrimage of sorts, though her quest is not a narrowly spiritual one. She does not reunite with Christ, nor is she granted a personal guardian spirit of the kind sought by Plains Indians in their coming-of-age vision quests across the prairies before she arrived there. Her tasks involve such matters as learning the rules of adult reciprocity and becoming self-possessed of the vessels of power already attached to her person. The implication is that if she can continue to use her powers rightly she may be able to move through adulthood much as she has moved through Oz, "gently wreaking order and distributing love."[22]

The message of *The Wizard of Oz* is coded into polyvocalic symbols open to many different readings. But one of the morals in Lyman's legacy appears to be the idea that becoming a bigger person is a mixed blessing in which the emeralds are strewn in the dust.

Adults in Kansas are able to operate in accord with the "useful tyranny of the normal" (to steal a phrase from Edward Sapir). They have learned a reality principle, and it has freed them from the bewitchments that hold the infra-humans of Oz in thrall. But in ridding the world of magic they put the torch not only to the impossible dreams but to the possible ones as well. And the conflagration has left them desiccated. Perhaps—just perhaps—we can escape this Kansas Syndrome of core melt-down. Perhaps we can become Glindas and not just low-level Munchkins, *if* we can keep a light on in that show window that displays the improved humans we would hope and like to be.

It takes brains, heart, and courage to stay that course, especially when there no longer is a road to follow because nobody in Oz ever wants to go that way. Dorothy melds this trio of qualities with a solid sense of balance and proportion. No patsy to culture shock, no Pollyanna when made prisoner by witchery, she is energized rather than enervated by the tension between the way things are and the way they might become—an Unsinkable Molly Brown as staged by Junior Achievement.

Dorothy can appeal to the better self in others, such as talking scarecrows and lions manqué, without losing sight of who they actually are. She is no Don Quixote compulsively demanding that Aldonza play only the role that his private script casts for a Dulcinea. Dorothy also can discard the hypothesis of childish weakness and adult omnipotence, slay her innocent past, and agree that life is not a free lunch, without falling into dismay. (Since she has no visible father she can't learn as most American children do that Santa Claus is only one's father in disguise.)

With that, she can begin to shoulder the burdens of judgment and power. She realizes that only she can unscramble her own ambiguities of choice, aware that the power to choose is the power to destroy, that any choice is likely to bring harm upon somebody, and that reasoned choice thus should be tempered with compassion. There is no Throne Room where she can go to ask for absolute guidance, no cosmic center of noncontingent Good. Bad wizardry, for example, ought to be exposed as a matter of honesty—but then the Ozmians would lose all joy in living. A souvenir doll might at last bring a smile to Aunt Em's face—but the china-person taken from its habitat would suffer catatonia.

Recognizing these things, Dorothy is ready to return to her own habitat. She has not been indoctrinated into some new code of morality. Rather she has learned to hold a critical purchase upon morality. She can entertain two (or more) contradictory notions of what might be good to do, without being the slave of either. When she turns the power of both shoes toward the same direction she will do so by sophisticated judgment. She has, so to speak, signed the blank check of responsibility for whatever good or evil her judgments may produce in the years to come. Her palms are truly open to experience, no longer gripped tightly around the security blanket of childhood.

What is it that Dorothy experiences once she is back home in her own habitat? An American reader could envision her growing into the kind of Pioneer Woman we celebrate with statues in city parks all across the prairie states. Attebery, taking a more literary approach,[23] projects her into the strong, bronzed protagonist of Willa Cather's novel *My Ántonia*. De-parochialized, she would become the sturdy peasant mother sketched in folk models of adulthood all over the world.

The later Oz books never come to grips with the issue. In his subsequent volumes Baum loaded Dorothy onto a space shuttle between Kansas and Oz as he responded to audience demand for encores of whimsy. Eventually she gave up American citizenship, was naturalized in Oz, and turned into a plastic if not china doll, a sort of ancestral Barbie without Ken. I leave it to a clever deconstructionist to interpret this as a new level of the play of symbolism: merging the Dorothy and Wizard of these later books into a single personage, who actually is Glinda transformed, continuing to age normally while at the same time remaining kindly and young at heart.

Staying within book one, we find that Baum offers a principle for sustaining vitality through the years but not a paradigm of life span change. Viewed through the rangefinders of current developmental theory the story is off target with regard to the crises of growth now predicted as normal. Dorothy apparently was not at home when the identity crisis blew across Kansas, for example, so she skipped that grade. Not even into puberty she already is studying for post-graduate degrees in "becoming one's own person," à la Gould or Levinson, and in "generativity" and "integrity" à la Erikson. At times she mounts the Mesa Verde of middle age, where the climate of meaning is shaped (to use Bernice Neugarten's phrase) by issues of "conscious self-utilization rather than the self-consciousness of youth."[24]

Perhaps this indicates a weakness in our life span models. After all, they are drawn from the study of only a few samples of upper-middle-class urbanites; country girls such as Dorothy may go through a different agenda entirely. Perhaps, on the other hand, we can sustain the theory by addressing it not to Dorothy but to her author instead, and psychologizing *him*. Recall that Lyman was in his forties when he wrote the first Oz book. So Dorothy is not really a child at all; she is only his child-self, his way of venting fears that his powers of illusion may soon fall victim to the prairie dogs of literary desiccation. A more nearly normal author would have been able to get the whole thing out of his system by writing a novel about a man taking a young lover.

The middle aged Lyman, however, was also editor of a journal on how to appeal to mass hopes and fears. Successful popular tales require not only talent with symbols but also market sense, the gift for translating one's private problem into public puzzlement. Baum may have realized that in 1900 he was standing on the hinge of history between two grand notions of life course nightmare in popular consciousness in America (and, if the success of *Wizard* overseas is any measure, in industrial mankind generally.)

The Victorian nightmare—a fear of being orphaned, and so

having to become one's own parent—was becoming passé. On the rise was the modern nightmare—a fear of being bereft as an elder, and so having to become one's own child. Note that Dorothy's parentage is never even mentioned. At issue is a plausible old age foreshadowed by a childless, wizened aunt and uncle. Dorothy does not return home bearing a sheepskin from Emerald City University, certifying that she will escape their fate. But she does return with her four-legged furry playfulness intact. And for Lyman that seems to be the best predictor of one's ability to adjust realistically to the agendas of normal change without becoming tyrannized by them.

Baum is credited with being the first to Americanize effectively the European tradition of the fantasy tale. He was a dedicated student of that tradition, and the care that he put into crafting *The Wizard of Oz* suggests that his motives were more than merely pecuniary or patriotic. Craftsman of illusion, he seems to have been disturbed that in their eagerness to rid the world of witchcraft his contemporaries, proud of their scientific rationalism, were in danger of exorcising as well their capacity for wonderment and joy.

Baum may be quintessentially American in his faith that whimsy is more powerful equipment for living than dogma. Oz is in the great tradition of an Ogden Nash ("Life is not having been told that the man has just waxed the floor") or a Mark Twain ("I am an old man and have known many troubles, most of which never really happened"). But before we leap to claim a national patent on self-irony let us note the reports of Australian troops (Aussies, pronounced Ozzies) marching into battle in World War II singing, "We're off to see the Wizard. . . ."[25]

With all of its whimsy, *The Wonderful Wizard of Oz* is a form of literature as equipment for living. In it Baum cerebrates about the life course, as I have tried to demonstrate, but he is even more intent on celebrating its promise. In our era of mass longevity we need new life-giving myths every bit as much as new cerebral paradigms. So we ignore vernacular narratives at our own peril, for no matter how high our heads may rise, our feet are rooted in popular culture. I can hear Glinda telling us that we only need to realize the fabulous power that already is at those feet.

Christine K. Cassel

The Meaning of Health Care in Old Age

Editor's Introduction. The meaning of aging, its value and place in human existence, would seem to be the pivotal concept determining the quality of health care older people receive. But what is that meaning according to health professionals? Physician Christine Cassel maintains that there can be no univocal meaning, nor need there be. "The individual differences between human beings grow more profound, more interesting and more particular with age," she asserts. A more emphatic affirmation of subjectivity could hardly be formulated, since it is precisely the elaboration of the self and its individuality that accounts for the growing distinctness Cassel recognizes. In her case study of William Carlos Williams's "English Grandmother," she illustrates the fragility of such radical subjectivity and the unlikelihood of its surviving institutional care. Health professionals thus are charged with the difficult task of approaching aged patients without having in hand categorical, predetermined meanings of aging. Yet health care institutions—the professionals within them as well as the public policies behind them—presuppose a particular view of infirmity as the basis for their existence. That view necessarily objectifies frailty in order to respond to it. The dilemma of the professional becomes the problem of attending to the "objectness" of persons without reducing them to the moral status of objects by imposing upon them institutional meanings of frailty and aging. It is that dilemma, arising at the intersection of meanings, which ultimately concerns Cassel.

S.G.

1

Why talk about health care in a conference on aging and
meaning? Epidemiological data tell us that a vast majority of the
elderly are vigorous, healthy, living on their own, and not in need
of intensive medical attention.[1] Those are not the people, however,
that I see as a physician. In this essay I take the stance of my quite
particular and practical experience in working with people of advanced age. That experience, more often than not, involves illness,
disability, hospitalization, and sometimes death. That experience
leads me often to philosophical inquiry, including at least two
questions of meaning: the meaning of work and the meaning of
life. Thus one aspect of the question of meaning and health care
in old age is the meaning to me as a physician and in particular as
a geriatrician. But I prefer, for two reasons, to begin with an attempt to look at the meaning of health care to the older person
himself or herself. Although this may be presumptuous on my part,
since I am only aging and not yet aged, it is necessary to understanding the meaning of the work of health professionals. First,
the health care endeavor is intensely relational—the meaning of
my interaction with persons who are patients is strongly influenced
(if not determined) by the subjective experience of the patient as
I perceive it. Second, even for those elderly persons who are not ill,
the specter of advanced age holds the image, the strong possibility,
of progressive chronic disease and disability.[2] Thus both the reality
and the stereotype of aging include interaction with the health care

system and health care workers. The meaning of health care and aging to our society, moreover, is an area of great public discussion at the moment, and probably of even greater professional discussion. The implications extend far beyond the world of health care, because the dramatic demographic shift of this century will affect all aspects of our economy and social structures, and its meaning will be expressed in our culture.[3]

To seriously contemplate the notion of *meaning* and its relationship to the enterprise of medicine is to be poised delicately between the theoretical and the concrete. In order to maintain that balance, the theoretical considerations must be grounded in reality. In a poetic mode, however, it is possible that the most concrete images are suffused with a fullness of life and its mystery (its meaning) so that the specific grounded reality becomes symbolic, taking us the full circle to the theoretical considerations of meaning. A poet who dealt masterfully with this relation between the concrete and the symbolic is the physician William Carlos Williams. To maintain this delicate balance between abstract concepts and grounded reality, I shall use a Williams poem as a "case study" in the consideration of the three loci of meaning in health care and aging: the elderly person as patient, the physician as health professional, and the larger society in which they live.[4]

The Last Words of My English Grandmother

> There were some dirty plates
> and a glass of milk
> beside her on a small table
> near the rank, disheveled bed—
> Wrinkled and nearly blind
> she lay and snored
> rousing with anger in her tones
> to cry for food,
>
> Gimme something to eat—
> They're starving me—
> I'm all right I won't go
> to the hospital. No, no, no
>
> Give me something to eat
> Let me take you
> to the hospital, I said
> and after you are well

you can do as you please.
She smiled, Yes
you do what you please first
then I can do what I please—

Oh, oh, oh? she cried
as the ambulance men lifted
her to the stretcher—
Is this what you call

making me comfortable?
By now her mind was clear—
Oh you think you're smart
you young people,

she said, but I'll tell you
you don't know anything.
Then we started.
On the way

we passed a long row
of elms. She looked at them
awhile out of
the ambulance window and said,

What are all those
fuzzy-looking things out there?
Trees? Well, I'm tired
of them and rolled her head away.

2

The meaning of health care to the elderly patient is portrayed poignantly in Williams's poem, and this is the aspect of the caring professions about which we understand the least. The English grandmother is "wrinkled and nearly blind," probably demented, as indicated by the "rank, disheveled bed" (suggesting incontinence) and the snoring and anger (suggesting disinhibition). For many old people, this image evokes fear and disgust. They will tell you clearly, "Never let this happen to me." They fear dependency and, even more, the loss of control which makes one strange and disgusting to other people. The state of cognitive deterioration, in particular, is fearful. Senile people appear somewhat inhuman, perhaps because they are often treated thus by caregivers who them-

selves find the condition fearful and personally threatening. As
with insanity, a natural tendency is to withdraw, to look away, to
avoid getting involved. This may fuel a latent paranoia in the patient ("They're starving me"), which further alienates people. As
with insanity, however, trained professionals and caring family or
friends can learn to relate to the person *who is there* rather than
see the void left by the person *who used to be there*.[5] Communication and the exchange of human affection are possible on very
basic levels, and dehumanizing isolation is not inevitable. The condition of cognitive deterioration puts severe stresses on relationships, however, and changes the entire meaning of what can be
done by health professionals. What the contact and the caring
mean to the demented person is undoubtedly an affirmation of
basic humanity, reducing isolation and paranoia. It may contain as
well a mystery, to which the code is not yet broken.

It is essential to note before going further that mental deterioration is not an integral part of aging, but in fact a disorder affecting only 5 to 10 percent of those over age sixty-five.[6] In general,
the most important precondition for an examination of the question of the meaning of health care to the elderly patient is the
statement that there is no such thing as "the elderly patient." The
individual differences between human beings, in fact, grow more
profound, more interesting, and more particular with age. Therefore, any generalizations about what old people want or do not
want in medical care are bound to be false. One wants to be respected, not pitied for one's frailties. Yet if the "frail" quality is
more or less a consistent quality of aging, should it be treated as a
disease?[7] Is all sadness in old age a depression needing treatment?
One person wants comfort and help in confronting pain and frailty,
and another is more interested in pride and independence than in
treatment for swollen ankles. In a stage of life where some things
will go wrong no matter what, the threshold for seeking treatment
is widely variable and distinctively individual. Likewise, many patients do not follow doctors' advice even if it is sought;[8] this is an
extension of the same ambivalence.

Different old people have different desires about how to live
out their lives and about their relationship to the wonders and disasters of medical care. This spectrum is very clearly described in
Williams's poem, at the point when it says, "by now her mind was
clear." This lady wants food and respect, not medical treatments in
a hospital. These are social needs, not medical needs, and they may

require more collaborative and human intervention than the strictly medical.

There are several ways to interpret this statement. Perhaps she had a fear of being abused and kept alive by machines—an image vividly described in the lay press[9] and, sometimes, true—and was asking to "die with dignity." Perhaps she was depressed and her rejection of help was a sign of potentially treatable psychopathology. Perhaps some simple intervention would have helped, and her life would have regained its meaning.

The tension between paternalism and autonomy is succinctly described in the grandmother's declaration: ". . . Yes / you do what you please first / then I can do what I please." She wants no ambulance and no hospital to be part of the final scene, even if this means that she may die before she gets to the hospital. For others, the fight to continue living has intrinsic meaning in itself, and should continue as long as there is breath; these people believe doctors should be helpers in that fight. Miracles do happen, and in fact eighty-eight-year-old people do sometimes return to life from the intensive care unit. One is almost always dealing in probabilities, rather than certainties, in medicine. Since the probabilities of successful treatment of life-threatening disorders generally decrease with advancing age, some would propose therefore a policy in which decisions to withhold heroic or costly interventions be based on criteria of age. However, when we cannot offer certainty in a prognostic statement and must weigh relative risks, it has been our cultural bias to turn to the patient for an individual opinion.[10]

The meaning of health care to the patient is called sharply into question when the issue of quality of life is raised. While severe disabilities occur at all stages of life that lead one to question that life's quality, undeniably this occurs more often in extreme old age. Degenerative brain disease, Alzheimer's disease, and the like raise this specter particularly often. In addition, motor disability caused by stroke, arthritis or multiple fractures, end-stage cardiac disease, or lung disease impairing mobility and energy can make it appear that life at that level is not worth living and can, therefore, call into question whether the meaning of health care intervention is a positive meaning or is, in fact, merely prolonging the suffering of the patient.

Life's meaning, and its value to the one whose life is in question, are the important data here. The health professional as well as the patient must engage in an epistemological and existential inquiry. The meaning of health care to the patient may vary depending on whether the goal of treatment is improvement in functional status or prolongation of life span. To some, health care offers hope and succor; to others, futile and embarrassing resistance to the natural end of life.[11] To act in the best interest of the patient may be to conflate paternalism and autonomy. To assume responsibility for the caring response to an individual's needs requires no such adversarial dichotomy. It does require, however, an ability to distinguish functionally the meaning of my activity to me, and its meaning to my patient. This is empathy, bolstered by respect for an individual.

3

In a study by the Rand Corporation in 1980, Robert Kane and his colleagues estimated that approximately nine thousand geriatricians were needed by the end of this century to care properly for the illnesses of the elderly in this country.[12] Written at a time when less than two hundred physicians in the entire country declared themselves as geriatricians, this was a striking and startling projection. While one can argue with the methodology of this study and with its effects on health care planning, its premises are sound. One cannot argue with the phenomenon that is now occurring in American medical schools. Geriatrics is becoming a part of the curriculum and thus of the language of medical education and standards of practice. Graduate physicians are taking fellowship training in geriatrics, new programs are starting up, self-study and continuing education programs are increasing, and students are learning geriatrics in their classrooms and on the wards.

One of the assumptions made by those who are doing the teaching is that there are "attitude problems" toward the elderly patients, especially among young trainees.[13] It is not uncommon for a patient who is simply hard of hearing, for example, to be diagnosed as having dementia because he does not answer the questions in the mental status examination briskly enough. It is not uncommon to see on the problem list in an excellent teaching hospital the fact that a patient has suffered a stroke listed secondary to "old age," equating disease process with the aging process, giving the latter no other meaning. It is not uncommon for the elderly to be considered uninteresting patients and for the complexity of their problems to be neglected in favor of some younger, "more redeemable," and more interesting patient.

If the English grandmother were to reach the hospital, chances are she would be seen by physicians and nurses less than half her age, to whom her life experience is completely unintelligible and uninteresting because it isn't "modern."[14] Moreover, her "eccentricity" and dishevelment probably signify behavior that doesn't fit well in the institutional schedule. She has an excellent opportunity of being dubbed a "gomer,"[15] a term (*Get Out of My Emergency Room*) that refers to a patient who is disliked, usually because he or she is old, is poor, is mentally ill, or has a chronic and uninteresting disease. In this case even previously existent avenues of communication, respect, and meaning close down. She becomes a victim of the dehumanization of this labeling.[16]

Health care institutions are geared toward dramatic, technological interventions. Many elderly people need the interdisciplinary continuing care of chronic disease, viewed by some professionals as tedious and unrewarding.[17] This dichotomy reflects a major idiosyncratic attitudinal component, since the personal rewards of successful care of chronic disease can be great. Less personal, more technical interventions rely on factors external to the therapeutic relationship for a sense of reward. There must be more to it than the statistical likelihood of success—given reasonable expectations of success. But medicine is taught through an implicit prime-of-life standard; the seventy-kilogram man in every medical textbook is a very misleading paradigm for a future practice in which forty-kilogram women will be much more common.

In the clinical medical care of very elderly people, the goals of treatment have not been very clear. Dramatic cures are distinctly unusual, although not unknown. Treatment of chronic disorders must be geared toward functional improvement or even, in some cases, slowing the rate of disease progression. This means the patient will never be "free of complaints," and success (the "meaning" of our work) must often be viewed in a much more personal and qualitative way than can be demonstrated by laboratory tests or twenty-four-hour cardiac monitoring. This is inconsistent with the role model of the heroic physician technocrat. Many nurses seem to have a more realistic sense of the rewards of their work in relation to chronic disease, and it may be professionally threatening to some physicians to identify too closely with this model.[18]

There is an even more threatening aspect to the clinical care of a very elderly and very sick person; this is the ethical dimension. How often, in making a decision to pursue aggressive therapy in a very frail and critically ill elderly person, do we hear the question, "Why are we doing this?" The decision to be aggressive is often made first, the question posed later. On the surface this question is looking for a technical response such as, "There is a 5 percent chance of complete recovery according to three studies published last year in the *New England Journal of Medicine.*" What I sometimes also hear in that question, "Why are we doing this?" is the search for meaning. The answers to that question are generally not found in the *New England Journal* and are rarely discussed on rounds. We fight death, even someone else's, at least partly because we fear it for ourselves. We also seek success. We are trained to be heroes, and anything less than heroic success feels like failure. If the patient doesn't get better and doesn't die, this is the worst case because there is a persistent reminder of the limits of one's power or, to put it more bluntly, there is evidence of impotence. This phenomenon is the source of Fat Man's truism, "Gomers never die," in *The House of God.*[19] If a patient dies, one can look away. If a patient lives on with chronic disease and disability, this is frustrating evidence of professional inadequacy. It is not uncommon for us to turn away from the personal threat to our own self-image that is presented by the face of aging and the image of death lurking behind it.

The answer to why are we pursuing aggressive therapy is almost always complex, and almost always includes the personal psychodynamics of the health care team. The statistics of success and failure are rarely known, but the meaning of the successes and failures are often intuitively obvious to the physician if there has been a substantial relationship with the patient. It may not matter at a certain point whether or not the life can be prolonged another day or week, but what matters is something about the quality of that relationship, a respect for fate and shared humanity. Such existential confidence is not seamless, however, for there is *always* that haunting "what if." What if I had not decided to recommend an operation for this woman's abdominal aortic aneurysm? Would she still be alive and home today instead of dead, or instead of being a permanent resident of a custodial nursing home having suffered a stroke during surgery? What if I had pushed harder for that old man to receive chemotherapy for his lymphoma? Would he have been one of the successes? Would he have thanked me for it? Or would his final weeks have been spent in the throes of infection and bleeding secondary to drug toxicity? Would it have been better to push the English grandmother into the ambulance sooner? Or not at all? The meaning of being a physician in health care of the elderly is partly the sense of veracity in the acknowledging of ambiguity.

An article in the *New Yorker* describes in typical and almost painful detail the year-long recuperation of an elderly woman after hospitalization for an ill-defined illness.[20] An extraordinarily complex array of social and health care services is required to allow her to stay at home, to avoid the awful fate of permanent institutionalization. The family squabbles, and doesn't offer much support. She herself is "crabby" and demanding of the home health aides. Very little joy is depicted in this very long story. At the end of the year, she is able to move around her own kitchen with a walker, hardly a heroic measure of success. The meaning in her struggle for recovery seems to have little to do with pleasure or happiness, and a great deal to do with strength and survival. She may only have a few more months to remain in her apartment, or perhaps a few years. The meaning of her struggle is, however, unrelated to the duration of its measurable success, but rather is bound up in its significance to her. This story is about ambiguity and authenticity; its strength is tensile.

Working in health care with the elderly evokes an understanding of the extent and the limits of one's own power. It teaches one to seek meaning more in the interactional aspects of struggle with these realities than in the outcomes. There is a seventy-year-old alcoholic woman with a complex forty-year-long dependency relationship with a husband who will not help her to stop her drinking but who continues to berate her for it. The task for the physician is to work at convincing this woman to take a stab at drying out, knowing that she will return to this encompassing, interpersonal relationship which is so much more strongly and complexly determined than her relationship with any health professional. The statistics weigh against success, even with expert help from social service and psychology professionals. One choice in such a situation is to say it is hopeless: "I cannot help you." This choice means focusing only on her other medical problems and joining her denial of the alcoholism. Once one realizes that choice, then the decision to attempt treatment of her alcoholism becomes an existential one and the choice of meanings is entirely one's own.

One can either look for meaning (search for it, discover it, elucidate it), or one can make it (create it, invent it, make it meaningful). These kinds of meanings are not the same. It is possible for others to join in a creation, but they can only witness a discovery. A meaning that one is creating can be shared in a way that a more static "found" meaning cannot.

In developing curriculum programs for medical students in geriatrics, one common ideal is that the students should be exposed as much as possible to ambulatory, healthy, community-dwelling elderly—the splendid, the charming, the delightful eighty-six- or ninety-five-year-olds.[21] If we show them the nursing home patients who are disabled, who cannot speak, walk, or control their bodily functions, according to this theory we will turn them off to geriatrics, we will turn them off to a career in health care for the elderly. It is true that approximately 90 percent of those over sixty-five years of age are in relatively good health and living independently, but with some degree of chronic disease that needs understanding and persistent care. Working with this group has potential benefits in developing positive relationships which could help to restore an intergenerational matrix to our society. It is also true, however, that those most in need of good medical care and good nursing care are the much smaller percentage who are more severely afflicted. One of the meanings of a profession of medicine is to care for those in need, not preferentially for those who are the most fun to be with. To be a physician is to be committed to the care of suffering on some level. It is probably not necessary to be a saint; to care for the sick and even the dying should not be supererogatory for a physician. It is, in fact, part of the job. Therefore, learning the active creation of meaning in the contextual world of ambiguity, frailty, and human finitude should also be part of the curriculum.

It is difficult, however, within many health care institutions to show the truly compassionate care of the elderly and to reap its rewards and its meanings. With institutions that constantly frustrate compassionate health care in the name of efficiency, it is indeed a struggle to create meaningfulness. Yet working together with students, house staff, and families in these situations can be an ideal situation in which to develop a personal sense of the profession. In order to do this (as has been noted many times), it is necessary to face head-on our own abilities to deal with suffering and disability. What kind of meaning can we give to it in our own lives? David Rabin, M.D. has recently written eloquently of this unfinished business in describing his own increasing disability from amyotrophic lateral sclerosis, and the pain of being abandoned by his former friends and colleagues.[22] His theory for this abandonment is that they truly cannot give meaning to suffering, cannot find any meaning in suffering, and would sooner avoid it when it occurs in one of their close friends because the customary professional distance is not there to protect them. This suggests a vacuum of deeper meaning in the relationships and behaviors of professionalism. In the subculture of medical care as it exists today, therefore, finding meaning is much, much less likely than creating it. Or, to put it another way, what one finds is significantly noumenal: highly dependent on internal structures of meaning.

All of the foregoing discussion describes difficulties in general with the practice of adult medicine. Increasingly, the majority of patients seeing internists and general surgeons are over age sixty-five. Thus the problem of the shift in needs from acute to chronic care in part describes a demographic shift in the patient population. But there are other aspects to the problem of health professionals' attitudes toward care of the elderly, related to both a quantitative and qualitative assessment of the value of the remaining life belonging to an old person. This is not often clearly articulated in medical decision-making, unless a situation of real scarcity arises. For example, if two patients are competing for one intensive care bed, the quantitative measure of "length of time remaining" will be raised if one of them is significantly older than the other. If health care is a product, and the measure of its outcome is length of life, or relative degree of life prolongation, then the elderly lose in this calculation.

It is interesting in this regard that younger persons with diseases such as metastatic malignancy or chronic heart failure may have a statistically shorter life expectancy than an older person without these diagnoses, and yet aggressive treatment is more often seen as justified in the former patients. Thus there must be a real void in the meaning of life in old age per se as viewed by younger health workers who are making these decisions.

Interpretations of the *meaning* of an old person's life—regardless of how many days, weeks, months or years remain—must come from either or both of the following sources. First, there can be meaning to life itself—in a perception often based in a spiritual context, one sees the person as deontological evidence of value. Ironically, the decision to allow death to come is often more consistent with a moral sense in this context. One asks about the meaning of remaining life to the person whose life it is, understanding that the significance of the life is not necessarily directly proportional to its duration. One doesn't grapple with betrayal or failure but rather sees the meaning of death as congruent with the meaning of life. Too often, instead, the values of the young, energetic, and future-oriented physician are projected onto the elderly patient. My own fears of aging and disability influence my decision about the quality of another, older person's life experience. That experience is something I truly cannot know until it is mine. Perhaps we should not see people as in a state of decline relative to what their previous condition of life was, but rather should judge the quality of their current life experience, of the essential reality compared to that of others who are like them.[23] To accomplish this would require extraordinary empathic imagination, moving beyond pity or sympathy. To act on it would require a new context of moral courage and respect for individuals.

Second, one can see the meaning of an old person's life as it contributes to the meanings of culture, a recognition of the life cycle in our worldview. In a society where historical perspective, extended family networks, the intergenerational matrix, and survivorship itself are valued for their contributions to the meaning of life in that society, one can see the need for health care as simply one aspect of that reality. Progressive frailty and chronic disease do not of themselves negate the value of life, except in a society where physical vigor as represented by youth is an overriding value. The Hill Farmer's wife, in Blythe's *The View in Winter*, says, "Old age was once a privilege, but it has now become a condition."[24]

When I announce that my specialty is geriatrics, two kinds of responses are common. In one, disbelief occurs in a statement such as, "Oh, how can you do that? It's so depressing." This reaction is most common from medical professionals, and suggests a negative attitude toward care of the aged patient. It also suggests that there is no transcendent or even prevailing meaning to the activity which might give value to it in spite of (or because of) the "depressing" aspects of it. It accepts a passive relationship to meaning. In the second, a kind of distant admiration is voiced in words such as, "Oh, good for *you*. It is such a needed specialty." This response comes most often from non-physicians and laypersons. It may also imply the "depressing" assumption of the first kind of response; that is, "Someone has to do it—I'm glad it's you." The positive aspect of this response, however, hints at a *virtue* in the geriatrician, as if some supererogatory task had been enjoined. The geriatrician then becomes either saint or hero, in Urmson's terms,[25] which is another active mode in which to infuse the activity of health care for the aged with meaning.

In a just and compassionate health care system, however, it should not be necessary to be saint or hero in order to make the care of the elderly a meaningful experience. The meanings would derive from those inherent in any kind of health care activity (caring for one's fellow human beings, bringing relief of suffering, discovering causes of disease and new treatments, etc.) and also from close involvement with aged persons (enlarging one's sense of personal and communal history, forging ties in the intergenerational tapestry, gaining perspectives in self-knowledge about one's own relationships to aging and to the end of life). There are many ways, however, in which our health care system is neither just nor compassionate, especially as regards the needs of elderly persons who become ill or suffer chronic disability. This reality exists within a culture where negative attitudes toward aging and toward aged persons are generally prevalent. In such a setting, a physician may in fact need some saintliness or heroism in order to work with the most disadvantaged of this group, and to give meaning to the work. It is a drawback of sophistication to sell this reward short.

The modern American form of this profession has been determined by a combination of the professional dominance of medical science, the entrepreneurial activities of corporate medicine, and the incentives toward acute and technologic interventions that are fostered by third-party payers. Medical students today learn the concept of marginal utility—of diminishing returns which come from increasing ordering of laboratory tests or interventions at a certain point. They often rely on unrealistic and binary measures of success (such as win or lose). The conceptual basis has only begun to exist for giving meaning to more ambiguous and more realistic outcomes.[26] These sorts of outcomes cannot be quantitatively measured; therefore, research in, for example, social and interactional interventions is rarely counted as rigorous.[27] If respected persons and institutions support work in these areas, their value to the profession will increase. Conditions which determine the meaningfulness of health care as work can be changed, through both education and political activity. Thus one way to actively *create* meaning in this realm is to work toward the social and institutional changes which will enlarge the scope of potential meaning.

4

It has become a familiar incantation that the portion of our population over the age of sixty-five accounts for close to 25 per-

cent of our $280 billion health care budget. In the last ten years
the Medicare portion of that budget has quadrupled. There are
more nursing home beds than hospital beds in the country today,
while ten years ago, before federal funding for them began, there
were one-tenth as many.[28] The Medicare budget and the Social
Security budget of which it is a part are constantly under threat of
bankruptcy. The increasing proportion of the population over the
age of sixty-five, coupled with the lack of full employment, has
raised real questions as to what degree the working young who
are paying taxes can, or want to, support the elderly who are collecting Social Security.

Concern about this unprecedented shift in the dependency
ratio is a question ripe for an answer about meaning. The dependency ratio thus described is not going to go away, although aspects of the so-called dependency could very well change. It is not
necessary that everyone stop working at the age of sixty-five if, in
fact, the economy is healthy enough to support enough workers.
It is not necessary that elderly people, even those who do not work
for monetary compensation, should be viewed as noncontributors
to society. It is not necessary that expenditures on health care be
viewed only as a drain on the economy, considering that both
service-provider and technology-production corporations are among
the fastest-growing issues on the stock market. Health care institutions provide much-needed jobs, at a higher rate per dollar spent
than many other federally funded enterprises. Thus the meaning
of health care is not only intrinsic but also extends into the opera-
tional aspects of our social economy.

A concern about waste and unnecessary spending is of course
valid. But is spending on old people wasteful simply because of
their age? If one defines wasteful spending as that which brings no
benefit or unacceptably low benefit, the question about health care
spending must be phrased carefully in terms of realistic outcome
measures. The value of various outcomes must be assessed, and
who should do this?

The burden presented by the elderly is talked about at great
length. Their value is rarely addressed. We live in a remarkably
ahistorical culture, in which even the history of a decade ago becomes clouded in the obsession with the present.[29] This may represent an anxiety about the future as well, as shown by economic
inflationary trends reflecting an unwillingness to make long-term
investments. Thus the lack of history goes forward as well as
backward, and we are locked in the present. The oral history which

enriches the meaning of an intergenerational culture is meaningless to us if not trusted, not believed, not even heard. Its relevance to the future likewise diminishes and we think we have nothing to learn from the aged. The English grandmother asserts with a clear mind, "Oh you think you're smart, you young people . . . but I'll tell you you don't know anything." We have an existential choice, in a situation where the numbers are not going to change (short of a form of social engineering which would be intolerable to our society), and therefore we must both look for and probably also create the meaning of this demographic revolution. If the demographic revolution presents us with difficult social choices, those choices should be grounded in the fullness of society and should thus include in large measure the perspective of the aged.

This challenge to the health care system could have implications that are truly radical in a positive sense. In all of the statements of the booming costs of medical care and the need for triage and allocation of scarce resources, we find an assumption about medical care which has not been examined. This assumption concerns the meaning of medical care. Let's assume health care is a basic good of society. Every major address at every major medical meeting starts with an assertion that we must cut health care expenditures, that 10 percent of the Gross National Product is too much for this country to be spending on health care. This assertion is rarely examined. Has anyone asked our society what it wishes to spend on health care? How much is too much and how do we know? What is the right amount? Should this be decided by majority vote of the citizenry? Of the medical profession? Of lobbying groups? Of medical care entrepreneurs? How are social values translated into policy? Are they? Are we prevented from buying other things we need because we are spending too much on medical care? Or the converse? What do we need the money for? Vast resources are going to the development of weapons whose only possible use is indiscriminate annihilation of civilization as we know it. Roger Evans has asked, "What is the relative good that medical care poses in our society and, therefore, the value that we are willing to spend on it compared to other, less clear goods to which great, vast quantities of resources are given?"[30] (He is referring here to military spending.) What is the meaning of such choices? The risk and the expense that such social choices represent suggest to Evans that we are not yet at a point of needing a triage mentality for people who truly need medical care. All such statements must be considered relative to some explicit standard, and this is an opportunity for meaningful examination of standards and priorities.

In a broad sense, we must decide the principles of taxation and income distribution. We tend to favor individual freedoms over a sense of obligation to the community.[31] To alter this preference for respecting the rights of individuals in favor of the more general "good of the community" would imply a major reordering of cultural and legal premises. Also, we cannot be sure that this way of conserving fiscal resources is necessarily "good for the community" in a more general sense. The meaning of the aged in our population, *and* of the aging in ourselves, must be considered seriously in order to include noneconomic values in a scheme of distributive justice.

Perhaps in an affluent and advanced society it is the norm to have large numbers of aged persons. Perhaps that is a positive value if we can figure out how to use the wealth that they have to give us, which is not necessarily future economic productivity but the economic contribution of a lifetime, along with experience, perspective, and some sort of sagacity. Perhaps the elderly are not overusing our health care; perhaps, instead, we have become distracted from the purpose of those health care facilities. If we ask a simple question, "What is medical care for?" and we answer not that "it is for the enrichment of corporations," nor that "it is for the career advancement of research scientists," nor that "it is for the furthering of an industry which employs millions of people," but rather that "it is for the treatment of the sick, the relief of pain, and when all else fails, for the humane care of the dying," then what possible objection could there be to the elderly taking a great share of health care resources? We know empirically that old age is more prone to disease. We have not yet drawn a fine enough line between the concepts of aging and the concepts of disease to know if, in fact, anyone ever dies simply of old age,[32] but we do know that all of the diseases that afflict adult human beings occur more often and their consequences are often more severe as people get older. Is it not then appropriate that these are the people for whom our health care services should be designed? The radical implications of this question are that our health care institutions are not designed to offer the kinds of health care services most needed by the elderly, and that economic incentives encourage the development of expensive interventions that are likely to benefit fewer people at the cost of neglecting more basic needs of larger numbers of people. What is needed is access to continuous care for chronic disorders, often including day hospitals for long-term care and attentive and well-trained professionals from many different areas of expertise. Professional and financial rewards are few in this realm. If we are to use the medical care system for those who need it the most, then it must be redesigned. It must become efficient in the care of the sick.

Viewed from a sociological perspective,[33] the development of hospitals is a history of institutions created initially as workhouses for the indigent, used later for the expression of professional dominance of physicians, and now in transition as corporate enterprises in the health care system. The meanings of hospitals to investors and physicians cannot help but conflict with the meaning to the patient. Society receives no consensus on this issue. In a single week at an academic medical center, there may be endless meetings and negotiations which include discussions of billing, admitting privileges, beds, and utilization, and may never once hear a mention of patient care. There can be no doubt that waste and overspending exist in medical care. Are we being overcharged? Are we getting what we pay for? Some have been so bold as to suggest that health care institutions, in particular nursing homes, should be reimbursed according to a functional assessment of the clinical outcomes of their work: that is, are the patients feeling better or worse?[34] The meaning that the health care needs of the elderly can give to the institution of medicine and to society is to ask these questions again and to formulate them in a new and more creative way which reflects a true efficiency in maximizing the meaning of this work, not simply maximizing the corporate profits.

An intern at one hospital described a patient with end-stage respiratory failure whose family wanted to take him home with a portable, mechanical ventilator. She spoke in exasperation, saying, "This family is terrible; they are around here *all* the time!" Why is this terrible? Certainly it is not inherently terrible that a family should be with a patient who is so desperately ill. What is terrible about it is that there is no place in the hospital for them to be, that they clutter up the patient's room and the hallways, and that they get in the way of this harassed intern completing her daily chores.

Stories like this one reflect a concept of the institution of the hospital and the broader institution of medical care as being intended for something other than the care of the sick. No wonder the English grandmother didn't want to go there. She saw what was

offered by the ambulance and by the hospital as meaningless, because it was ahistorical, disrespectful, anonymous, and irrelevant
to her needs.

It has often been pointed out that our technical sophistication
in medicine has surpassed our moral capabilities to deal with its
potential. The meaning of taking seriously the health care of the
aged could be a fundamental step in the moral development of
society and its institutions. In the best of worlds the meaning of
health care to the patient is an integral part both of its meaning to
me, the physician, and in a larger sense of its meaning to the
benevolent society.

Natalie Rosel

Growing Old Together: Communality in a Sarasota Neighborhood

Editor's Introduction. Each of the authors in the second half of this book is concerned with the relationship between meaning as given, discovered, or imposed, and meaning as created, an act of the imagination, an expression of subjectivity. The fragility of subjective, individual meanings is nowhere more evident than in aging, when the person is surrounded by forceful social meanings. The preceding chapter documents the vulnerability of older persons within health care institutions, where social meanings are compelling. Yet in that discussion lies a clue to the problem of individual frailty. As Christine Cassel observed (pp. 189–90 above): "It is possible for others to join in a creation whereas they can only witness a discovery." An act of the imagination, the creation of meaning, need not be a solitary work; it can be the expression of persons together.

It is just such a community of individuals creating meaning that Natalie Rosel portrays in the following chapter. Describing the intricate life-world of a neighborhood, she details the tangible, daily forms of meaning as it is created between people. Frailty in aging becomes the occasion for "something common and fundamental—human connectedness." The forms of connectedness are the shapes that meaning takes when the essence of an individual's aging is relationship. In the scenes that Rosel re-enacts, the concept of a support network, typically schematic and arid, stirs, comes to life, and stretches into every imaginable shape. Frailty and aging in Rosel's neighborhood are continuous acts of the imagination, though not carried out in the solitude of poetry or the privacy of reminiscence. Now the imagination is directed outward toward another person, mobilized in the perception of the other's particular frailty and in the creating of a response to that particularity. Meaning here is not the fragile product of single individuals but the more resilient outcome of subjectivity shared.

S.G.

According to Alfred Schutz, there are, among contemporaries, people who share a community not only of time but of space. To share a community of space means that certain dimensions of the larger world are available to each contemporary equally, and that the world contains objects of common interest and relevance. Contemporaries in this special situation view even each other's bodies as meaningful in gesture, gait, and facial expression. Schutz says,

> Sharing a community of time—and this means not only outer (chronological) time, but of inner time—implies that each partner participates in the onrolling life of the other, can grasp in a vivid present the other's thoughts as they are built up step by step. They may thus share one another's anticipations of the future as plans, hopes or anxieties. In brief, such contemporaries are mutually involved in one another's biography; they are growing older together.[1]

The following narrative account describes as accurately as possible the everyday lives of my elderly neighbors in Sarasota, Florida, who have literally grown older together. My purpose is to use the "language of reality"[2] to demonstrate how meaning is created (and maintained) in ongoing activity. It should become evident through the characterization of each neighbor and the interaction patterns among them that meaning is created and shared through direct, face-to-face encounters—the bedrock of the social world.[3] Before turning to the neighborhood and its communality, it is appropriate to comment on the spatial and temporal structuring of the life-world, as this structuring will be used to introduce particular neighbors.

Y. F. Tuan defines "place" as an organized world of meaning.[4] He says, "Abstract space becomes concrete place, filled with meaning."[5] For the elderly, places lived in a long time become laden with meaning in relation to a life history. In a 1980 study of rural elderly in Appalachia, Graham Rowles found that "place becomes a scrapbook, a repository for the drama of one's life as selectively construed with the vision of hindsight—it conveys ongoing identity."[6] In other words, place is imbued with a temporal depth of meaning when lived in as a mosaic of "incident places" from the past. Setting, then, is not only the physical context of the present, but an arena in which one's life has been lived. In the present study we will be looking at neighborhood as such a setting for its elderly residents.

Time and space are as crucial to patterning the lives of the elderly as they are fundamental. In commentary on the longevity attributed to the Soviet Georgians, Walter Cain emphasizes the regularity of their daily activities.[7] The retired workers living in Les Florialies on the outskirts of Paris comment on the importance of routine shopping, no matter how small the purchase.[8] And of course for the frail elderly, routine is essential: "in later years people often have to learn to compensate for losses in hearing or vision by maintaining a routine which will permit them to move in familiar ways and surroundings. This maneuver, which appears to be rigidity, may simply be a survival technique."[9] Just as knowing where one is spatially serves to provide confidence and security, so too orientation in time provides for the meaningful structuring of experience.

"Above all we are oriented," says Tuan.[10] Aging and frailty are situations requiring considerable orientation. In other cases of temporal uncertainty, such as terminal illness, individuals construct their own timetables.[11] The point is the fundamental nature of the structuring of time. Temporal structure is apprehended in both daily agenda and overall biography. The clock and the calendar are more than household objects. They "mark time." For many older people, routine and regularity are extremely important; for others they are not. For the older people described in this study, familiarity regarding both spatial and temporal experience is crucial.

Routine and ritual will be used to introduce an elderly couple, just as spatial orientations will introduce two elderly widows. Through these short vignettes, it should become apparent that time and space are measured, and that these measurements provide anchorage in a safe harbor of familiarity. The tempests in this case are frailty and despair, underplayed perhaps in the depiction of individual coping and neighborhood communality. The point here is simply to present something common and fundamental— human connectedness and its consequences. The means to this end include the basic frameworks of space, time (everyday routines and extraordinary events) and neighborliness. Let's begin with a view of the life-worlds of two neighbors who are relatively house-bound and then two who are "doers" by comparison.

Home base: Mrs. Winter

It is 8:30 on a Wednesday morning, and a partially blind woman, Mrs. Winter, stands in her carport feeding the birds in front of her house. She has done this every morning for the last twenty-eight years. One block away, an infant is fussing at its mother, just as the father leaves for work and an older sibling for school. The infant's day revolves around its home and mother. The old woman's day revolves around her home and neighborhood. Both the infant and the old woman heed the different noise and activity levels of a weekend compared to a weekday, but for the old woman, in particular, most days begin like Wednesday morning.

The birds gather on the front lawn, and after scattering bird seed Mrs. Winter goes inside to watch the birds from her kitchen window. She frequently eats breakfast standing at her kitchen window. In good weather, she brings her breakfast to a TV tray on the carport and sits there while the birds eat. The carport extends partially across the front of the house. It is covered with vines and greenery, so that it is barely distinguishable as a carport. Rather, it looks like a spacious sitting area with porch furniture and a front entrance to the house. It is shaded with big trees, as is the entire front yard. It is a good vantage point for bird-watching as well as neighbor-watching. Mrs. Winter's kitchen window also looks across her corner lot to the intersection beyond. She spends much time at this kitchen window; it is a point of surveillance of the immediate neighborhood. Mrs. Winter can hear the activities of others in the neighborhood, even though she can no longer survey them visually. Mrs. Winter also has a side porch from which she listens to birds, children, and the neighborhood street noises. An ample supply of cookies for children, wine for adult visitors, and of course bird seed are always close at hand. Mrs. Winter enjoys visitors immensely, and she is a gracious hostess to all who stop by. Her house is well-situated for neighborhood surveillance, and she takes advantage of it.

The inside of Mrs. Winter's house also speaks of convenience and handy arrangement. Items are placed, and left, within easy reach. This is especially true for the kitchen window area and the middle of the living room, two places where Mrs. Winter spends most of her time. In the living room, for instance, the phone, television, tape recorder, and record player for "talking books" are all clustered near a favorite chair. Visitors sit on the living room sofa; Mrs. Winter sits in her centrally placed chair. Many frequently used items sit on a sizable round table next to this chair—phone numbers, tapes, small change, etc. The handiness of items enhances the comfort of Mrs. Winter's living room. It is a homey place, arranged with convenience in mind.

The kitchen, too, is a frequented room, especially since Mrs. Winter likes to nibble on food throughout the day. The same dishes are used repeatedly, and they are left out rather than put away in cupboards. In fact, all items of frequent use are placed handily on counters beneath the kitchen window. Mrs. Winter works slowly in the kitchen. Food preparation is time-consuming when eyesight is poor. A passer-by in the street at any time of day is very likely to see Mrs. Winter in her kitchen window.

Mrs. Winter says she prefers to spend time "out and about" rather than indoors, yet she revels in the self-sufficiency allowed by her intimate relationship with the space around her. To say that Mrs. Winter's spatial experience is one of support would be to understate the obvious implications of this detailed description. She thrives in her environment, its familiar space and meaningful content.

Housebound: Mrs. Fliszek

Mrs. Fliszek does not pick up her feet; she shuffles from place to place. Usually in bedroom slippers, she moves from one chair to another during the course of a day—usually from a sitting chair in the living room to a sitting chair in the bedroom. Most of her day is spent in the two sitting chairs, between napping on her living room sofa or bed. A path could be traced on Mrs. Fliszek's carpeting to suggest the short radius of her movement from the living room chair, a place where she can usually be found, a central spot in her house.

The house is a small wood frame "cottage," and Mrs. Fliszek uses roughly half of it. The small kitchen in which she fixes endless pots of coffee is used primarily as an entrance to the living room area. (She does cook Sunday dinner for herself, as Meals-on-Wheels does not deliver on Sundays.) A large table is just inside the living room from the kitchen; this is an eating table on which numerous plastic flowers and doilies are arranged, and above which the walls are covered with pictures, photographs, calendars, and various little doodads taped flat or dangling loosely. Mrs. Fliszek's sitting chair is a few feet from the table, across from an oil heater and electric fan. Winter or summer, she sits just a few feet from sources of heat or ventilation. Unused sources—an air conditioner and a fireplace—are also located along that wall, but the mantle for the unused fireplace serves nicely to enhance a display of more pictures, photographs, meaningful objects, and still more doodads. (Walls and surfaces are virtually covered with objects, an unthinking stranger might even say cluttered.) Also there are house plants; they sit on shelves near the table and sitting chair and otherwise (literally) fill the small sun porch at the front end of the house. The "unused" portion of the living room contains two more chairs and a TV set (turned on periodically for the noise, rarely watched). A living room sofa completes the furnishings; it is used only for naps.

When Mrs. Fliszek does leave her house (usually five or six times a day), she goes to one of three places: the Cains' house (her landlord and landlady in an adjacent house), the outdoor sitting chair, or the garbage can. The Cains' back door is probably thirty feet from Mrs. Fliszek's back door, on good days an "easy shuffle," on bad days a trek requiring stops to rest (a car parked in the driveway or tree en route become good places to lean and rest). This distance is usually traversed once a day, sometimes twice. The garbage can is roughly twelve feet from Mrs. Fliszek's back door, and Mrs. Fliszek deposits garbage after each meal, small bundles wrapped in paper towel. The outside sitting chair, at the foot of her back steps, is used infrequently. On exceptionally nice days, Mrs. Fliszek will sit in it for a few minutes, but rarely for longer periods of time. Plants on the back steps (and stoop), however, receive lengthy daily attention, and Mrs. Fliszek will often stand there for several minutes at a time, taking in her surroundings while tending her plants. Other than rare occasions (to be discussed in the section on outings and unusual events), Mrs. Fliszek traverses only the immediate space surrounding her house, and that only a handful of times a day (at most).

Mrs. Fliszek lives in a small circle of space, but unlike people confined or incarcerated, she does not think of herself as a prisoner of space, or even as housebound. Yet she rarely moves beyond a circumscribed half of her house. While Mrs. Fliszek could walk farther from her house (on good days) than she does, she chooses not to, and this underscores the fact that her spatial world is chosen—it is familiar, it is home and security to Mrs. Fliszek.

Both Mrs. Fliszek and Mrs. Winter dwell in measurable spaces in and around their homes. While they live within a much shorter radius than previously in their lives, they are not marooned on islands of memory. Rather, they have bridges and walkways to keep them securely involved with their surroundings. The lives of Mr. and Mrs. Cain, by contrast, are anchored more through patterns of time than of space.

A day in the life: Mr. Cain

Most lives have "daily rounds," activities as habitual as getting dressed in the morning or eating supper in the evening. These can be dictated by external demands (cows to be milked, babies to be fed) or by internal impetus—the sheer force of habit. Mr. Cain's day-to-day pattern of activities is predictably consistent from day to day.

Arising at 7:30 A.M. on a Wednesday for breakfast, Mr. Cain helps his wife with the meal preparation by fixing the toast and pouring the tea. (She gets their cereal and juice ready.) Variations in breakfast come from the particular fruit that's in season or the next flavor of jam to be opened, not from the "division of labor" between them. He always fixes the toast and pours the tea, both at breakfast and for the evening supper as well. Breakfast is a relatively quiet meal, as he claims to be "still waking up" at that hour. After breakfast, as after each meal, he goes into the living room (or sun porch, depending on the season) and smokes his pipe. This habit varies only when there are guests at a meal, in which case the pipe will be smoked at the table during extended conversation, more leisurely when interspersed with talking.

The morning's daily rounds begin in the vegetable garden (see photo one). Each small crop's progress is checked, and the garden surveyed slowly and meticulously (as if to estimate what the day's garden work might amount to). The second daily round will be a trip to the grocery store, and for this a three-wheeled tricycle is used (see photo two). The store is roughly half a mile away, "down the line" as the Cains call it. This literal making of daily rounds is a habit based on several considerations: Mr. Cain's former work role as a grocer; his interest in shopping for bargains put on sale each morning; and his (now routine) socializing with others who frequent the store as it opens for business each morning.

Returning from the store usually by mid-morning, Mr. Cain briefly sits to rest before working in the yard or garden until lunchtime. Sometimes he has projects to work on such as home repair (and repair of their rental house next door) and very light construction—making a compost box, a garden fence, or indoor shelving. Other times it is simply a matter of puttering. Indeed, puttering consumes most of the time spent outdoors, as many as four or five hours a day.

Dinner is the big meal of the day, served at noon and followed by pipe-smoking, reading, napping, or just relaxing. The day seems divided and slightly changed in pace by this leisurely meal. The afternoon's activities rarely begin before 2:30, and then they usually consist of continuations from the morning's project-work (if there is any) or simply puttering for an hour and a half (till 4:00 P.M.). If there are televised football or baseball games on weekends, these provide for variation in the afternoon routine. Otherwise, it changes little except for possible repair work being done for a neighbor instead of at home. The afternoon is punctuated by a four o'clock snack, and the next hour or so is spent reading or doing crossword puzzles. Five to 5:30 is the time for an evening bike ride. The Cains usually go for a ride together unless she is detained by chores or simply can't go. He *always* goes for a bike ride before supper, and when the season and weather permit, he takes a bike ride after supper as well.

During daylight savings, he putters in the yard after supper, retiring to the house around 8:30, having locked up the garage for the night. Evenings are spent reading or watching TV—reading includes magazines, newspapers, mystery novels (Mr. Cain's favorite), or crossword puzzle work. Evenings last until 11:00 or 11:30 P.M.; staying up to this hour assures an unbroken sleep until morning, or at least this is Mr. Cain's reasoning.

From several years' observation, and especially from noting Mr. Cain's declining physical capacities, it appears that routine

Photo one: Mr. Cain

Photo two: Mr. and Mrs. Cain

Photo three:
Mrs. Fliszek and Mrs. Cain

Photo four: Mrs. Fliszek and the author

serves him in two ways. First, his daily rounds of gardening and grocery shopping maintain the continuity of his life's work. At one time, he was a professional berry farmer, and since then he has continued as a small-scale home gardener. He now organizes the planting and tending so that his gardening can be managed easily on a daily basis, even with a year-round growing season. The grocery business is also one that he identifies with daily as he checks for bargains. Charting prices over time is as much of interest to him as the daily charting of his vegetables' growth. Both kinds of daily checking keep him in touch with lifelong interests, using manageable expenditures of energy in doing so.

The second way in which routine serves Mr. Cain's current capacities is by allowing him to do things in short spells, resting in between. Morning rounds are followed by a brief period of sitting and reading, and afternoon puttering is begun only after a rest (and is broken again by an afternoon snack). The entire day, in fact, consists of alternations of activity and resting. Several years ago, meal times were the only breaks in the day. Now, however, it is essential for Mr. Cain to sit frequently throughout the day. His routine basically allows him to maintain the activities of on-going interest while not "overdoing it" at any one time. The daily organization of his time is well-suited to Mr. Cain's physical capacity and keen interest in the food business.

Mr. Cain's daily routine is noticeably lacking in variation. He doesn't seem to mind this, and he never speaks of wanting to go anyplace else or do anything differently. Happy moments are brought on by a crop's doing exceptionally well (he weighs vegetables of unusual size and shows them off before cutting them), or by a store bargain he has found and brought home. Unhappy times are few. They have been related to ill health—periods of time when he was unable to get about very well or was confined to the house. Recently his health has been good; his only trouble comes when he "overdoes it." He seems genuinely content with his routine, and while he appreciates a change in the form of visitors or outings, he usually prefers to stay at home and never complains about the sameness of his daily routine.

A week in the life: Mrs. Cain

Mrs. Cain's life is probably less altered by retirement than Mr. Cain's (they owned and ran the grocery store together). She has "done for others" all her life, and she continues to do that now.

She has kept house, canned food and maintained several flower beds all her life, and she does that now, in addition to the home-making tasks she does for others. She has a daily life no less organized than Mr. Cain's, but her tasks seem more varied, more social, and more demanding.

Sunday mornings are devoted to cooking and baking. A large noon dinner is prepared with extra vegetables and casseroles, so that the first few days of the week are taken care of as well. Homemade pie is fixed for both the Cains and two others—Mrs. Fliszek and Mrs. Winter receive smaller pies and look forward to this weekly treat. The smell of Sunday morning cooking fills the atmosphere, spilling out into the yard area when the house is open. Mrs. Cain rarely sits down until the noon meal is served. Once in a while, she invites Mrs. Winter to join them for dinner. After dinner the dishes are stacked at the sink for later washing. Sunday afternoon naps are taken as soon as the leftovers are stored. Sunday afternoons are more leisurely than other afternoons. Relaxing, letter-writing, visiting, and taking a longer bike ride in the late afternoon make Sundays a welcome change from weekdays.

Monday is frequently wash day (or sometimes Saturday and Monday), and all the wash is done by hand. Seasonal washings of blankets and curtains make this chore an unusually time-consuming one, but ordinarily it's a morning's job. (Mrs. Cain must get her own housework done in the morning, as afternoons are spent helping Mrs. Winter with hers.) After the noon meal and afternoon nap, Mrs. Cain spends weekday afternoons away from the house. Mrs. Winter's needs determine the afternoon's variety; often it includes simply letter-writing or visiting with her. Weekday evenings invariably include short bike rides (half an hour compared to an hour or two on weekends), watching television, and either reading to or visiting with Mrs. Jones (another older neighbor) for an hour or so. In the extremes of cold or hot weather, the evenings include covering plants (using numerous blankets and clothespins) or watering them. In dry weather, watering the plants takes roughly an hour's time every other evening. Mrs. Cain used to work on sewing projects (making clothes for herself and mending clothes for others) in the evening, but now that her eyesight is declining, she must find time during the day for her sewing. Mondays, like most weekdays, are dominated by daily tasks and necessities (the Cains' and others'); weekly routines vary at the beginning and end of each week, starting with Thursdays.

Thursday morning grocery shopping for others is as institutionalized a routine as Sunday morning cooking. Mrs. Cain gets grocery lists from Mrs. Fliszek and Mrs. Winter, and fills her tricycle baskets with their weekly orders. (This is no mean feat, considering that both food orders are sizable.) If it weren't for Meals-on-Wheels, Mrs. Cain would probably have to shop for both ladies twice a week or more. Sometimes Mrs. Winter goes along to the store with Mrs. Cain, in which case the entire morning is spent at the grocery store making selections. This weekly routine takes place rain or shine, and in cold or stormy weather it is a particularly arduous task. During the months of November through April, Thursday afternoons are spent in preparing meals for the evening, as the Cains have friends who visit weekly during that time. (These "snow birds" from Pennsylvania first met the Cains on a fishing bridge in the 1950s, and they've been close friends ever since.) Thursdays can be busy days for Mrs. Cain, or at least somewhat more hectic than the rest of the week.

Fridays are distinguished only by the morning's weekly soup-fixing—a vegetable soup made almost exclusively from homegrown produce. It is made on Friday morning to tide the couple over until Sunday's cooking replenishes the ready-to-heat meal supply, and it also leaves Saturday mornings free for running longer-distance errands (using the author's car).

Saturdays are delegated as errand days, and Saturday mornings are usually spent going to hardware, department, garden, and discount stores. This weekly round varies considerably, but the use of Saturday mornings to do "car shopping" does not. Usually home in time to heat up soup for dinner, Mrs. Cain spends the remainder of each Saturday on her own projects (frequently sewing), as Mrs. Winter likes to listen to classical music on the radio on Saturday afternoons. Saturdays (like Sundays) can also include visits from friends. Saturday, in this respect, is less routinized than the weekdays, and like Sunday it provides a welcome change in the week's basic pattern.

In contrast to Mr. Cain's, Mrs. Cain's pace is anything but slow. She works steadily, not in haste, but rarely with moments of sitting or relaxing. Afternoon napping is essential for this reason. Her mornings, afternoons, and evenings tend to be full of activity. She frequently sighs deeply as she sits down to dinner or supper, and equally frequently she falls asleep in the early evening during the news. Time is filled with activity for Mrs. Cain. Observation suggests that she has slowed down little in the past ten years. She has no complaints about her life-style, and she, like Mr. Cain, is unhappy only when health problems slow her down. Mrs. Cain is probably served by the routinized nature of her week in basically one way: it allows her to get everything done. This routine serves both of the Cains well. He is served by the pacing of a day's routine, and she is served by a familiar pattern of days which allows her to accomplish a great deal for herself and others. Both live comfortably (not to mention compatibly) with this habitual usage of time. Daily rounds and weekly routines are lived experiences— an adjustable familiarity and a taken-for-granted life-style for the Cains.

As the spatial world constricts in advancing age, familiarity and routinization allow these older people to have life-styles of their own choosing. For them, independent living in the community depends on adequate neighborly support. Old-fashioned "neighboring" makes a world of difference, particularly to the frail elderly. Perhaps these people are recreating the neighborhood experiences of their own pasts (in Margaret Mead's phrase, they are immigrants in time). Whatever the causes of neighborliness, the consequences are clear. I turn now to the background and emergence of the neighborhood communality that supports the independent living of its participants.

The long-term residents

When Mrs. Jones moved into the neighborhood in August 1940, she didn't like it. The climate was hot and rainy, and the swarming mosquitoes got her down. (This was before the days of pest control.) Mrs. Jones had to walk several blocks to pick up the mail each day (mailboxes were clustered on a nearby "through street" at that time), and she ventured out only after wrapping herself in towels for protection against mosquitoes. Then there were the snakes. Rattlesnakes were common then, and people gladly protected the area's black snakes because they preyed on the rattlers. One large black snake, "Old Percy," was a neighborhood pet; people waited patiently for him to cross the road if they met him while traveling. Houses were sparse in the neighborhood then. In fact, Mrs. Jones recalls a "park area" on one side of her and a swamp (complete with an alligator whose grunting could be heard from the house) on the other. Neighbors gathered in the park area (vacant lots) for picnics on holidays, and people shared a general good humor about the challenges of dealing with their tropical wildlife.

Mrs. Jones was the youngest person on the street when she arrived. Now she is the oldest. Her parents had bought (and actually finished building) their retirement home during the Depression; after her father died ten years later, Mrs. Jones came here "temporarily" to help her mother relocate. But neither woman ever moved from the place, and Mrs. Jones's mother died in it shortly after celebrating her hundredth birthday. While caring for her mother, who was blind during most of that period, Mrs. Jones drove and did errands for three older couples in the neighborhood. As the youngest and only driving resident, she kept busy helping others; now she comments on the appropriateness of "being on the receiving end" of neighborly assistance.

Mrs. Jones, who is ninety, grew up in a small town in Iowa; she has lived almost all her life in rural Iowa and once-rural Sarasota. Her closest neighbors currently are Mrs. Stone and Mrs. Cain, and aside from family in other parts of Florida, she turns to these neighbors for assistance and companionship. Widowed since 1971, Mrs. Jones has recovered from a serious fall in recent years, and other than coping with poor eyesight she considers herself to be in generally good health. Walking a mile a day (with Mrs. Johnson), Mrs. Jones hopes that she will stay reasonably fit and continue living in her own home for a long time.

In February 1942 the young Glick family moved into the neighborhood. They had been living close to the downtown area and now sought the relative remoteness of the then-undeveloped neighborhood. Buying a section of six lots, they moved into the only house on the property. In these spacious surroundings they planted a grape arbor and citrus trees, and they kept chickens for their own use. As a young working couple, they didn't get to spend much time socializing with their new neighbors, and their small son missed having playmates his own age. At that time, the few neighbors around the Glicks were much older than themselves.

Now Mrs. Glick keeps her grandchildren during periodic visits, and otherwise lives alone in a house next door to their first location on the property. Her newer home was built by the Glicks' son in 1961. Mrs. Glick has been widowed for four years and now spends much of her time on domestic projects (sewing, gardening, baking) and visiting. Primarily she entertains herself, recalling that she grew up on a farm without little girls to play with; she has been self-sufficient all her life. A retired school teacher and native Floridian (whose parents were also Floridians), Mrs. Glick still drives a car, and aside from back trouble is in generally good health. She frequently takes neighbors on errands and enjoys visiting in the neighborhood. Mrs. Glick is pleased with the neighborhood, with both its new younger families and its older long-term residents. She hopes to continue living in it for a long time.

Mrs. Stone also recalls that her small children had no playmates in the neighborhood when the family first arrived in December 1974. Like Mrs. Glick, she sent her son to kindergarten a year early for that reason. The Stones bought their corner lot and built a home on it, living nearby in a cottage and then a trailer until it was ready. There was just one house (across the street) near them at the time. The vicinity was all sand and trees—very quiet. Periodically, pieces of shells would be dumped and spread on the narrow dirt road, and one day a city official came to Mrs. Stone's door to ask for ideas in the renaming of her street. Since most of the well-known plant names had been used elsewhere in town, she luckily hit upon Turk's Cap when looking around her yard for an idea. Mrs. Stone's shrubbery thus named the short (two block) street on which she lives, and over the years, she has watched the street change to its current "built up" state (it is even paved at this point).

Having moved here from a small town in Pennsylvania, Mrs. Stone recalls both good changes and bad changes in this once small-town neighborhood. Although she is happy with all her nice neighbors, she regrets that houses must be locked and protected from break-ins (she experienced two recently). The good changes—nice young families moving in—outweigh the bad ones, and Mrs. Stone plans to stay in the neighborhood indefinitely.

Mrs. Stone is a relatively young widow of sixty-six, who cares for a handicapped daughter living at home. In addition, she does some of the driving for older neighborhood residents and babysits periodically for younger ones. An outgoing person, Mrs. Stone has lived all her life in small towns—one in the North and one in the South. This neighborhood is now the one in which she has lived most of her life, and she is contentedly looking forward to staying here.

Unlike those of the other long-term residents in the neighborhood, Mrs. Winter's overwhelming first impression was one of complete enchantment. After twenty-five years of renting a New York City apartment, the Winters decided to buy land in Florida and build a house there. Mrs. Winter remembers little of her joy in having a home. In fact, Mrs. Winter spent so much time working in the yard that her new neighbors teased her about it at first. Using their front yard for "carport parties," the Winters enjoyed entertaining their neighbors, she fixing sandwiches and Mr. Winter serving drinks. People were very social in those days she recalls, the atmosphere was different then. Everybody visited outdoors because it was before the days of air conditioning. While the neighbors are all still helpful, there are no more outdoor parties like the ones Mrs. Winter remembers from the late 1950s. Mr. Winter was newly retired then and Mrs. Winter was still working. Widowed since 1972, Mrs. Winter now lives alone. She appreciates all the help and visiting of her neighbors, but still misses the parties of the earlier days.

Born in Switzerland in 1894, Mrs. Winter immigrated to New York City in 1927 after living in several European cities. She still corresponds (via tape recordings) with Swiss relatives, but since her husband's death she has no family living in this country. (Mrs. Winter has no children.) Having lost most of her eyesight in the last few years, Mrs. Winter is completely dependent on others in her determination to remain living at home. She returns favors in many forms, and she continues to enjoy the socializing of neighbors who frequently drop by to visit. She also still enjoys her yard as much as ever, reveling in the fact that she still keeps up her yard and its appearance with very little help. Mrs. Winter is extremely social and happy in the neighborhood. Her only continuing struggle is self-sufficiency—a struggle against the decline of age itself. She succeeds despite the setbacks (such as a recent hard fall), primarily with the assistance and encouragement of neighbors.

Mrs. Fliszek's first response to the question of when she arrived in the neighborhood was that it was "too far away" to remember. Using photo albums and old clippings, however, we traced the Fliszeks' arrival to December 1957. Mrs. Fliszek recalled how happy she and her husband were to be away from the winters in Ohio and how much they enjoyed their neighbors. Widowed for eleven years, Mrs. Fliszek is ninety years old and in poor health. Several ailments make it difficult for her to get around very well, and she socializes very little with those around her. Most of her time is spent sitting in her house. Mrs. Fliszek is both frail and housebound. Her days consist of everyday chores/activities and much reminiscing. While she does take care of her housework and entertains herself, Mrs. Fliszek is dependent on others for shopping and other forms of assistance. Two constant forms of assistance for her are (1) memory and information when she forgets things, and (2) medical attention during her "spells" (usually related to diabetes). The Cains, from whom she rents, provide assistance and generally watch out for her, and Mrs. Fliszek insists repeatedly that she doesn't know what she'd do without them.

Subsequent interviews with residents fairly new to the neighborhood revealed that they shared common perceptions of the physical setting of this qualitatively defined space. All agreed on a description of four rectangular blocks of homes "nestled back" from the highway and "in from the bay." The cross streets are both dead ends, and residents all think of the area as a quiet one. (Within these common boundaries, houses vary in age and style, although the neighborhood itself is an older one in the larger community. Streets are narrow and curbless, homes are maintained by middle-class standards, and car traffic is exceedingly light.) Residents were asked to describe their first impressions of the neighborhood, and then to comment on ways in which they felt it had changed since they moved into it. The summaries are derived from highly detailed and often enjoyable sessions of reminiscing on the "then" versus "now" neighborhoods. The following interviews were done with three couples. All are actively involved in the neighborhood, although the Cains are more involved currently than either the Townes or the Browns.

The Townes moved into the neighborhood in August 1963. Living temporarily in the Fliszeks' house while theirs was being built, they looked after the Fliszeks and helped other neighbors who needed transportation and assistance. The Townes, initially the youngest couple in the neighborhood, are still relatively young. Both were forced to retire early due to health problems. They recall the earlier socializing and high rate of activity among neighbors and notice the evident decline in health of older neighbors. In fact, there have been several deaths in the twenty years they've lived here. More than the lessened activity and neighboring, however, they regret the recent installment by a young couple of a solid wooden fence in the yard behind them. It interrupts neighboring and makes them feel as though they are snooping when they go in the back yard to check on a neighbor. Otherwise, the neighborhood is still friendly and quiet. "It's a home," they observe.

The Browns moved to the neighborhood from suburban New Jersey in 1968, and they were initially struck by the quiet and friendly atmosphere. Both are still socially and physically active. He is seventy-five, she is seventy-two. He drives for neighbors when they need assistance, but not on a regular basis. Both are eager to help or to socialize informally, and they both miss the earlier outdoor parties and gatherings in the neighborhood. Mr. Brown summarized the change in the neighborhood in recent years, including himself in this wistful complaint: "The old people around here are getting older." The Browns are the only older couple in the neighborhood still driving north each summer for a vacation.

When the Cains moved into the neighborhood in 1969, Mrs. Cain was very ill. It was almost a year before she became acquainted with neighbors and began actively keeping house. Mr. Cain was busy with the two rental houses on their property, one of which was occupied by the previous owner, Mrs. Fliszek. Having lived near downtown Sarasota for several years, the Cains were glad to be on the outskirts of town, yet close to a shopping center. Like the other neighbors, the Cains appreciated both the quietness and friendliness of their new surroundings. Mrs. Cain still corresponds with a couple of neighbors who subsequently moved elsewhere, because the people they met in this neighborhood were not just acquaintances but close friends. The Cains are both avid gardeners, and they met many people in the vicinity through their gardening advice and some exchanging of plants. Most of their attention recently, however, has gone to people living in the block around them. Both geographically and socially, the Cains' house is what she describes as "the hub of a wheel." They live in the middle (both literally and socially) of the neighborhood.

Having met some of the older residents individually, it is appropriate at this point to look at the physical arrangement of the neighborhood within which the people interviewed have evolved a pattern of mutual support. The area along Turks Cap Place between 41st and 42nd Streets is the focus of interest for us. If footprints and bike tires could leave traceable markings in this area, they would reveal a literal webbing of repeated lines between most of the houses. The table below shows the arrangement of houses in the neighborhood support network.

Neighborhood communality

The phenomenological dimensions of neighborhood are captured dramatically and sensitively by Kai Erikson in his study of the 1972 Buffalo Creek flood disaster. For our purposes, it is the survivors' loss of communality which so aptly, even if painfully, demonstrates the subjective experience of neighborhood. To quote Erikson:

I use the term "communality" here rather than community in order to underscore the point that people are not referring to particular village territories when they lament the loss of community but to the network of relationships that make up their general human surround. The persons who constitute the center of that network are usually called "neighbors," the word being used in its Biblical sense to identify those with whom one shares bonds of intimacy and a feeling of mutual concern.[12]

And:

Communality on Buffalo Creek can best be described as a state of mind among a particular gathering of people, and this state of mind, by definition, does not lend itself to sociological abstraction. It does not have a name or a cluster of distinguishing properties. It is a quiet set of understandings that become absorbed into the atmosphere and are thus a part of the natural order.[13]

The long-term residents of this neighborhood in Sarasota take their communality for granted. Responsiveness and mutual assistance are facts of life. One neighbor's chores and activities

Table 1   Neighborhood Diagram

Name	Age	Length of residence	"Family status"
Mrs. Jones	90	44 years	Children in Florida
Mrs. Glick	75	42 years	Children and grand-children in town
Mrs. Stone	67	37 years	Children in town
Mrs. Winter	90	29 years	No children; relatives in Switzerland
Mrs. Fliszek	90	27 years	No children; relatives in town
The Townes	66/63	21 years	Children and relatives in the North
The Browns	76/73	16 years	No children; relatives in the North
The Cains	84/79	15 years	No children; relatives in the North

include much that is relevant to others. Interdependence is so pervasive as to go largely unrecognized by participants. Emotional, physical, and practical ties are often undefinable yet observable as a kind of body language. It is the way they "move through" a day, a week, a year, a crisis, or a celebration. In fact, these older people label themselves neither friends nor neighbors. Instead, they think of themselves as distinct personalities with particular needs and attributes. In this way they resemble family members. It takes "consciousness-raising" to draw people's attention to the communality as such. It is *there*. It is the "general human surround" referred to by Erikson.

Just as categories of space and time were useful in introducing the long-term residents and their lifestyles, the concepts of communality and neighborhood enhance our understanding of their collective experience and its setting. Basic connections of mutual help and moral support crisscross the neighborhood every day—by hand, telephone, tricycle. However, something more like an encompassing social world exists in this neighborhood. Just when the transition from neighboring to intensified mutual support took place would be difficult to pinpoint, as would the degree to which the neighborhood for some residents forms the entire social world. Nevertheless, some general changes in the neighborhood and its residents can be traced, changes which have intensified the network of relationships among them.

Over time the neighborhood has become relatively densely built up. Numerous vacant lots have been filled in with houses, many of them built or bought by younger people. The area in which these long-term residents live is now twice as dense and half as old. The homes of older residents are now bordered by those of younger ones; demographically it is a core/periphery arrangement reflecting both age and length of residence. While the younger people do interact with the older residents, the quantity and quality of their exchange is casual rather than constant. The added neighborhood children are enjoyed for the most part, and the area as a whole continues to be relatively quiet. Older residents in our survey unanimously agreed that the biggest change in the neighborhood since their arrival has been the increased density of it.

Another obvious demographic change in the neighborhood is that, indeed, the old people are getting older. Slowing down both physically and socially, the residents who recalled lively outdoor parties and constant activity are now coping with arthritis and loneliness. And they *are* coping. Nonetheless, they miss the socializing of earlier years, and the widowed women, especially, miss their husbands. All five widows interviewed lost their husbands after moving into the neighborhood. Mrs. Cain recalled Mrs. Winter's despondence when her husband died and she approached Mrs. Cain for comfort and friendship. Their friendship has since emerged into a supportive exchange, as neither woman travels or socializes as widely as she used to (Mrs. Cain has discontinued her summer trips north to visit relatives due to her husband's increasing frailty).

The same shrinking of the social world accounts for the increased visiting and socializing among the widows themselves. Once they were friendly as neighbors, living independent lives in close proximity. Now these people remain independently in their own houses largely due to their interdependence on one another. As the long-term residents in the neighborhood have grown older (and some of them frail) the neighborhood friendships have evolved into supportive connections of an essential sort.

All of the residents interviewed were once in good health despite intermittent illnesses. Now most have numerous health problems. This decline, more than their shrinking social worlds, makes them dependent on other people. Mrs. Stone, the youngest resident interviewed, is one of the very few in completely good health. Three of the oldest residents have suffered bad falls in recent years, and only one has fully recovered. Many experience the typical losses of hearing, eyesight, and ease of mobility (usually due to arthritis). Those with failing eyesight rely on others with better eyesight to read the fine print. Those with limited mobility rely on others for help with shopping or errands. Those who are relatively housebound rely on others for visits and everyday social exchange. Proximity makes this interreliance convenient, but like aging itself, proximity is a condition and not a cause of mutual assistance.

Supportive exchanges benefit the giver and the receiver, though not necessarily in the same way.[14] Shared values also play a role in mutual helping patterns. Doing for oneself and doing for others become inseparable empirically. In fact, as Barbara Myerhoff and others have found,[15] it is interdependence among supportive peers that promotes independence on the individual level. To support—or sustain—in social interaction is to enhance the integrity of the individual. In a system such as neighborhood communality, this is done over time and in a regular (patterned) fashion.

In his 1925 study of four preliterate societies, Marcel Mauss found an archaic form of exchange—the gift and the return gift.

The exchanges were not simply of objects, but of each person's spiritual essence, and indeed these exchanges created spiritual bonds of intrinsic value between them.[16] In the exchanges of time and treasure in the present study, "treasure" is often something rich in personal meaning—if not a valued object, then straightforwardly the verbalized expression of caring. Thus the relationships themselves become highly valued.

Everyday exchange and assistance

Mrs. Fliszek frequently goes through her possessions to sort them out, usually rearranging and straightening them into piles, boxes, and corners. In a note to Mrs. Cain dated January 1981, she wrote, "Mrs. Cain really likes this one plant. So I want her to have it." She proudly bestowed the plant upon Mrs. Cain, and told whoever she saw for the rest of the day about her special gift-giving. (See photo three.) At other times her gestures include more mundane items, such as collected rubber bands and old pencils. And after each delivery from Meals-on-Wheels, Mrs. Fliszek takes her salad or unwanted food items over to the Cains (via myself if I'm available to save steps).

Mrs. Fliszek receives both informational and material assistance on a daily basis. "What day is it?" she will ask anybody who happens to be within earshot, and "Would you get me such-and-such from the store the next time you go?" she asks Mr. Cain when she sees him in the yard. She also *provides* an important item of assistance by being the only household of the three on the property with a phone. Both the Cains and I borrow Mrs. Fliszek's phone, and she seems happy about the arrangement (happier when it includes a few minutes of visiting). Mrs. Fliszek is a frequent receiver of medical advice and moral support, and on a daily basis she needs information and errands run.

Practical assistance dominates Mrs. Jones's requests for help. With failing eyesight, she depends on others for shopping assistance, reading, and sewing alterations. Mrs. Stone takes Mrs. Jones shopping each week, and of course, Mr. Cain fills in with any midweek errands to be run. Mrs. Jones still gets out quite a bit (bridge games, visits to relatives, short travels), and she brings back things to share from her outings. Mrs. Cain reads to Mrs. Jones each evening, and Mrs. Jones dreads the day she will have to give up her home and neighbors. "Who would read to me in a nursing home?" she asks Mrs. Cain when the subject of failing health comes up.

Mrs. Jones, Mrs. Stone, and Mrs. Cain used to take evening walks together, but since Mrs. Cain has been going on bike rides with her husband, Mrs. Jones and Mrs. Stone go by themselves as the evening walkers. As one of the younger (and still driving) neighbors, Mrs. Stone frequently helps others with transportation, and to Mrs. Jones she is a particularly close friend. Mrs. Jones needs help in practical matters, but in friendship and social support she is well-supplied.

Everyday assistance comes in a variety of forms, ranging from help with a household task to moral support during a time of sadness. A small sample will suffice to represent this constant flow of assistance. On any given day errands will be run, information exchanged, items shared or borrowed, emotional or moral support provided, and a home remedy applied to a health problem. Participants do not seem conscious of the give and take per se. While gratitude is invariably expressed for assistance, it is not expected—each person is simply responding to the needs of others, whether these are large or small, practical or personal.

Every form of assistance mentioned above is utilized by Mrs. Winter to maintain her independence. She also is quick to share with others whatever resources she has, usually in the form of gifts (uncalled for by any special occasion)—food of various kinds, or simply household items which she knows others can use. Listen to the following exchange between Mrs. Winter and Mrs. Cain: "How do you open this?" (It is a package of sliced bacon.) "You have to use a knife." Mrs. Cain opens it for her. The conversation then proceeds to which pan (of Mrs. Winter's) should be used in cooking a meat loaf. Specific cooking instructions are followed by Mrs. Cain's asking, "Do you want me to come down after a while and check?" "No, no. I can do it myself." (Standard response.) Mrs. Winter next thanked the author for offering to take her shopping, but refused because she needs to prepare far in advance for her shopping. She didn't want to go on short notice. The Sunday meal just discussed and prepared on her own is a good example of assistance which allows independence. She can fix food and do a great deal of housework with simply some instruction, label-reading, and encouragement. Mrs. Winter is a constant presence—at the Cains', taking walks, visiting others, working in her yard, giving or receiving everyday items, or just sitting in her breezeway. Constant interdependence quite literally keeps her going.

With their tricycles, tool shed, and indispensable willingness, the Cains are certainly the center and fulcrum of everyday assistance. Their everyday know-how is applied to household and health problems. Mr. Cain is handy and experienced in the former area, and Mrs. Cain is knowledgeable in both. Neighbors make use of her medical knowledge (acquired mainly from books and practical experience) on an almost daily basis. She gives advice, acupressure treatments, or simply a "talking to" about health habits, primarily diet. In addition to practical know-how, the Cains are relatively younger than the widows in the neighborhood, and she in particular is energetic ("too busy to get old"). Running errands and dispensing information constitute the bulk of the Cains' daily "doing for others," although they consider many tasks of various sorts to be everyday—filling out medical and tax forms for others, for example. Just as they assist others freely and continuously, so too they receive assistance in the forms of transportation and moral support (provided mainly by the author). The Cains' outpouring of assistance is unselfconscious, like their routines for getting things done. It all seems to be a matter of life-style and choice, meaningful interaction and preferred involvement.

Assistance is not measured or directly repaid; it is diffuse. If friends are people you do things *with*, and neighbors are people you do things *for*, then these people are both friends and neighbors interchangeably. People who live in close proximity have grown closer still through their socializing and mutual assistance. From day to day observation, what is most impressive is the *assumed* nature of the help and the socializing. Support extends in several directions among neighbors, and it moves "inward" and "outward" as well. The sharing of food especially goes "outward" from a central tree, garden, or kitchen. Conversely, the rallying of support in time of need goes "inward" either directly or indirectly to the individual who has suffered a blow. For the most part, exchange and support are constantly flowing in various directions simultaneously. The following sequence involving the author illustrates the spontaneous exchanges between residents.

On Saturday, July 31, 1982, the author helped Mrs. Glick pick avocados (the second or third picking). On Sunday Mrs. Winter called the author to ask if she would like some drink glasses which had been treasured in the past but were now sad reminders of the present lack of entertaining and parties. The author went to Mrs. Winter's the next day (to convince her to store the glasses away somewhere), and in the process discovered that the record player was broken. On the next day, arrangements were made for a shopping trip with the Cains, stopping for the record player's repair and any other errands needed at the time. Orders came from several long-term residents for items from the health food store, and when these were purchased and distributed by the Cains, another round of exchanges began again. (Any starting point is arbitrary.) Avocados "make the rounds"—a phrase aptly implying repetition, regularity, and coverage. Hand-to-hand exchanges resemble a well-used spider web of continuous communal thread. This communality—practiced, palpable, and pervasive—is the framework within which these elderly neighbors' lives seem rich in shared meaning.

Everyday socializing

Everyday socializing ranges from spontaneous exchanges with a mailman or delivery person to lengthy conversations with close friends. Though there is no conscious patterning to it, every older person in the neighborhood has some daily contact with others. What does everyday socializing look like to its participants?

Sometimes everyday socializing looks like companionship: people watching others work, standing together to guess the weather (or simply experience it), and lingering long after conversation has stopped. Merely being together is an important form of socializing for many who live alone—they value taking in the activity of another household. This silent socializing is typical. Mrs. Winter likes to sit in the Cains' yard or kitchen when there are projects going on, such as food canning or painting the house. The Cains, in turn, enjoy riding abreast on their tricycles through lightly trafficked streets. Many moments of lingering at a day's end or on Sundays seem to include the pleasures of being together—the presence of people rather than of conversation. Mrs. Winter says, "I hate to be alone in the evenings. That's why I come and just sit here [the Cains'] after my walk."

Telling someone about an important phone call, a new flower blossom, a new ache or pain, a special entity of any sort—just the telling—is a typical form of everyday socializing. A phone call will be made to tell about a letter received. A milkman will be detained to tell him about a new plant (or old arthritis pain). A neighbor will be invited in to see a new home furnishing, a jigsaw puzzle completed, a rearranged shelf space. Unlike the sharing involved in companionship, the emphasis in telling is on self-affirmation. The receiver of the news is often less important than the news itself. When no one is in sight to tell something to, Mrs. Fliszek talks to her dog (this is easily mistaken for talking to herself). Usually, however, a neighbor is available, willing, and interested. At 7:40 A.M., for example, Leo Moses interrupts Mr. Cain's breakfast to show him new tricycle tires. Mr. Cain comes to the door, toast in hand, and admires the tires. Similarly, after each visit to the doctor, Mrs. Jones goes to the Cains to report. Mrs. Winter calls local friends to tell about a long distance call from a relative. These exchanges are endless unprompted "showing and telling," but done in a way that commands attention.

Conversation is abundantly commonplace, and it too varies in quantity and context. Often conversation is referred to as "visiting"—catching up on one another's news. Frequently it focuses on a topic of common concern. Day in and day out it is "staple socializing." Of course, people share personal thoughts and feelings at some length; conversations may begin one day in someone's home, and pick up again at another place and time. Talking is a mainstay activity for Mrs. Winter. She loves to visit in person or on the phone. It is a rare day when Mrs. Winter has not spent most of it talking—from morning till night, not compulsively, but characteristically; she is gregarious. Visiting with people defines her life-style, and others enjoy visiting with her. A good listener as well as an interesting conversationalist, Mrs. Winter is a full-time socializer. While other people in the neighborhood are equally outgoing, they spend different portions of their time socializing. All speak with each other frequently—indoors or out, short exchanges or long, spontaneous or planned.

Everyday socializing and everyday assistance have an unreflective dimension for these neighbors. The talking and/or helping are so ingrained in the daily to's-and-fro's as to go unnoticed by the participants. This unreflective dimension is made conscious by the disruptions of untoward events. Drama, as opposed to routine and ritual, is an intense experience of either joyous or tragic coloration which superimposes a perspective of life's meaning on both clock and calendar. In this neighborhood context, drama is the opposite of routine; it is the extraordinary.

When a need arises, such as a medical emergency, neighbors are there on the spot. Neighbors comprise what Carol Stack calls the "domestic network" of people one can count on: predictable resources in time of need. The neighborhood network in the present study resembles the "stability and collective power of family life" which Stack found among blacks.[17]

Bad falls

Friends of Mrs. Jones provide her with transportation to and from church each Sunday. One Sunday almost four years ago, Mrs. Jones fell while getting out of the car. Her hip was broken before she reached the ground. Neighbors rushed her to the hospital where she remained for three weeks having her hip set by a new method. After the hospitalization, Mrs. Jones spent an additional three weeks recuperating in a nursing home before going to stay with her daughter. During her six weeks of hospitalization and nursing home confinement, Mrs. Jones received daily visits from her neighbors. Mrs. Stone visited daily and frequently brought Mrs. Cain or Mrs. Winter. Ongoing relationships intensified to keep Mrs. Jones's spirits up until she was well enough to return home, walker and all. Once home, she quickly progressed past the need for a walker. Since her bad fall, Mrs. Jones walks more slowly, and her daily exercise walks are interspersed with frequent rest stops.

Mrs. Winter tried to keep her bad fall a secret from others, but this was impossible. Mrs. Cain commented the fall just made her all the more "ornery" to try to help. She snapped at Mrs. Cain to help her and then rejected the assistance. She was equally ambivalent about seeing a doctor. Mrs. Cain expressed exasperation over this: "I knew I had something on my hands when she fell." Indeed, Mrs. Cain's concern has been borne out. Mrs. Winter has never completely recovered. Much support has to be directed to helping her accept her increased limitations—a difficult task, since Mrs. Winter rejects limitations of any kind. She says, "I know I'm an old lady, but I don't want to be treated like one."

Dependency is a fact of life for the frail elderly in the present study. The three elderly widows, in particular, would not be in their own homes without the assistance of others. The late eighties for all three widows have been marked by an increasing rate of physical decline. The last two or three years have required more assistance of a physical sort than was necessary when the women were still in their early eighties. Five years ago they could take care of themselves almost entirely; now they need help on a daily basis.

Pet death

In addition to physical setbacks, there are occasions when special attentiveness is called for on emotional grounds. Deaths of family or friends are obvious occasions, but the loss of a pet can be a devastating event. The weekend of May 24 and 25, 1980, was a long one for Mrs. Fliszek and her old dog Rex. The dog was dying, and although it lived through the weekend, it was decided that it was best for the dog to have it put to sleep on Monday morning. Mrs. Fliszek's niece Edith came on Monday to take the dog to the vet, and Mrs. Fliszek was agreeable about it because she didn't want the dog to suffer. Another relative in town brought a baby over to Mrs. Fliszek's house to cheer her up. "She loves babies," the relative announced, and indeed Mrs. Fliszek did seem cheered for a while. Mrs. Winter came later that day to express her regrets about the dog. "I know it must be hard for you," she said. Mrs. Cain and the author kept a close watch on Mrs. Fliszek for the next couple of days. She seemed to manage all right. The author took Mrs. Fliszek a jigsaw puzzle to work on, but this once favorite activity sparked no response at that time. Instead, Mrs. Fliszek showed visitors the plastic flowers in her bedroom, a tribute she had arranged for Rex.

Almost a year later Mrs. Cain's parakeet died of old age; Mrs. Fliszek was very responsive to Mrs. Cain's grief. Mrs. Cain buried the parakeet in a favorite flower bed and spent the next few days trying to decide whether to get another bird. A week later the author took the Cains to get a new parakeet. Mrs. Cain was surprised that Mr. Cain wanted to go along. "I didn't know he was that interested," she said. They picked out a bird and talked to it all the way home. Once in the house, they set the cage on the kitchen table. "Nice to have a bird," they agreed.

Fiftieth wedding anniversary

At first the Cains were reluctant to plan a celebration for their fiftieth wedding anniversary, but gradually the encouragement and helpful suggestions of neighbors won them over. An afternoon open house was planned. Neighbors became involved in the advanced planning and preparations. A long list of guests was drawn up, and food suggestions weighed and considered at length. Various punch recipes were reviewed, along with those for cake, cookies, and "dieter's" possibilities. The same peach ice cream cranked at the Cains' wedding reception would be hand-cranked again. Before the special day arrived, the Cains even decided to notify the local paper and have an anniversary photo taken. Forty or so people made the afternoon of July 18, 1977, a memorable one, and neighbors stayed for the entire day to help with serving, cleaning up, and the general sharing of responsibility for everyone's enjoyment.

Relatives from Switzerland

In a neighborhood where few relatives visit from out-of-state, a visit from overseas relatives is a rarity indeed. Mrs. Winter was delighted that a Swiss niece and her husband planned to see her on their way to California. She spent weeks anticipating their arrival and many, many days getting her house in order. But she could not have done this alone. Mrs. Glick took her shopping for new linens for her guests, and Mrs. Cain reassured her that other household items (dishes, utensils, etc.) were good enough for her special visitors. Mrs. Winter frequently became dismayed in the midst of her preparations: "What will they think of my house, my yard, my housekeeping . . . ?" Mrs. Winter was in a "tizz" (as Mrs. Cain would say) when preparations did not suit her. Yet she managed to anticipate the relatives' visit with joy. Once arrived, the relatives were taken to various neighbors' homes. Photographs were taken—copies to be sent in numerous directions. The sharing of these special visitors lasted well into its aftermath of anecdote-telling and general recuperation. Rare occasions are savored, shared, and recalled for months on end.

Sharing and support during extraordinary events revolve around joy and celebration, as well as grief and bereavement. The drama and need for assistance are no less intense in happy events than in instances of loss or physical setback. All provide opportunities for the giving and receiving of one's spiritual essence referred to by Mauss. Neighborhood communality is a means and an end in the present context, and the drama of joy or sorrow brings both these dimensions into high relief. Not only is collective life landscaped by drama, but also the structuring of time is punctuated by the dips and bumps of emotional peaks and valleys. Drama, routine, and ritual are the frameworks of meaning superimposed on these elderly neighbors' day-to-day lives. One more viewpoint on their growing old together needs attention, namely the relationship of these elderly people to the neighborhood as a whole.

Time plays a role in the collective life of these neighbors, just as it does in their individual lives. Two basic conditions giving rise to this neighborhood's communality revolve around time. One is the fact that the long-term residents are indeed people who have lived in the neighborhood a long time, twenty-nine years on the average. The other basic condition is best captured by a resident's observation that "the old people in the neighborhood are getting older." Substantial length of residence and substantial length of life are shared by a small number of people who in recent years have "cashed in" these similarities for support from each other. People of similar age not only live in close proximity today, but have done so for years.

Residents' first impressions of a "quiet and friendly neighborhood" held up over the years. Thus people stayed in the neighborhood and contributed to a core of stability around which the newer residents grew. This stability, the handful of older residents, is not a necessary condition for communality's emergence, but in this case it provided a natural base. Also, the neighborhood setting in which communality emerged has been structurally conducive in various ways—short dead-end streets (quiet with respect to traffic), old neighbors in close proximity, and little change in the residence patterns at the core of the neighborhood.

Neighbors—partly fated and partly chosen—trust each other on provincial grounds. Neighbors are those people living close by, who have come to play an important role in each other's lives. Neighbors respond to need, and usually this involves asking for help. In the present instance, little time is spent asking for help. It is there, every day. Assistance and socializing constitute the lifestyles of these older people, perhaps to some extent because of the fact that they have so literally grown old together. Their social worlds have shrunk considerably in the last few years, so that older people getting still older together is a pervasive fact of life for the long-term residents. Aging, and aging together, provide conditions for a support network's emergence.

Needs have been exemplified in two categories, physical assistance and moral support. Frailty is difficult to appreciate in the abstract. One needs to experience its constancy to realize how many adjustments are involved when strength and physical capacity are on the wane. Sometimes one must get help reaching for things in high places because standing on a stool is too treacherous, or wait for help with lifting a heavy object, fastening a button, or opening a jar. This list includes help with reading or writing when there is failing eyesight, or getting someone to take a phone message because the caller is speaking too rapidly or softly for a listener with hearing impairment. The residents in their upper eighties need constant help and reassurance in order to maintain their independent life-styles, and they get it. Most of the help comes from people who are themselves over seventy-five. Moral support is most frequently needed to combat loneliness or depression. Both physical and emotional needs are equally demanding. They account for most of the activities and socializing among the elderly neighbors discussed here.

Closely related to the dependencies brought on by advanced age are the values shared by these people with respect to where and how they want to live out their lives. The entire network's existence reaffirms each individual's striving to live as independently as possible for as long as possible. Doing for oneself and doing for others are inextricably linked. Independence is treasured. It is enacted, articulated, and supported. This value, along with the desire for security—equally fervent in its expression—are the common emotional bases on which the mutual support emerged. Observation suggests that these shared values are no less important than the structural conditions or the physical needs. This communality is more than simple homogeneity based on age or frailty; these people believe in what they're doing—helping each other maintain their own homes. It is as if an ideology or age-old tradition were being fulfilled in each act of exchange or support.

Thus, a support network emerged where neighboring already had existed. Stability (long-term residence), similarity of need, shrinking social worlds (as exemplified by widowhood), and shared values (especially independence and security) constitute the conditions facilitating the network's emergence. The network not only serves the purposes of individual members, it has also become an end in itself, a valued social entity.

The two most significant consequences of the network are making it possible for members to live independently in their own homes, and providing twofold integration into the community—age homogeneous and age heterogeneous. Successful functioning on a practical level has led to social integration.

These people are not isolated in their homes, and even if their social participation is largely through surveillance, it is essential nonetheless. Blythe says,

> It is not nosiness but nourishment. The old woman left alone in her four walls is starved and parched, and what goes on on her [television] set, however sensational, is never going to be as interesting as a neighbor taking a short cut, or a stranger entering number eight without knocking. The old become their own novelists when they fall into abstract street watching.[18]

The people in the present neighborhood setting are indeed nourished by their surroundings, and, in turn, they remain part of the community, however indirectly or vicariously at times. They belong. They are connected to each other, to a place, and to a socially meaningful life-style.

Eight-thirty A.M. or P.M.—on any day of the week—the long-term residents will be in predictable places engaged in a predictable range of activities. No one complains about monotony, but rather each seems to appreciate the security that accompanies routine. The present study has been almost exclusively concerned with everyday interaction and routine. The way these people live from morning till night and from week to week has been our subject matter. What behavior is typical for each resident? What things are taken for granted? What events are ordinary and which are extraordinary for these people?

The answer is that a trip to the store for someone else's prescription is typical. The sharing of flowers, fruit, or a homemade dessert is routine. The telling of news from long-distance relatives, or reports on a plant's progress or a visit to the doctor—these are everyday conversations. The errands, the sharing, and the telling go in all directions. Everyday interaction is not repetitious in this sense; it is multipurpose and multidirectional. This interaction appears consciously organized to a participant observer, yet it is taken for granted by its members. Older long-term residents of the neighborhood share the self-evident routines of everyday life in a network of relationships that has emerged unselfconsciously over time. Interdependencies are a way of life for these people, and no one is apologetic about it.

In fact, the long-term residents illustrate a 1976 finding by Lowenthal and Robinson that the old old "may have less trouble accepting the dependency needs which are inevitable consequences of the increasing frailties of very old age, than those persons who come after them."[19] After all, this is the age cohort which took care of its own aging relatives at home. Taking mutual assistance for granted is one finding of this study; the second (and not less important) is that the assistance exists among the elderly themselves. The support network in this neighborhood emerged gradually in response to needs shared by aging neighbors. This we-relationship has been characterized in other studies by observers as primary, communal, *gemeinschaft*, and mechanical solidarity. In this case we are adding the observation that the sharing has led to a support network which allows elderly neighbors to grow old together in settings where they have lived for years and want to continue living for as long as possible.

Sally A. Gadow

Frailty and Strength: The Dialectic of Aging

Editor's Introduction. The imposition of meaning upon individuals is the most powerful method of devaluing subjectivity and reducing persons to the moral status of objects. As social objects of special contemporary interest, aging persons indeed may have become so special as to be considered a separate species. But the most severe reduction of individuals to objects occurs in the *self*-categorization of persons. "Old" is the objective meaning used to organize and interpret various phenomena; it does not describe a self-evident state that individuals find in themselves. Being old, like being alluring or loathsome, expresses an external judgment which the self may adopt as its identity without experiencing it first as an inward reality, with the immediacy of pain, energy, or joy. The category of old is, in Sartre's term, "an unrealizable." It is impossible to experience, from within, one's identity for others; it is a falsification—and an inestimable loss—to substitute that identity for subjective meanings and so *make of oneself* an object.

The choice of meanings to interpret physical frailty is an example of the power of categories over experience. In the following chapter Gadow contrasts two meanings of frailty in aging: one based upon a rationalist approach in which the body is adversary; the other, upon an existentialist acceptance of the body as part of the self. As in Rosel's neighborhood described in the preceding chapter, frailty serves as opportunity and occasion at the same time that it operates as constraint. In the existentialist view that Gadow develops, frailty is both a limit and a freedom—the freedom to lavish intensity upon the body as upon a beloved whose idiosyncrasies—amusing, endearing, or disgusting—are by now valued as part of a cherished whole.

S.G.

Aging often is categorized as frailty—despite the insistence of elders like Florida Scott-Maxwell who lay aside categories to examine experience itself and conclude that aging is "a place of fierce energy," of "wild life that is almost incommunicable," "a place I had no idea existed until I had arrived here."[1] How could she have known, when the dominant image of aging is weakness, disengagement, and a stylized serenity?

The danger of discussing frailty as a characteristic of aging is the distortion of isolating an experience as a fragment apart from the whole. A narrow focus has value for isolating pathology in order to eliminate it, and gerontology has contributed greatly in this regard, making conspicuous the specialized forms of discrimination practiced upon the elderly for the purpose of removing those phenomena from the experience of aging. But the risk of the fragmenting approach is that it may distinguish aging so vividly from the rest of human experience that the elderly become a separate species. The danger of examining one category of persons as objects of interest is that the examiner defines the parameters of study and so imposes upon the persons studied a view of experience that may not be theirs. They are thus estranged from their own reality as well as from those whose object they are. John Berger describes one outcome of addressing individuals as objects of scrutiny: "The fact that they can observe us has lost all significance. They are the objects of our ever-extending knowledge.

What we know about them is an index of our power, and thus an index of what separates us from them. The more we know, the further away they are."[2]

An alternative to the "separate species" approach is the view of aging as a crystal through which experiences common to all persons are the most clearly identified, becoming—like colors through a prism—purified and intensified. In this light, the frailty of older persons is not a feature setting them apart from younger persons but an opportunity for both to address the frailty that each experiences. An unalterable given in human existence is the possibility of injury and destruction, the quality of frailty. As Edith Wyschogrod observes, "To be as embodied existence, as flesh, is to be fragile."[3]

The *meaning* that frailty has is not a given, however, although the phenomenon itself is intrinsic to human experience. To appreciate this, one only need contrast the prevalent meanings of frailty at opposite ends of the age spectrum. The exquisite vulnerability of even the healthiest infant calls forth tender concern and devotion, while the same degree of dependence in an elder often is found burdensome if not revolting. (These opposite meanings meet in the middle in the ambivalence typically felt by mid-life adults when they encounter their own frailty: they cherish the physical expressions of concern that are permitted in the form of sick care but at the same time are terrified of being found disgusting.)

The meaning that is given to frailty reflects the overall approach of a culture to understanding the human condition. The two approaches with the clearest interpretations of frailty are the rationalist and the existentialist views. In the following comparison of these perspectives, it will be proposed that, of the two, the existentialist view offers the greater freedom to experience dignity and integrity through frailty.

From the rationalist perspective, the human condition is essentially intelligible. That which cannot be understood rationally is not essential but contingent, accidental. In metaphysical terms, the essential is the pure, the enduring, while the contingent is the corruptible, the decaying. Thus, in rationalist metaphysics, flesh and spirit divide: spirit is essence, indestructible; flesh is frail, irrational, and transient. The experience of frailty is the testimony to finitude, imperfection, and eventual death. "When a new disability arrives," confesses Scott-Maxwell, "I look about to see if death has come, and I call quietly, 'Death, is that you?' "[4]

As long as frailty does not disrupt an otherwise rational and seemingly infinite life, the finitude of the flesh can be ignored. But when the body thwarts the projects of the self, erupting into conscious experience with the brute objectness of the physical, frailty becomes thematic. More important, the very dignity of the person as a self-defining subject is destroyed if the body's objectness overwhelms the self. Frailty then is no longer a background, a horizonal boundary marking the remote limits of human endeavor; it has overtaken the self at its very center.

Regarded strictly as object, part of the material world of decay, the aging body can only destroy the dignity that consists in the self remaining at the center of its experience, freely determining the nature of its relation with the body. When experience is dominated by the body's dysfunction and disfigurement, dignity seems salvageable only through a sharp distinction between body and self to prevent the person's being defined in toto as disabled: the self repudiates the body to escape being contaminated by its deterioration. The body becomes a mere shell, a disguise, as in the description by Ray Bradbury: "A body like this is a dragon, all scales and folds . . . the dragon ate the white swan. I haven't seen her for years. I can't even remember what she looks like. I *feel* her, though. She's safe inside, still alive; the essential swan hasn't changed a feather."[5] The swan-dragon dichotomy expresses symbolically what Simone de Beauvoir mourns as "the insoluble contradiction between the inward feeling that guarantees our unchanging quality and the objective certainty of our transformation."[6] The contradiction between subject and object, self and body, is not a logical as much as a lived contradiction cultivated by the self in order to avoid becoming one with the frail and failing body. The indignity of being swallowed by a dragon is at least alleviated if the swan is indigestible and survives to denounce its host as its enemy.

But the dignity purchased by disowning the frail body is ultimately self-defeating, for the self thereby surrenders its most essential freedom, that of deciding how it shall regard itself. In fearing that it will be defined, like the body, as an object in the world of decaying objects, the self gives up the very essence of its *not* being an object, namely, the essence of a subject as self-defining, capable of transcending external definition and being-for-other. No longer does the contradiction lie between self and body; now the contradiction exists *within* a self, a subject that regards itself as an object.

The indignity of frailty is insoluble in the rationalist view because the integrity of the self-body relation is destroyed and, more important, the self—in fleeing the body's failure as an object—makes of itself an object. Moreover, the rationalist view of the body not only precludes a self-body unity in aging by forcing the self to renounce the body, it also undermines the relation between the self and its world. As a physical and social object, the body—in good health or ill—belongs to the world as well as to the self. It is the face of the self toward the world and thus the most intimate connection between self and world. Repudiation of the body as a failed object or, worse, as an enemy, jeopardizes that connection of persons and their world—for example, the individual who refuses to eat in the company of others because of her own disgust at her lack of coordination or her fear of others' disgust. The result is alienation. But to withdraw from the body when its limitations become pronounced is no more alienating than the alternative, which is to deny its limitations in order to prevent isolation. In the latter situation a true relation between self and world is not achieved, but rather a facsimile is created based upon denial of the individual's frailty. Scott-Maxwell laments, "Real pain is there, and if we have to be falsely cheerful, it is part of our isolation."[7]

The combined alienation from both the body and the world generated by the rationalist view would seem grounds for the most profound despair in aging. Yet Ronald Blythe observes, "the old often have amused eyes and are not necessarily desperate. Serviced with dentures, lenses, tiny loudspeakers, sticks and hip-pins, the flesh has become absurd and can no longer be taken seriously. The body has become a boneshaker which might just about get you there, if you are lucky."[8] The "amused eyes" are not those of the rationalist but the existentialist. There are, however, two types of existentialist to be carefully distinguished. The first is the grim, unsmiling one, for whom the lack of rationality eliminates all black-white distinctions, only to replace them with a gray and aimless ambiguity: Camus's fable of Sisyphus's eternal and futile labor, Sartre's freedom that sits like a stone at the heart of being, de Beauvoir's dirge of insoluble contradictions. The second type is the laughing, dancing existentialist who can say:

> My formula for greatness is *amor fati*: that one wants nothing to be different, not forward, not backward, not in all eternity . . . this ultimate, most joyous, most wantonly extravagant Yes to life represents the highest insight that . . .

nothing in existence may be subtracted, nothing is dispens-
able . . . a Yes-saying without reservation, even to suffering.[9]

This from Nietzsche after a decade of unrelieved ill health, excru-
ciating pain, and professional failure. Frailty here is not reason for
despair. Despair is the no-saying spirit of rationalism and other
forms of idealist metaphysics. Decay and weakness are manifest
not in the body's decline, but in the lack of vitality in the self to
embrace one's life, including the life of the body with its unceasing
tides of strength and frailty. The boneshaker is absurd but not a
negation of life or an irreconcilable opponent of the self. On the
contrary, it is the opportunity—greater in aging than at any other
time—to cultivate a conscious integrity of self and body, to cherish, not renounce, the body, to care for it as one would a beloved
with whom one has laughed and danced and from whom one soon
will be parted.

In the existentialist view, frailty is not a cause for despair but
neither is it to be celebrated in a "cult of suffering." Nietzsche, who
urged more emphatically than any philosopher before him that one
becomes a "free spirit" through embracing the body in all its finitude, held in utmost contempt the cultivation of suffering. The
danger in infirmity is that it be experienced as tragic and therefore
as entitlement. Nietzsche's well-known abhorrence of privilege as
the reward of the weak is based not on a contempt for weakness
but on a regard for suffering as dialectical, as containing within it
the *possibility* for still greater strength, energy, and vitality. The
cult of suffering is based on the view of weakness as the *impossi-
bility* of strength and thus serves as much a closure to part of existence as does the worship of strength. It is that closure, the no-
saying spirit, that amounts to true weakness. Physical frailty is
simply one of the colors that an existence will have, and an especially strong color at that, neither black nor white, and certainly
not gray. "Perfect brightness . . . even exuberance of the spirit,
is compatible in my case," insisted Nietzsche, "not only with the
most profound physiological weakness, but even with an excess of
pain."[10] In his last writing, only weeks before his collapse, he could
affirm the "sweetening and spiritualization which is almost insepa-
rably connected with an extreme poverty of blood and muscle."[11]

If frailty is dialectical, containing within it its apparent opposite—new life and strength—the potential should be even more
vivid in aging than in the experience of illness. This is exactly the

claim that Scott-Maxwell offers, in elucidating both the negative level of dialectic—the level of contradiction—and the positive level of synthesis.

At the negative level, frailty and energy are experienced in sharp antagonism to one another. Scott-Maxwell observes, "Inside we flame with a wild life that is almost incommunicable. . . . The sad fact is this vivid life cannot be used. If I try to transpose it into action I am soon spent."[12] Frailty and energy here are so antithetical that the subjective dimension of frailty is clearly its primary meaning. That meaning is distinct from the objective, clinical concept of vulnerability as the statistical probability of new or increasing dysfunction. At the personal level of free, subjective aim, where probabilities do not reach, frailty is defined not statistically but dialectically, as the degree to which one's intensity cannot find expression. Frailty alters the immediacy with which a person's energy and passion are expressed completely, with none "left over" to enter consciousness. When intensity surpasses the capacity to communicate it, it becomes the conscious contradiction between self and body, between life and aging. Scott-Maxwell finds that "it is a place of fierce energy. . . . It has to be accepted as passionate life, perhaps the life I never lived, never guessed I had it in me to live. . . . It is just life, the natural intensity of life, and when old we have it for our reward and undoing."[13] The loss of immediacy is the "undoing," the intrusion into consciousness of purpose and frailty at opposite poles. What then is the "reward"?

Energy and frailty are themselves the reward, but only when seen at another level of dialectic, where they no longer merely limit and define one another negatively but also are mutually affirming— that is, where the positivity as well as the limit of each one derives from the other. At this level, the consciousness of "fierce energy," of the "natural intensity of life" becomes possible through frailty: "It may be a degree of consciousness which lies outside activity, and which when young we are too busy to experience."[14] When physical strength is sufficient for one's aims, when vitality is fully actualized without remainder, there is no conscious access to that intensity. The body expresses it and the world absorbs it before it can become conscious. It is of course always present to consciousness in specific forms, as the projects and tasks which it fuels and which convey a sense of activity, of busy engagement with the world. But only when those forms are absent can the pure intensity, the life-force per se, appear in all its strength.

At this point the very frailty which made possible the encounter with intensity is itself suffused with new life and rendered intense: *it becomes the new form for the life;* it is itself experienced with the passion that once was directed into other forms. To the extent that it is the focus of energy, frailty becomes in turn the source of still more life. Scott-Maxwell notes repeatedly that pain brings new energy: "It is the possibility that all intense experience is an increase of energy."[15] Frailty, then, is not simply the antithesis of energy. It is itself an intense experience and brings with it new life.

Frailty and vitality at this point are so nearly fused that the contradiction between them is overcome. Frailty becomes a positive rather than negative limit, a needed boundary against dissolution, indeed, as Blythe observes, "one of the most subtle pleasures of the very old, . . . the utilization of one's frailty and slightness, the knowing how short a distance one can go—and then going it. The knowing that one need not do more because it is impossible to do more."[16] Frailty is at once a limit and a freedom—the freedom to lavish all of one's intensity upon the creation of a new self-body relation in which the body is not a mere object but a subject, a beloved whose so-called imperfections are an essential part of the whole. "How strange," exults one of Blythe's elders, "my new life is my old age."[17]

With her simple eloquence, Scott-Maxwell crystallizes the difference between rationalist and existentialist views of frailty: "It may not make sense but it makes me!"[18] The rationalist can make no sense of frailty. The somber existentialist can make neither sense nor self out of the ebb of energy. But for the yes-saying philosopher, frailty is essential to the making of a self and—far from being an indignity in aging—is a source of intensity and life without which no self is whole.

Appendix

A Select Bibliography of Aging and Meaning

————————

Harry R. Moody and Thomas R. Cole

Aging and Meaning: A Bibliographical Essay

The problem of meaning

Many writers who have thought about meaning and aging have sensed something missing in literature on old age. It is as if we have inquired about almost every imaginable aspect of late life—sex, death, politics, religion—but somehow missed what is all-important, perhaps the very thing we wanted to understand in the first place. The question, or at least the concern, is felt. But there is no well-defined or even articulated body of thought that responds to this concern. In surveying what has been written on the subject, then, it is necessary to look into many different kinds of contributions from many different disciplines.

An approach to meaning and aging is inevitably an interdisciplinary one. That fact in itself underscores a problem in surveying the literature on the subject. How is meaning to be understood? Is it a psychological problem—"a sense of meaning in life"? A philosophical question—"does life have a meaning"? Or is it to be seen from a sociological or historical viewpoint: that is, through the diverse "social constructions" of meanings attached to old age? All of these views are legitimate, but each raises serious substantive questions. In this brief bibliographical essay, these substantive issues cannot be treated. Still, one problem is apparent in the literature itself, a problem which reflects the diversity and fragmentation of modern experience. What we have are specialized studies by the different disciplines which often entirely lose sight of the problem of meaning as an issue in old age.

The phenomena of aging and the life course have been treated in extensive detail by specialized disciplines. Since World War II, a vast empirical literature of gerontology has grown up. The dominant methodology in that literature has been inspired by a positivistic view of the natural and social sciences, a view that makes it difficult even to think of meaning as a legitimate object of inquiry. In addition, most studies of aging and the life course proceed from within a single specialized discipline—sociology, psychology, history, and so on. Given such an approach within a single discipline, it is inevitable that broader issues of meaning tend to be eclipsed. But will a multidisciplinary approach be any better? Combining all the specialized perspectives—each of which ignores the problem of meaning—will not result in a picture that is satisfactory. Apparently, deeper reflection on meaning and aging is called for in the very methods and assumptions that the specialized disciplines use to illuminate the last stage of life.

This bibliographical essay suggests four broad themes within gerontology that seem to call for deeper reflection about the problem of meaning and aging. These themes—the life cycle, modernity, death, and time—have all been treated in the gerontological literature. But they stand in unarticulated relationship to questions of meaning and it is this deeper set of questions that remains to be explored. An overview of these themes is followed by a brief suggestion of some emerging questions that will demand attention:

The Life Cycle. One of the distinctive achievements of scholarship in aging is attention to the idea of the human life course from an interdisciplinary point of view (Neugarten, 1979; Back, 1980), including the views of developmental psychology, autobiography, social history, etc. In such an enterprise the disciplines of the humanities must have a central place (Spicker, 1978; Van Tassel, 1979). For a variety of reasons, it is now becoming clear that a purely empirical study of the human life course cannot dispense with attention to value, meaning, and ideology.

Modernity. Within the gerontological literature there has been a persistent concern with the relationship between modernity and the social meaning of old age (Cowgill and Holmes, 1972; Achenbaum and Stearns, 1978). Modernity often entails a loss of traditional sources of meaning ascribed to old age, as illustrated by the problematic status of wisdom in modern, technological societies (Byrne, 1976). Again, the desirability of disengagement versus activity in late life is clearly a value-laden topic of controversy (Gustafson, 1977; Sill, 1980). Modern societies appear to have little room for values that formerly sustained a sense of meaning in the last stage of life. Indeed, only in modern societies does old age pose a distinctive question about meaning at all.

Death. The problem of meaning in old age is, to some degree, intertwined with the meaning of death (Aries, 1981; Choron, 1964). Does death make life meaningful or does it signify the end of meaning? The question can no longer remain speculative. With advances in biomedical technology and life-prolongation, the timing of death becomes increasingly a matter of explicit decision (Veatch, 1979; Kass, 1983). Bioethical decision-making cannot take meaning for granted in trying to weigh competing values such as welfare, justice, or autonomy.

Time. Gerontologists have been interested in questions of time and the self (Gubrium, 1976; Hazan, 1980; Kastenbaum, 1966). Issues of meaning and aging are bound up with the consciousness of time (Cottle and Klineberg, 1974) and the problematic nature of time for modern man (De Grazia, 1964; Dunne, 1973). Time consciousness seems tied to the "mid-life crisis" widely discussed in the literature of life span development psychology (Jacques, 1965; Eichorn, 1981). The meaning of time evidently has multiple implications for the study of human aging (Hendricks in Gubrium, 1976; and Hendricks, 1982).

In addition to the four broad themes cited above, a cluster of issues will command attention by scholars in the future:

(1) The interpretation of autobiography and reminiscence, life stories and personal narrative (Brockelman, 1980; Burrell and Hauerwas, 1977; Churchill, 1979).

(2) The dialectical, or contradictory experience of old age (Scott-Maxwell, 1979; Gadow, 1983) as disclosed by phenomenological or biographical methods.

(3) The changing historical configuration of the human life course (Hareven, 1976, 1978; Mayer and Muller, 1984), including implications for public policy (Nelson, 1982).

(4) The role of ideology and values in shaping our view of old age (Reigel, 1973; Cole, 1979, 1983).

(5) The nature and meaning of development over the life span (Kastenbaum, 1965; Peck, 1968; McCulloch, 1981; Pascual-Leone, 1983).

Disciplinary perspectives

A variety of disciplines—including philosophy, psychology, religion, history, the arts, and the social sciences—offer perspectives on the problem of meaning and aging. The references suggested here identify for the most part writers who have given explicit attention to problems of meaning in late life. Since meaning is inherently relational, we have also included certain important works which bear on the problem without directly addressing it. There are obviously many other references in which the meaning of old age is implicitly treated. By what criterion are such references to be included or excluded? A working criterion is illustrated in the field of biomedical ethics, in which we can find a fast-growing literature that considers issues such as autonomy, competency, quality of life, and choices about life-extension. But in this literature it is rare to find examples where the meaning of freedom or self or quality of life is treated with any detailed inquiry about the special position of old age. In our bibliography we have attempted to confine our selections from the vast literature on bioethics to those references where explicit reflection on meaning is to be found. The same criterion has been applied to other disciplines.

Philosophy. Philosophers have considered the problem of the meaning of life from a variety of methodological perspectives. Both Continental philosophy and, more recently, analytic philosophy have made contributions. The existential view acquired prominence in the work of Simone de Beauvoir (1972). There have been more rigorous efforts to use phenomenological methods (Philibert, 1974; Ainlay and Redfoot, 1983) in the qualitative study of aging: for example, the idea of intentionality (Lowenthal, 1971); in biography (Starr, 1983); or through the framework of hermeneutics (Watson, 1976). One methodologically fruitful result of the phenomenological approach has been renewed attention to the concept of meaning in narrative (Ricouer, 1984), a perspective applied to life span development (Cohler, 1982; Prado, 1983). The study of narrative and autobiography is a major current in contemporary literary theory, where, again, Continental perspectives are dominant (Olney, 1980).

Anglo-American analytic philosophers have also been willing to explore the problem of meaning in life (Britton, 1969; Klemke, 1981; Sanders, 1980). Certain philosophers have examined the structure of the human life course as a philosophical problem (Philibert, 1968; Norton, 1976). The problem of meaning obviously reaches far deeper than the concept of "life satisfaction" that has become a commonplace in the gerontological literature (McKee, 1981). In the domain of practice, problems of meaning are related to dilemmas of ethical choice (Lesnoff-Caravaglia, 1984): for example, in geriatric health care decisions, a subject of attention in biomedical ethics (Caplan, 1981; Engelhardt, 1977). Similar questions of meaning arise in older adult education (Moody, 1976, 1978).

Psychology. Psychology in the twentieth century long neglected questions of meaning and aging, despite the significant early work by Charlotte Buhler (1935). Among depth psychologists, Freudian psychoanalysis has at times illuminated issues of meaning in late life (Gutmann, 1981). Jungians have long been interested in the archetypes of wisdom and age (Hillman, 1975; Weaver, 1964) as well as the meaning of modern youth culture (Von Franz, no date).

Ego psychology, notably through the work of Erik Erikson (1950, 1975, 1976), early drew attention to the structure of the human life cycle as a whole (Roazen, 1976). This approach has become very prominent in the last decade (Levinson, 1978). Psychologists concerned with self-actualization in late life (Maslow, 1962; Landua and Moaz, 1978; May, 1982) have pointed to positive dimensions of meaning in old age. These preoccupations are closely linked to the study of creativity in later life (Gedo and Pollock, 1984; McLeish, 1976) and the nature of wisdom (Staude, 1981; Clayton, 1980).

Gerontology has been concerned with the question of meaning through life span development psychology (Breytspraak, 1982). Gerontologists have displayed particular interest in the ideas of reminiscence and life review (Butler, 1963; Lieberman and Falk, 1971; Merriam, 1980; Gerfo, 1981; Kaminsky, 1984). The idea of moral development has been extended beyond childhood to include a life span perspective (Kohlberg, 1973).

Religion. The problem of meaning in old age has evident kinship with religion (LeFevre and LeFevre, 1981). Sociologists of religions have examined spiritual well-being in connection with late-life meaning (Moberg, 1979). Others have written about the problem of meaning from the standpoint of pastoral theology (McClellan, 1977; Clements, 1981). Aging and the life course have also been examined from the standpoint of comparative religion (Kakar, 1968).

Perhaps a more significant development in recent years has been the application of life span development psychology to the stages of faith or to religious development itself (Fowler, 1981). This psychological emphasis can be juxtaposed with comparable explorations in theology, explorations undertaken sometimes from a classical viewpoint (Hiltner, 1975), sometimes from the viewpoint of depth psychology (Whitehead and Whitehead, 1979; Bianchi, 1982).

Arts and Literature. The meaning of old age is of particular importance in the arts. Art historians have identified a distinctive "late style" of artists in their old age (Arnheim, 1978; Clark, 1972; O'Conner, 1979; Munsterberg, 1983). Issues of meaning and aging cut across the fields of literature, philosophy, and visual arts (Lefcowitz and Lefcowitz, 1976; Berg and Gadow, 1978) and across different cultures (Maduro, 1974). A similar pattern of late styles can be discerned in literary artists (Grene, 1967; Woodward, 1980). Some students of gerontology have used literary sources (Merriam, 1980) for empirical investigation; others have collected an extensive range of those literary sources (Lyell, 1980). Literary criticism has examined the meaning of aging in fiction (Loughman, 1977; Sohngen, 1977; Berdes, 1981) and in poetry (Sohngen, 1978; Clark, 1980; Zavatsky, 1984).

History. Although some intellectual historians have emphasized the importance of meaning (Bouwsma, 1981), such an approach has not yet seriously influenced the history of aging and old age, which is barely a decade old. Several works (Fischer, 1978; Stearns, 1976; Thomas, 1977) connected early modern European and American systems of authority with ideas about old age. Other work (Haber, 1983; Cole, 1983, 1984; Gratton, 1984; Gruman, 1979; Hareven, 1976) has emphasized the importance of scientific expertise in shaping late nineteenth- and twentieth-century understandings of old age. For the most part, historians have been more concerned with sociological questions of changing roles, status, and behavior (Achenbaum, 1977; Demos, 1978; Graebner, 1981; Kleinberg, 1982; Laslett, 1977) than with questions about the intellectual vitality and cultural power of ideas about old age. Important work has been done on changing configurations of the life course (Chudacoff, 1980; Hareven, 1978; Elder, 1978; Smith, 1982) in the light of economic and family history.

The recent historical studies of old age have approached the aged almost exclusively as objects of society's veneration or contempt, recipients of its benevolence or neglect, and as products of the historical forces of demography, social structure, and political economy. We are just beginning to see scholarly attention to old people as centers of meaning and value (Premo, 1983; Cole and Premo, forthcoming); the increasing attention to the personal writings of old people presages the growth of a dialectical phenomenology in which historians explore the moral, spiritual, and psychological experience of aging in its many ideological and structural contexts.

Anthropology. In cultural anthropology, the question of meaning and the life course grew out of the use of biographical methods (Langness, 1981), a concern shared by some sociologists (Berger, 1974; Bertaux, 1982; Rosenmayr, 1978, 1981). This concern is of obvious importance in cross-cultural studies of aging (Plath, 1980). Anthropologists have long been interested in rites of passage signalling life course transitions (Van Gennep, 1909); today, this work is often informed by theories of age differentiation (Keith, 1982) and motivated by a desire to demonstrate and understand our own as well as other ways of growing old (Amoss, 1981; Kertzer and Keith, 1984). Recently, anthropologists have also focused on the role of myth and ritual in shamanism (Halifax, 1981) as well as in contemporary cultural communities (Myerhoff, 1975, 1980).

Sociology. The study of aging in modern societies has confronted the fact that succeeding generations show shifts in values and meanings attached to the different life stages. The study of social and cultural changes underscores the concept of generations, an idea prominent in the work of Mannheim (1952) and one that continues to be a central concept in studies of aging (Bengtson and Cutler, 1976; Wuthnow, 1976). Sociological research has increasingly often utilized historical and anthropological perspectives in following the aging of cohorts through historical time, family time, and the life course (Riley, Abeles, and Teitelbaum, 1982; Riley, Hess, and Bond, 1983). The issues of intergenerational obligations have been examined as a problem of ethics and social policy (Daniels, 1979). A few sociologists, such as Rosenmayr (1983), have explored questions of meaning in the very broadest context of culture and history.

A Select Bibliography

I. History and Public Policy

Achenbaum, W. Andrew. *Old Age in the New Land; the American Experience since 1790*. Baltimore: Johns Hopkins University Press, 1978.
———. *Shades of Gray*. Boston: Little, Brown, 1983.
Achenbaum, W. Andrew and Peter N. Stearns. "Old Age and Modernization." *The Gerontologist* 18 (1978): 307–12.
Aries, Philippe. *Centuries of Childhood; a Social History of Family Life*. Trans. by Robert Baldick. New York: Alfred A. Knopf, 1962.
———. *The Hour of Our Death*. Trans. by Helen Weaver. New York: Alfred A. Knopf, 1981.
———. *Western Attitudes Toward Death: From the Middle Ages to the Present*. Trans. by P. M. Ranum. Baltimore: Johns Hopkins University Press, 1974.
Bertman, Stephen, ed. *The Conflict of Generations in Ancient Greece. and Rome*. Atlantic Highlands, N.J.: Humanities Press, 1976.
Binstock, Robert H. "Responsibility for the Care of the Geriatric Patient: Legal, Psychological, and Ethical Issues—Fantasies and Facts about Social Policy and Aging." *Journal of Geriatric Psychiatry* 5 (1972): 148–59. Discussion: 160–73.
Bouwsma, William J. "Intellectual History in the 1980s: From History of Ideas to History of Meaning." *Journal of Interdisciplinary History* 12 (1981): 279–91.
Carlton, Charles. "The Widow's Tale: Male Myths and Female Reality in Sixteenth and Seventeenth Century England." *Albion* 10 (1978): 118–29.
Chew, Samuel Claggett. *The Pilgrimage of Life*. New Haven: Yale University Press, 1962.
Chudacoff, Howard. "The Life Course of Women: Age and Age Consciousness, 1865–1915." *Journal of Family History* 5 (Fall 1980): 274–92.

Cohen, Elias S. "Civil Liberties and the Frail Elderly." *Society* 15 (July/August 1978): 34–42.
Cole, Thomas R. "Aging, Meaning, and Well-Being: Musings of a Cultural Historian." *International Journal of Aging and Human Development* 19 (1984): 329–36.
———. "The 'Enlightened' View of Aging: Victorian Morality in a New Key." *Hastings Center Report* 13 (June 1983): 34–40.
———. "The Ideology of Old Age and Death in American History." *American Quarterly* 31 (Summer 1979): 223–31.
———. "The Prophecy of *Senescence:* G. Stanley Hall and the Reconstruction of Old Age in America." *The Gerontologist* 24 (August 1984): 360–66.
——— and Terri L. Premo. "The Pilgrimage of Joel Andrews: Aging in the Autobiography of a Yankee Farmer." *International Journal of Aging and Human Development* (forthcoming).
Demos, John. "Old Age in Early New England." In *The American Family in Social-Historical Perspective,* edited by Michael Gordon, 2d ed., 220–56. New York: St. Martin's Press, 1978.
Engelhardt, H. Tristram. "Treating Aging: Restructuring the Human Condition." In *Extending the Human Life Span: Social Policy and Social Ethics,* edited by Bernice L. Neugarten and Robert J. Havighurst, 33–39. Chicago: University of Chicago Press, 1977.
Estes, Carroll Lynn. *The Aging Enterprise.* San Francisco: Jossey-Bass, 1979.
———, et al. *Political Economy, Health, and Aging.* Boston: Little, Brown, 1984.
Fischer, David Hackett. *Growing Old in America.* (Expanded edition) New York: Oxford University Press, 1978.
Graebner, William. *A History of Retirement: The Meaning and Function of an American Institution, 1885–1978.* New Haven: Yale University Press, 1980.
Gratton, Brian. "The Infant Geriatrics." *International Journal of Aging and Human Development* 19 (1984): 253–56.
———. "Social Workers and Old Age Pensions." *Social Service Review* 57, no. 3 (September 1983): 403–15.
———. *Urban Elders: Family, Work, and Welfare Among Boston's Aged, 1890–1950.* Philadelphia: Temple University Press, 1985.
Gruman, Gerald J. "A History of Ideas about the Prolongation of Life." *Transactions of the American Philosophical Society,* n.s. 56, pt. 9 (December 1966): 3–102.
———, ed. *The 'Fixed Period' Controversy: Prelude to Ageism: An Original Anthology.* New York: Arno Press, 1979.
Haber, Carole. *Beyond Sixty-Five: The Dilemma of Old Age in America's Past.* New York: Cambridge University Press, 1983.
Hareven, Tamara K. "Family Time and Historical Time." *Daedalus* 106 (Spring 1977): 57–70.
———. "The Last Stage: Historical Adulthood and Old Age." *Daedalus* 105 (Fall 1976): 13–27.
———. "The Search for Generational Memory: Tribal Rites in Industrial Society." *Daedalus* 107 (Fall 1978): 137–49.
———, ed. *Transitions: The Family and the Life Course in Historical Perspective.* New York: Academic Press, 1978.
Kleinberg, Susan J. "The History of Old Age." *Convergence in Aging* 1 (March 1982): 124–37.

Kriegel, Annie. "Generational Difference: The History of an Idea." *Daedalus* 107 (Fall 1978): 23–38.

Laslett, Peter. *Family Life and Illicit Love in Earlier Generations.* Cambridge: Cambridge University Press, 1977. Chap. 5: "The History of Aging and the Aged," 174–213.

———. *The World We Have Lost*, 2d ed. New York: Scribners, 1971.

Nelson, Douglas W. "The Meanings of Old Age for Public Policy." *National Forum* 62 (Fall 1982).

Neugarten, Bernice L., ed. *Age or Need?: Public Policies for Older People.* Beverly Hills: Sage Publications, 1982.

Neugarten, Bernice L., and Robert J. Havighurst, eds. *Extending the Human Life Span: Social Policy and Social Ethics.* Chicago: University of Chicago, Committee on Human Development, 1977.

———, eds. *Social Policy, Social Ethics, and the Aging Society.* Committee on Human Development, University of Chicago. Washington, D.C.: Superintendent of Documents, U.S. Government Printing Office, 1976.

Premo, Terri L. "Like a Being Who Does Not Belong: The Old Age of Deborah Norris Logan." *Pennsylvania Magazine of History and Biography* 107 (January 1983): 85–112.

Roebuck, Janet. "When Does Old Age Begin? The Evolution of the English Definition." *Journal of Social History* 12 (Spring 1979): 416–28.

Smith, Daniel Scott. "Historical Change in the Household Structure of the Elderly in Economically Developed Societies." In *Aging: Stability and Change in the Family*, edited by Robert Fogel et al. New York: Academic Press, 1981, 91–114.

Sprandel, Rolf. *Alterschicksal und Altersmoral.* Stuttgart: Anton Hiersemann, 1981.

Stannard, David E. *The Puritan Way of Death.* New York: Oxford University Press, 1977.

Stearns, Peter N. *Old Age in European Society: The Case of France.* New York: Holmes and Meier, 1976.

———. "Toward a Historical Gerontology." Review of *Growing Old in America*, by David Hackett Fischer. *Journal of Interdisciplinary History* 8 (Spring 1978): 737–46.

———, ed. *Old Age in Pre-Industrial Society.* New York: Holmes and Meier, 1983.

Thomas, Keith. "Age and Authority in Early Modern England." *Proceedings of the British Academy* 62 (1976): 205–48. London: Oxford University Press, 1977.

Tobriner, Alice. "Almshouses in Sixteenth-century England: Housing for the Poor Elderly," *Journal of Religion and Aging* 1 (4), (Summer 1985): 13–41.

———. "Honor for Old Age: Sixteenth-Century Pious Ideal or Grim Delusion?" *Journal of Religion and Aging* 1 (3), (Spring 1985): 1–21.

Trimmer, Eric James. *Rejuvenation: The History of an Idea.* London: Hale, 1967.

See also:

II. *Philosophy:* Choron, 1963.

IV. *Medicine, Nursing, and Health Care:* Cole and Winkler, 1985; Fox, 1972; Grant, 1963.

V. *Psychology:* Erikson, 1975; Riegel, 1973; Runyan, 1982.
VI. *Sociology and Anthropology:* Cowgill and Holmes, 1972; Demos and Boocock, 1978; Elder, 1978, 1982; Hendricks, 1982; Spanier and Glick, 1980; Uhlenberg, 1978.
VII. *Gerontology:* Freeman, 1979; Gruman, 1979; Hareven, 1982; Hendricks, 1975; Philibert, 1965.

II. Philosophy

Amoss, Pamela T., and Stevan Harrell, eds. *Other Ways of Growing Old.* Stanford: Stanford University Press, 1981.
Becker, Ernest. *The Denial of Death.* New York: Free Press, 1973.
Berg, Geri, and Sally A. Gadow. "Toward More Human Meanings of Aging: Ideals and Images from Philosophy and Art." In *Aging and the Elderly,* edited by Stuart F. Spicker, Kathleen M. Woodward, and David D. Van Tassel, 83–92. Atlantic Highlands, N.J.: Humanities Press, 1978.
Bertaux, Daniel. "The Life Course Approach as a Challenge to the Social Sciences." In *Aging and Life Course Transitions,* edited by Tamara K. Hareven, 127–50. New York: Academic Press, 1978.
Britton, Karl. *Philosophy and the Meaning of Life.* New York: Cambridge University Press, 1969.
Brockelman, Paul T. "Myths and Stories: The Depth Dimension of Our Lives." *Philosophy Today* 24 (Spring 1980): 73–88.
Burrell, David, and Stanley Hauerwas. "From System to Story: An Alternative Pattern for Rationality in Ethics." In *Knowledge, Value and Belief,* edited by H. Tristram Engelhardt and Daniel Callahan, 111–52. Hastings-on-Hudson, N.Y.: Hastings Center, 1977.
Byrne, Edmund. "Death and Aging in Technopolis: Toward a Role Definition of Wisdom." *Journal of Value Inquiry* 10 (Fall 1976): 161–77.
Callahan, Sidney and Drew Christiansen. "Ideal Old Age." *Soundings* 57 (Spring 1974): 1–16.
Caplan, Arthur L. "Is Aging a Disease?" In *Vitalizing Long-Term Care,* edited by Stuart F. Spicker and Stanley R. Ingman, 14–28. New York: Springer 1984.
————. "The 'Unnaturalness' of Aging—A Sickness Unto Death?" In *Concepts of Health and Disease,* edited by Caplan et al., 725–37. Reading, Mass.: Addison-Wesley, 1981.
Charme, Stuart L. *Meaning and Myth in the Study of Lives: A Sartrian Perspective.* Philadelphia: University of Pennsylvania Press, 1984.
Choron, Jacques. *Modern Man and Mortality.* New York: Collier Books, 1964.
————. *Death and Western Thought.* New York: Collier Books, 1963.
Churchill, Larry R. "The Human Experience of Dying: The Moral Primacy of Stories Over Stages." *Soundings* 62 (Spring 1979): 24–37.
Daniels, Norman. "Justice Between Age Groups: Am I My Parents' Keeper?" *Milbank Memorial Fund Quarterly. Health and Society* 61 (Summer 1983): 489–522.
Engelhardt, H. Tristram, and Daniel Callahan. *Knowledge, Value and Belief.* Hastings-on-Hudson, N.Y.: Hastings Center, 1977.
Erwin, Edward. *The Concept of Meaninglessness.* Baltimore: Johns Hopkins University Press, 1970.

Gadow, Sally A. "Frailty and Strength: The Dialectic in Aging." *The Geron-tologist* 23 (April 1983): 144–47.

Gustafson, James M. "Extension of the Active Life: Ethical Issues." In *Extending the Human Life Span*, edited by Bernice L. Neugarten and Robert J. Havighurst, 27–32. Chicago: University of Chicago Press, 1977.

Havice, Doris Webster. "Old Age: The Possibility of Enlightenment." *Soundings* 57 (Spring 1974): 70–79.

Hepburn, R. W. "Questions About the Meaning of Life." In *Religious Studies* 1 (April 1966): 125–40.

High, Dallas M. "Is 'Natural Death' an Illusion?" *Hastings Center Report* 8 (August 1978): 37–42.

Hustedde, Germaine. "Authentic Living—Graceful Aging." *Humanitas* 13 (February 1977): 53–68.

Joske, W. D. "Philosophy and the Meaning of Life." *Australasian Journal of Philosophy* 52 (1974): 93–104.

Klemke, E. D., ed. *The Meaning of Life*. New York: Oxford University Press, 1981.

Koestenbaum, Peter. "The Vitality of Death." *Journal of Existentialism* 5 (1964): 139–66.

Kuypers, Joseph A. "Aging: Potentials for Personal Liberation." *Humanitas* 13 (February 1977): 17–38.

Landsberg, Paul Ludwig. *The Experience of Death; the Moral Problem of Suicide*. London: Rockliff, 1953.

Langford, Thomas Anderson, and William Hardman Poteat. *Intellect and Hope; Essays in the Thought of Michael Polany*. Durham, N.C.: Duke University Press, 1968.

Leveton, Alan. "Time, Death and the Ego-Chill." *Journal of Existentialism* 6 (Fall 1965): 69–80.

McGee, Charles Douglas. *The Recovery of Meaning: An Essay on the Good Life*. New York: Random House, 1966.

MacIntyre, Alasdair C. *After Virtue*. Notre Dame, Ind.: University of Notre Dame Press, 1981.

McKee, Patrick L. *Philosophical Foundations of Gerontology*. New York: Human Sciences Press, 1982.

Moody, Harry R. "Reminiscence and the Recovery of the Public World," in *Uses of Reminiscence*, edited by Marc Kaminsky, 157–66. New York: Haworth Press, 1984.

Nielsen, Kai. "Linguistic Philosophy and 'The Meaning of Life.'" *Cross Currents* 14 (Summer 1964): 313–34.

Norton, David L. *Personal Destinies*. Princeton: Princeton University Press, 1976.

Orr, John B. "Aging, Catastrophe, and Moral Reasoning." *Soundings* 57 (Spring 1974): 17–32.

Philibert, Michel A. J., et al. "The Phenomenological Approach to Images of Aging." Trans. by John Orr, Erika Georges, Suzanne DeBenedictis, et al. *Soundings* 57 (Spring 1974): 33–49.

———. "Philosophical Approaches to Aging." In *Dimensions of Aging*, compiled by Jon Hendricks and C. Davis Hendricks. Cambridge, Mass.: Winthrop, 1979.

———. *L'echelle des ages*. Paris: Le Seuil, 1968.

Pieper, Josef. *Leisure, the Basis of Culture.* Trans. by Alexander Dru, rev. ed. New York: Pantheon Books, 1964.

Prado, C. G. "Ageing and Narrative." *International Journal of Applied Philosophy* 1 (Spring 1983): 1–14.

Putnam, Hilary. *Meaning and the Moral Sciences.* London: Routledge and Kegan Paul, 1978.

————. "The Meaning of Meaning." In *Language, Mind and Knowledge,* vol. 7, edited by K. Gunderson. Minnesota Studies in the Philosophy of Science. Minneapolis: University of Minnesota Press, 1975.

Reichbenbach, Maria, and Ruth Anna Mathers. "The Place of Time and Aging in the Natural Sciences and Scientific Philosophy." In *Handbook of Aging and the Individual,* edited by James Emmett Birren. Chicago: University of Chicago Press, 1959.

Ricoeur, Paul. *Time and Narrative.* 2 vols. Trans. by Kathleen McLaughlin and David Pellauer. Chicago: University of Chicago Press, 1984.

Riley, Matilda White, Ronald P. Abeles, and Michael S. Teitelbaum, eds. *Aging from Birth to Death.* Vol. 2: "Sociotemporal Perspectives." Boulder, Colo.: Westview Press, 1982.

————, Beth B. Hess, and Kathleen Bond, eds. *Aging in Society.* Hillsdale, N.J.: Lawrence Erlbaum Associates, 1983.

Sanders, Steven, and David R. Cheney, eds. *The Meaning of Life: Questions, Answers and Analysis.* Englewood Cliffs, N.J.: Prentice-Hall, 1980.

Stern, Alfred. *The Search for Meaning: Philosophical Vistas.* Memphis: Memphis State University Press, 1971.

Tournier, Paul. *Learn to Grow Old.* Trans. by Edwin Hudson. New York: Harper and Row, 1972.

Wisdom, John. "The Meanings of the Question of Life." In his *Paradox and Discovery,* 38–42. Oxford: Basil Blackwell, 1966.

See also:

III. Religion: Heschel, 1965.

IV. Medicine, Nursing, and Health Care: Kass, 1983; Veach, 1979.

V. Psychology: Ainlay and Redfoot, 1982–83; G. May, 1982; R. May, 1981, 1983; Vischer, 1948, 1967; Yalom, 1974.

VI. Gerontology: Beauvoir, 1974; Gadow, 1983; Moody, 1976, 1978.

III. Religion

Bianchi, Eugene C. *Aging as a Spiritual Journey.* New York: Crossroad, 1982.

Bouwsma, William J. "Christian Adulthood." *Daedalus* 105 (Spring 1976): 77–92.

Browning, Don S. "Preface to a Practical Theology of Aging." In *Toward a Theology of Aging,* by Seward Hiltner, 151–67. New York: Human Sciences Press, 1975.

Clements, William M. *Ministry with the Aging: Designs, Challenges, Foundations.* New York: Harper and Row, 1981.

Downing, Christine. "Your Old Men Shall Dream Dreams." In *Wisdom and Age,* edited by John Raphael Staude. Berkeley: Ross Books, 1981.

Fecher, Vincent John, comp. *Religion and Aging: An Annotated Bibliography.* San Antonio: Trinity University Press, 1982.

Gatch, Milton McCormick. *Death: Meaning and Mortality in Christian Thought and Contemporary Culture.* New York: Seabury Press, 1969.

Gray, Robert M. and David Oscar Moberg. *The Church and the Older Person,* rev. ed. Grand Rapids, Mich.: Eerdmans, 1977.

Griffin, John J. "The Bible and Old Age." *Journal of Gerontology* 1 (October 1946): 464–71.

Heschel, Abraham Joshua. "To Grow in Wisdom." In his *The Insecurity of Freedom: Essays on Human Existence,* 70–84. New York: Farrar, Straus & Giroux, 1966.

———. *Who Is Man?* Stanford: Stanford University Press, 1965.

Hiltner, Seward. *Toward a Theology of Aging.* New York: Human Sciences Press, 1975.

Kakar, Sudhir. "The Human Life Cycle: The Traditional Hindu View and the Psychology of Erik Erikson." *Philosophy East and West* 18 (July 1968): 127–36.

LeFevre, Carol, and Perry D. LeFevre, eds. *Aging and the Human Spirit: A Reader in Religion and Gerontology.* Chicago: Exploration Press, 1981.

McClellan, Robert W. *Claiming a Frontier: Ministry and Older People.* Los Angeles: University of Southern California, Andrus Gerontology Center Publications Department, 1977.

Moberg, David Oscar. *Spiritual Well-Being: Background and Issues.* White House Conference on Aging: Background and Issues. Washington, D.C.: U.S. Government Printing Office, 1971.

———. "Spiritual Well-Being in Late Life." In *Late Life,* edited by Jaber T. Gubrium. Springfield, Ill.: Charles C Thomas, 1974.

North Texas State University. *Religion and the Aging: A Bibliography.* Denton: North Texas State University Press, 1981.

Nouwen, Henri J. M., and Walter J. Gaffney. *Aging.* Garden City, N.Y.: Doubleday, 1974.

O'Conner, G. *The Second Journey: Spiritual Awareness and the Mid-Life Crisis.* Ramsey, N.J.: Paulist Press, 1972.

Pruyser, Paul W. "Aging: Downward, Upward or Forward?" In Hiltner, *Toward a Theology of Aging,* 105–11.

Sill, John Stewart. "Disengagement Reconsidered: Awareness of Finitude." *The Gerontologist* 20 (1980): 457–62.

Thorson, James A., and Thomas C. Cook, eds. *Spiritual Well-Being of the Elderly.* Springfield, Ill.: Charles C Thomas, 1980.

Whitehead, Evelyn Eaton. "Religious Images of Aging: An Examination of Themes in Contemporary Christian Thought." In *Aging and the Elderly,* edited by Stuart F. Spicker, Kathleen M. Woodward, and David D. Van Tassel, 37–48. Atlantic Highlands, N.J.: Humanities Press, 1978.

Whitehead, Evelyn Eaton, and James D. Whitehead. "Spirituality and Aging." *Studies in Formative Spirituality* (November 1980).

———. *Christian Life Patterns: The Psychological Challenges and Religious Invitations of Adult Life.* Garden City, N.Y.: Doubleday, 1979.

See also:

I. *History and Public Policy:* Becker, 1973; Chew, 1962; Cole, 1983; Sprandel, 1981.

V. *Psychology:* Feifel, 1959, 1977; Fowler, 1981; Frankl, 1973.

VII. *Gerontology:* Tellis-Nayak, 1982.

IV. Medicine, Nursing, and Health Care

Avorn, Jerry. "Benefit and Cost Analysis in Geriatric Care: Turning Age Discrimination into Health Policy." *New England Journal of Medicine* 310 (May 17, 1984): 1294–1301.

Babb de Ramon, Pamela. "The Final Task: Life Review for the Dying Patient." *Nursing* 13 (February 1983): 44–49.

Barnard, David. "Psychosomatic Medicine and the Problem of Meaning." *Bulletin of the Menninger Clinic* 49 (January 1985): 10–28.

Barresi, Charles M. "The Meaning of Work: A Case Study of Elderly Poor." *Industrial Gerontology* n.s. 1 (Summer 1974): 24–34.

Bromberg, Shirley, and Christine K. Cassel. "Suicide in the Elderly: The Limits of Paternalism." *Journal of the American Geriatrics Society* 31 (November 1983): 698–703.

Caplan, Arthur L., H. Tristram Engelhardt, and James J. McCartney. *Concepts of Health and Disease.* Reading, Mass.: Addison-Wesley, 1981.

Chinn, Peggy L., ed. *Development and Aging.* Gaithersburg, Md.: Aspen Systems, 1983.

Christiansen, Drew. "Aging and the Aged: Ethical Implications in Aging." In *Encyclopedia of Bioethics,* edited by Warren T. Reich, vol. 1, 58–65. New York: Free Press, 1978.

Cole, Thomas R., and Mary G. Winkler. "Aging in Western Medicine and Iconography: History and the Ages of Man." *Medical Heritage* (September/October 1985): 335–47.

Einspruch, Burton C. "Helping to Make the Final Years Meaningful for the Elderly Residents of Nursing Homes." *Diseases of the Nervous System* 37 (1976): 439–42.

Fox, Sanford J. "Responsibility for the Care of the Geriatric Patient—Legal, Psychological, and Ethical Issues—Past, Present, and Future of a Child's Legal Responsibility for Support of His Parents." *Journal of Geriatric Psychiatry* 5 (1972): 137–47.

Fries, James F., and Lawrence M. Crapo. *Vitality and Aging.* San Francisco: W. H. Freeman, 1981.

Gadow, Sally A. "Advocacy Nursing and New Meanings of Aging." *The Nursing Clinics of North America* 14 (March 1979): 81–91.

———. "Medicine, Ethics, and the Elderly." *The Gerontologist* 20 (December 1980): 680–85.

Grant, Richard L. "Concepts of Aging: An Historical Review." *Perspectives in Biology and Medicine* 6 (1963): 443–78.

Grmek, Mirko Drazen. *On Ageing and Old Age; Basic Problems and Historic Aspects of Gerontology and Geriatrics.* Monographia Biologicae, vol. 5, 57–162. Den Haag: W. Junk, 1958.

Hamdy, R. C., and A. M. Braverman. "Ethical Conflicts in Long-Term Care of the Aged." *British Medical Journal* 280 (March 1980): 717. [Reply to an article by Astrid Norberg (February 1980): 377.]

Kass, Leon R. "The Case for Mortality." *The American Scholar* 52 (1983): 173–91.

Levine, Norman B., et al. "Existential Issues in the Management of the Demented Elderly Patient." *American Journal of Psychotherapy* 38 (1984): 215–23.

Libow, Leslie S. "The Interface of Clinical and Ethical Decisions in the Care of the Elderly." *Mount Sinai Journal of Medicine* 48 (November/December 1981): 480–88.

Margolis, Emmanuel. "Changing Disease Patterns, Changing Values—Problems of Geriatric Care in the U.S.A.: An Outsider's View." *Medical Care* 27 (1979): 1119–30.

Menkin, Eva Landecker. "Comment on Christiansen's Article: Dignity in Aging—Notes on Geriatric Ethics." *Journal of Humanistic Psychology* 18 (Spring 1978): 55–56.

Ratzan, Richard M. " 'Being Old Makes You Different': The Ethics of Research with Elderly Subjects." *Hastings Center Report* 10 (October 1980): 32–42.

Reich, Warren T. "Ethical Issues Related to Research Involving Elderly Subjects." *The Gerontologist* 18 (1978): 326–37.

Reiss, R. "Moral and Ethical Issues in Geriatric Surgery." *Journal of Medical Ethics* 6 (1980): 71–77.

Robertson, George S. "Dealing with the Brain-Damaged Old—Dignity Before Sanctity." *Journal of Medical Ethics* 8 (1982): 173–77. Commentary by F. J. Hebbert, 177–79.

Rogers, William R., and David Barnard, eds. *Nourishing the Humanistic in Medicine.* Pittsburgh: University of Pittsburgh Press, 1979.

Spicker, Stuart F. "The Role of Humanities in Geriatric Education." *The Gerontologist* 18 (1978): 578–81.

————, and Stanley R. Ingman. *Vitalizing Long-term Care: The Teaching Nursing Home and Other Perspectives.* New York: Springer, 1984.

Stanley, Barbara, ed. *Geriatric Psychiatry: Clinical, Ethical, and Legal Issues.* Washington, D.C.: American Psychiatric Press, 1985.

Thomasma, David C. "Ethical Judgments of Quality of Life in the Care of the Aged." *Journal of the American Geriatrics Society* 32 (1984): 525–27.

Veatch, Robert Marlin, ed. *Life Span: Values and Life-Extending Technologies.* New York: Harper and Row, 1979.

Watson, Wilbur H. "The Meanings of Touch: Geriatric Nursing." *Journal of Communication* 25 (Summer 1975): 104–12.

See also:

I. *History and Public Policy:* Engelhardt, 1977; Estes et al., 1984; Gruman, 1977; Haber, 1983; Trimmer, 1983.

II. *Philosophy:* Caplan, 1981, 1984; Daniels, 1979; Gustafson, 1977.

V. *Psychology:* Feifel, 1977; Kastenbaum, 1969; Vischer, 1948, 1967.

VII. *Gerontology:* Freeman, 1979; Gadow, 1984.

V. Psychology

Ainlay, Stephen G., and Donald L. Redfoot. "Aging and Identity-in-the-World: A Phenomenological Analysis." *International Journal of Aging and Human Development* 15 (1982–83): 1–16.

Baum, Willa. "The Therapeutic Value of Oral History." *International Journal of Aging and Human Development* 12, no. 1 (1980–81): 49–53.

Breytspraak, L. M. *The Development of the Self in Later Life.* Boston: Little, Brown, 1983.

Buhler, Charlotte. "The Curve of Life as Studied in Biographies." *Journal of Applied Psychology* 19 (1935): 405–09.

———. "Meaningful Living in the Mature Years." In *Aging and Leisure: A Research Perspective into the Meaningful Use of Time*, edited by Robert Watson Kleemeier, 345–87. New York: Oxford University Press, 1961.

———. "Old Age and Fulfillment of Life with Considerations of the Use of Time in Old Age." *Acta Psychologica* 19 (1961): 126–30.

———, and Fred Massarick. *The Course of Human Life*. New York: Springer, 1968.

Butler, Robert N. "The Life Review: An Interpretation of Reminiscence in the Aged." *Psychiatry* 26 (February 1963): 65–76.

———. "Successful Aging and the Role of the Life Review." In *Readings in Aging and Death*, edited by Steven H. Zarit, 13–19. New York: Harper and Row, 1977.

Clayton, Vivian P. "Erikson's Theory of Human Development as It Applies to the Aged: Wisdom as Contradictive Cognition." *Human Development* 18 (1975): 119–28.

Clayton, Vivian P., and James E. Birren. "The Development of Wisdom Across the Life-span: A Reexamination of an Ancient Topic." In *Life-span Development and Behavior*, edited by Paul B. Baltes and Orville Gilbert Brim, vol. 3, 103–35. New York: Academic Press, 1980.

Cohler, Bertram J. "Personal Narrative and Life Course." In *Life-span Development and Behavior*, edited by Paul B. Baltes and Orville Gilbert Brim, vol. 4, 205–41. New York: Academic Press, 1982.

Eichorn, Dorothy H., et al., eds. *Present and Past in Middle Life*. New York: Academic Press, 1981.

Elkind, David. "Age Changes in the Meaning of Religious Identity." *Review of Religious Research* 6 (1964): 36–40.

Eng, Erling. "World and Self in Ageing and Psychosis." *Journal of Phenomenological Psychology* 15 (Spring 1984): 21–31.

Erikson, Erik H. *Childhood and Society*. New York: W. W. Norton, 1950.

———. *Dimensions of a New Identity*. (Jefferson Lecture in the Humanities, 1973.) New York: W. W. Norton, 1974.

———. *Life History and the Historical Moment*. New York: W. W. Norton, 1975.

———. "Reflections on Dr. Borg's Life Cycle." *Daedalus* 105 (Spring 1976): 1–28.

Eurich, Alvin C., ed. *Major Transitions in the Human Life Cycle*. Lexington, Mass.: Lexington Books, 1981.

Feifel, Herman, ed. *The Meanings of Death*. New York: McGraw-Hill, 1959.

———, ed. *New Meanings of Death*. New York: McGraw-Hill, 1977.

Fowler, James W. *Stages of Faith: The Psychology of Human Development and the Quest for Meaning*. New York: Harper and Row, 1981.

Frankl, Viktor Emil. *Man's Search for Meaning: An Introduction to Logotherapy*. Trans. by Ilse Lasch, rev. ed. Boston: Beacon Press, 1962.

Gedo, J. E., and George H. Pollock, eds. *Psychoanalysis: The Vital Issues*. Vol. 1, sec. 3, "Creativity and the Life Course," 257–362. New York: International Universities Press, 1984.

George, Linda K., and Lucille B. Bearon. *Quality of Life in Older Persons: Meaning and Measurement*. New York: Human Sciences Press, 1980.

George, Linda K., Elizabeth J. Mutran, and Margaret R. Pennybacker. "The Meaning and Measurement of Age Identity." *Experimental Aging Research* 6 (1980): 283–98.

Giele, Janet Zollinger. "Adulthood as Transcendence of Age and Sex." In *Themes of Work and Love in Adulthood,* edited by Neil J. Smelser and Erik H. Erikson, 151–73. Cambridge, Mass.: Harvard University Press, 1980.

Gutmann, David L. "Psychoanalysis and Aging: A Developmental View." In *The Course of Life,* edited by Stanley I. Greenspan and George H. Pollock. Vol. 3: *Psychoanalytic Contributions toward Understanding Personality Development/Adulthood and the Aging Process.* Garden City, N.Y.: Adelphi University, Mental Health Study Center, Division of Mental Health Service Program, NIMH, 1981, 489–517.

Hall, Granville Stanley. *Senescence: The Last Half of Life.* New York: Appleton, 1922.

Hillman, James. "The 'Negative' Senex and A Renaissance Solution." *Spring* (1975): 77–109.

Jaques, Elliott. "Death and Mid-Life Crisis." *International Journal of Psychoanalysis* 46 (1965): 502–14.

Kastenbaum, Robert. "The Foreshortened Life Perspective." *Geriatrics* 24 (August 1969): 126–33.

———. "Is Old Age the End of Development?" In *New Thoughts on Old Age,* edited by Robert Kastenbaum. New York: Springer, 1964.

———. "On the Meaning of Time in Later Life." *Journal of Genetic Psychology* 109 (September 1966): 9–25.

Kastenbaum, Robert, and Ruth Aisenberg. *The Psychology of Death.* New York: Springer, 1972.

Kohlberg, Lawrence. "Stages and Aging in Moral Development: Some Speculations." *The Gerontologist* 13 (Winter 1973): 497–502.

Levinson, Daniel J. *The Seasons of a Man's Life.* New York: Alfred A. Knopf, 1978.

Lieberman, M. A., and Jacqueline M. Falk. "The Remembered Past as a Source of Data for Research on the Life Cycle." *Human Development* 14 (1971): 132–41.

Lifton, Robert Jay. *The Broken Connection: On Death and the Continuity of Life.* New York: Simon and Schuster, 1979.

———. *History and Human Survival.* New York: Random House, 1970.

———. "Protean Man." In his *History and Human Survival,* 311–31. New York: Random House, 1970.

Lowenthal, Marjorie Fiske. "Intentionality: Toward a Framework for the Study of Adaptation in Adulthood." *International Journal of Aging and Human Development* 2 (May 1971): 79–95.

Luce, Gay Gaer. *Your Second Life.* New York: Delacort Press, 1979.

McCulloch, Andrew W. "What Do We Mean by 'Development' in Old Age?" *Ageing and Society* 1 (1981): 229–43.

McGee, Charles Douglas. *The Recovery of Meaning: An Essay on the Good Life.* New York: Random House, 1966.

Marris, Peter. *Loss and Change.* London: Routledge and Kegan Paul, 1974.

May, Gerald G. *Will and Spirit: A Contemplative Psychology.* New York: Harper and Row, 1982.

May, Rollo. *The Discovery of Being: Writings in Existential Psychology.* New York: W. W. Norton, 1983.

———. *Freedom and Destiny.* New York: W. W. Norton, 1981.

Merriam, Sharan B. "The Concept and Function of Reminiscence: A Review of the Research." *The Gerontologist* 20 (1980): 604–09.

Munnichs, J. M. A. *Old Age and Finitude.* New York: Karger, 1966.

Nesselroade, John Richard, and Hayne W. Reese, eds. *Life-span Developmental Psychology: Methodological Issues.* New York: Academic Press, 1973.

Peck, Robert C. "Psychological Developments in the Second Half of Life." In *Middle Age and Aging,* edited by Bernice L. Neugarten, 88–92. Chicago: University of Chicago Press, 1968.

———. "Developmental Psychology and Society: Some Historical and Ethical Considerations." In *Life-span Developmental Psychology,* edited by John Richard Nesselroade and Hayne W. Reese. New York: Academic Press, 1973.

Riegel, Klaus F. "Toward a Dialectical Theory of Development." *Human Development* 18 (1975): 50–64.

Ruffin, Julian E. "The Anxiety of Meaninglessness." *Journal of Counseling and Development* 63 (September 1984): 40–42.

Runyan, William McKinley. *Life Histories and Psychobiography: Explorations in Theory and Method.* New York: Oxford University Press, 1982.

Sherman, Edmund, and Evelyn S. Newman. "The Meaning of Cherished Personal Possessions for the Elderly." *International Journal of Aging and Human Development* 8 (1977–78): 181–92.

Spence, Donald L. "The Role of Futurity in Aging Adaptation." *The Gerontologist* 8 (Autumn 1968): 180–83.

Vischer, Adolf Lukas. *Old Age: Its Compensations and Rewards.* Trans. by Bernard Miall. New York: Macmillan, 1948.

———. *On Growing Old.* Trans. by Gerald Orr. Boston: Houghton Mifflin, 1967.

Weisman, Avery Danto. *On Dying and Denying.* New York: Behavioral Publications, 1972.

———, and Robert Kastenbaum. "The Psychological Autopsy." *Community Mental Health Journal,* Monograph 4. New York, 1968.

Yalom, Irvin D. *Existential Psychotherapy.* New York: Basic Books, 1980.

See also:

I. *History and Public Policy:* Cole, 1984.

II. *Philosophy:* Ainlay and Redfoot, 1982–3; Becker, 1973; Tournier, 1972.

III. *Religion:* Bianchi, 1982; Bouwsma, 1976; Heschel, 1966; Kakar, 1968; O'Conner, 1972; Nouwen and Gaffney, 1974.

IV. *Medicine, Nursing and Health Care:* Barnard, 1985.

VI. *Sociology and Anthropology:* Berger and Berger, 1973; Rosenmayr, 1981; Schrader, 1982; Sill, 1980; Smelser and Erikson, 1980; Sorenson and Sherrod, 1984.

VII. *Gerontology:* Gubrium, 1976; Hoffman, 1977; Kaminsky, 1984; Rosenmayr, 1984.

VI. Sociology and Anthropology

Back, Kurt Wolfgang. *Life Course: Integrative Theories and Exemplary Populations*. Boulder, Colo.: Westview Press, 1980.

Bengtson, Vern L., and Neal E. Cutler. "Generations and Intergenerational Relations: Perspectives on Age Groups and Social Change." In *Handbook of Aging and the Social Sciences*, edited by Robert H. Binstock and Ethel Shanas, 130–59. New York: Van Nostrand Reinhold, 1976.

Berger, Peter L., Bridgette Berger, and Hansfried Kellner. *The Homeless Mind: Modernization and Consciousness*. New York: Random House, 1973.

Binstock, Robert H., and Ethel Shanas, eds. *Handbook of Aging and the Social Sciences*. New York: Van Nostrand Reinhold, 1976.

Cowgill, Donald Olen, and Lowell Don Holmes. *Aging and Modernization*. New York: Appleton-Century-Crofts, 1972.

Datan, Nancy. "The Life Cycle, Aging, and Death: Dialectical Perspectives." *Human Development* 20 (1977): 185–216.

De Grazia, Sebastian. *Of Time, Work, and Leisure*. Garden City, N.Y.: Anchor Books, 1964.

Demos, John, and Sarane Spence Boocock, eds. *Turning Points: Historical and Sociological Essays on the Family*. Chicago: University of Chicago Press, 1978.

Elder, Glen H. "Family History and the Life Course." In *Transitions*, edited by Tamara K. Hareven, 17–64. New York: Academic Press, 1978.

Elder, Glen H., et al. "Economic Crisis and Well-Being: Historical Influences from the 1930's to Old Age in Postwar America." Paper presented at the West Virginia University Conference on Life-Span Developmental Psychology, May 1982.

Faver, Catherine A. "Life Satisfaction and the Life-Cycle: The Effects of Values and Roles on Women's Well-Being." *Sociology and Social Research* 66 (1981/82): 435–51.

Francher, J. Scott. "American Values and the Disenfranchisement of the Aged." *The Eastern Anthropologist* 22 (1969): 29–36.

Fry, C., and J. Keith, eds. *New Methods for Old Age Research: Anthropological Alternatives*. Association for Anthropology and Gerontology, 1980.

Gennep, Arnold van. *Rites of Passage*. Trans. by Monika B. Vizedom and Gabrielle L. Caffee. Chicago: University of Chicago Press, 1960.

Hazan, Haim. *Limbo People: A Study of the Constitution of the Time Universe Among the Aged*. London: Routledge and Kegan Paul, 1980.

Kalish, Richard A. "Of Social Values and the Dying: A Defense of Disengagement." *The Family Coordinator* 21 (1972): 81–94.

Kaufman, Sharon. "Cultural Components of Identity in Old Age: A Case Study." *Ethos* 9 (1981): 51–87.

Keith, Jennie. *Old People as People*. Boston: Little, Brown, 1982.

Kertzer, David I., and Jennie Keith. *Age and Anthropological Theory*. Ithaca: Cornell University Press, 1984.

Lakoff, Sanford A. "The Future of Social Intervention." In *Handbook of Aging and the Social Sciences*, edited by Robert H. Binstock and Ethel Shanas, 643–63. New York: Van Nostrand Reinhold, 1976.

Langness, Lewis Leroy and Gelya Frank. *Lives: An Anthropological Approach to Biography*. Novato, Calif.: Chandler and Sharp, 1981.

Lasch, Christopher. "Aging in a Culture Without a Future," review of *No More Dying*, by Joel Kurtzman and Phillip Gordon and *Prolongevity*, by Albert Rosenfeld. *Hastings Center Report* 7 (August 1977): 42–44.

Laslett, Peter. "Societal Development and Aging." In *Handbook of Aging and the Social Sciences*, edited by Robert H. Binstock and Ethel Shanas, 87–116. New York: Van Nostrand Reinhold, 1976.

Lerner, Max. *America as a Civilization: Life and Thought in the U.S. Today.* New York: Simon and Schuster, 1957.

Marias, Julian. "Generations: I. The Concept." In *International Encyclopedia of the Social Sciences*, edited by David Sills, vol. 6, 88–92. New York: Macmillan and The Free Press, 1968.

Mayer, K. U., and W. Muller. "The Development of the State and the Structure of the Life Course." In *Lifespan Perspectives on Human Development*, edited by A. Sherrod Sorenson and F. Weinert, 1984.

Mizruchi, Ephraim H., Barry Glassner, and Thomas Pastorello. *Time and Aging: Conceptualization and Application in Sociological and Gerontological Research.* Bayside, N.Y.: General Hall, 1982.

Moore, Sally F., and Barbara G. Myerhoff. *Secular Ritual.* Amsterdam: Van Gorcum, 1977.

Mutran, Elizabeth, and Donald C. Reitzes. "Intergenerational Support Activities and Well-Being Among the Elderly: A Convergence of Exchange and Symbolic Interaction Perspectives." *American Sociological Review* 49 (February 1984): 117–30.

Myerhoff, Barbara G. "A Symbol Perfected in Death: Continuity and Ritual in the Life and Death of an Elderly Jew." In *Life's Career—Aging*, Myerhoff and Andrei Simic, 163–205. Beverly Hills: Sage Publications, 1978.

———. "Life History Among the Elderly: Performance, Visibility and Re-Membering." In *Life Course*, edited by Kurt W. Back, 133–53. Boulder, Colo.: Westview Press, 1980.

——— and Andrei Simic. *Life's Career—Aging: Cultural Variations on Growing Old.* Beverly Hills: Sage Publications, 1978.

———. *Number Our Days.* New York: Simon and Schuster, 1980.

———, and Virginia Tufte. "Life History as Integration: An Essay on an Experiential Model." *The Gerontologist* 15 (1975): 541–43.

Poteat, William H. "Myths, Stories, History, Eschatology, and Action: Some Polanyian Meditations." In *Intellect and Hope: Essays in the Thought of Michael Polanyi*, edited by Thomas Anderson Langford and William H. Poteat, 198–231. Durham, N.C.: Duke University Press, 1968.

Rex, John. *Sociology and the Demystification of the Modern World.* London: Routledge and Kegan Paul, 1974.

Riley, John W., Jr. "Dying and the Meanings of Death: Sociological Inquiries." *Annual Review of Sociology* 9 (1983): 191–216.

Riley, Matilda White. "Aging, Social Change, and the Power of Ideas." *Daedalus* 107 (Fall 1978): 39–52.

Riley, Matilda White, et al., eds. *Aging and Society.* Vol. 2, *Aging and the Professions.* New York: Russell Sage Foundation, 1969.

Robertson, Roland. *Meaning and Change: Explorations in the Cultural Sociology of Modern Societies.* New York: New York University Press, 1978.

Rosenmayr, Leopold. "Achievements, Doubts, and Prospects of the Sociology of Aging." *Human Development* 23 (1980): 46–62.

———. "Objective and Subjective Perspectives of Life Span Research." *Ageing and Society* 1 (March 1981): 29–49.

Schrader, William. "Demoralization in Modern Society: The Experiential Dilemma." *Contemporary Crisis* 6 (1982): 267–83.

Sill, John Stewart. "Disengagement Reconsidered: Awareness of Finitude." *The Gerontologist* 20 (1980): 457–62.

Smelser, Neil J., and Eric H. Erikson, eds. *Themes of Work and Love in Adulthood.* Cambridge, Mass.: Harvard University Press, 1980.

Sokolovsky, Jay, and Carl Cohen. "The Cultural Meaning of Personal Networks for the Inner-City Elderly." *Urban Anthropology* 7 (1978): 323–42.

Spanier, Graham B., and Paul C. Glick. "The Life Cycle of American Families." *Journal of Family History* 5 (Spring 1980): 97–111.

Uhlenberg, Peter. "Changing Configurations of the Life Course." In Tamara Hareven, *Transitions,* 65–98. New York: Academic Press, 1978.

Woehrer, Carol E. "Cultural Pluralism in American Families: The Influence of Ethnicity on Social Aspects of Aging." *The Family Coordinator* 27 (1978): 329–39.

Wood, Roy V., Joanne S. Yamauchi, and James J. Bradac. "The Communication of Meaning Across Generations." *Journal of Communication* 21 (1971): 160–69.

Wuthnow, Robert. "Recent Patterns of Secularization: A Problem of Generations?" *American Sociological Review* 4 (1976): 850–67.

See also:

I. *History and Public Policy:* Hareven, 1976, 1978.

II. *Philosophy:* Philibert, 1968.

V. *Psychology:* Cohler, 1982; Eurich, 1981; Feifel, 1959, 1977; Erikson, 1975; Giele, 1980; Lieberman and Falk, 1971; Marris, 1974; Munnichs, 1966; Riegel, 1973, 1975.

VII. *Gerontology:* Gubrium 1976; Hareven 1982; Rosenmayr 1984.

VII. Gerontology

Beauvoir, Simone de. *The Coming of Age.* Trans. by Patrick O'Brian. New York: G. P. Putnam's Sons, 1972.

Binstock, Robert H., and Ethel Shanas, eds. *Handbook of Aging and the Social Sciences.* New York: Van Nostrand Reinhold, 1976.

Birren, James E. *Handbook of Aging and the Individual.* Chicago: University of Chicago Press, 1959.

Borenstein, Audrey. "Chimes of Change and Hours: Views of Older Women in Twentieth–Century America." Madison, N.J.: Fairleigh Dickinson University Press, 1984.

Cahill, Pati. *The Arts, the Humanities, and Older Americans: A Catalogue of Program Profiles.* Washington, D.C.: National Council on Aging, 1981.

Chappell, Neena L. "Awareness of Death in the Disengagement Theory: A Conceptualization and an Empirical Investigation." *Omega* 6 (1975): 325–43.

De Grazia, Sebastian. "The Uses of Time." In *Aging and Leisure: A Research Perspective into the Meaningful Use of Time,* edited by Robert Watson Kleemeier, 113–53. New York: Oxford University Press, 1961.

Dychtwald, Ken. "The SAGE Project: A New Image of Age." *Journal of Humanistic Psychology* 18 (Spring 1978): 69–74.

Freeman, Joseph Theodore. *Aging: Its History and Literature.* New York: Human Sciences Press, 1979.

Gadow, Sally A. "Toward a Critical Gerontology: Curriculum Design in Philosophy and Aging." *Gerontology and Geriatrics Education* 4 (Fall 1983): 67–74.

————. "Humanities Teaching and Aging: Issues and Approaches in Medical Education." In *Vitalizing Long-term Care*, edited by Stuart F. Spicker and Stanley R. Ingman, 119–27. New York: Springer, 1984.

Gerfo, Marianne Lo. "Three Ways of Reminiscence in Theory and Practice." *International Journal of Aging and Human Development* 12 (1980/81): 39–48.

Gruman, Gerald J., ed. *Roots of Modern Gerontology and Geriatrics.* New York: Arno Press, 1979.

Gubrium, Jaber F., ed. *Time, Roles, and Self in Old Age.* New York: Human Sciences Press, 1976.

Hareven, Tamara K., and Kathleen J. Adams, eds. *Aging and Life Course Transitions: An Interdisciplinary Perspective.* New York: Guilford Press, 1982.

Hendricks, C. Davis, and Jon Hendricks. "Historical Development of the Multiplicity of Times and Implications for the Analysis of Aging." *The Human Context* 7 (1975): 117–29.

Hendricks, Jon. "Concepts of Time and Temporal Construction Among the Aged." In *Time, Roles, and Self in Old Age*, edited by Jaber F. Gubrium. New York: Human Sciences Press, 1976.

————, and C. Davis Hendricks. *Dimensions of Aging.* Cambridge, Mass.: Winthrop, 1979.

Hoffman, Adeline M. "Fulfillment in the Later Years." *Humanitas* 13 (February 1977): 5–15.

Kaminsky, Marc. *Uses of Reminiscence: New Ways of Working with Older Adults.* New York: Haworth Press, 1984.

Kastenbaum, Robert. "Gerontology's Search for Understanding." *The Gerontologist* 18 (1978): 59–63.

————. *New Thoughts on Old Age.* New York: Springer, 1964.

Kleemeier, Robert Watson. *Aging and Leisure: A Research Perspective into the Meaningful Use of Time.* New York: Oxford University Press, 1961.

Kleinberg, Susan J. "The Role of the Humanities in Gerontological Research." *The Gerontologist* 18 (1978): 574–76.

McKee, Patrick L. "Consummation: A Concept for Gerontologic Theory." *International Journal of Aging and Human Development* 12 (1980/81): 239–44.

Moody, Harry R. "Philosophical Presuppositions of Education for Old Age." *Educational Gerontology* 1 (January 1976): 1–16.

————. "Education and the Life Cycle: A Philosophy of Aging." In *Introduction to Educational Gerontology*, edited by Ronald H. Sherron and D. Barrey Lumsden. Washington, D.C.: Hemisphere Publishing, 1978.

Moss, Walter G. *Humanistic Perspectives on Aging: An Annotated Bibliography and Essay.* Ann Arbor: Institute of Gerontology, University of Michigan and Wayne State University, 1976.

———. "Humanities, Aging and the Public." *The Gerontologist* 18 (1978): 581–83.

Neugarten, Bernice L. *Middle Age and Aging.* Chicago: University of Chicago Press, 1968.

Philibert, Michel A. J. "The Emergence of Social Gerontology." *Journal of Social Issues* 21 (October 1965): 4–12.

Rosenmayr, Leopold. *Die Späte Freiheit* (The Late Freedom). Berlin: Severin and Siedler, 1983. See also review essay by Louis Lowy. *The Gerontologist* 24 (1984): 546–48.

Sherron, Ronald H., and D. Barry Lumsden. *Introduction to Educational Gerontology.* Washington, D.C.: Hemisphere Publishing, 1978.

Spicker, Stuart F., et al. *Aging and the Elderly: Humanistic Perspectives in Gerontology.* Atlantic Highlands, N.J.: Humanities Press, 1978.

Staude, John Raphael, ed. *Wisdom and Age.* Berkeley: Ross Books, 1981.

Tallmer, Margot, ed. *Thanatology and Aging.* New York: Columbia University Press, 1983.

Tellis-Nayak, V. "The Transcendent Standard: The Religious Ethos of the Rural Elderly." *The Gerontologist* 22 (1982): 359–63.

Van Tassel, David D., ed. *Aging, Death, and the Completion of Being.* Philadelphia: University of Pennsylvania Press, 1979.

Weisman, Avery Danto. "Does Old Age Make Sense? Decisions and Destiny in Growing Older." *Humanitas* 13 (February 1977): 111–20.

Wershow, Harold J., ed. *Controversial Issues in Gerontology.* New York: Springer, 1981.

Wesner, David O. "Aging as Loss and Decline," *Research Studies* 48(4) (December 1980): 183–97.

Zarit, Steven H., ed. *Readings in Aging and Death: Contemporary Perspectives,* 1977/78 ed. New York: Harper and Row, 1977.

See also:

I. *History and Public Policy:* Achenbaum, 1983; Cole, 1984; Gruman, 1979.

II. *Philosophy:* Berg and Gadow, 1978; Callahan, 1974; Caplan, 1981, 1984; Gadow, 1983; Hustedde, 1977; McKee, 1982; Philibert, 1968, 1974.

III. *Religion:* LeFevre, 1981.

IV. *Medicine, Nursing, and Health Care:* Freeman, 1979.

V. *Psychology:* Butler, 1963, 1977; George and Bearon, 1980; Kastenbaum, 1966; Merriam, 1980.

VI. *Sociology and Anthropology:* Kaufman, 1981.

VIII. *Art and Literature:* Ansello, 1977; Blythe, 1979; Charles, 1977; Morrow, 1979, 1983.

VIII. *Art and Literature*

Ansello, Edward F. "Old-Age and Literature: An Overview." *Educational Gerontology* 2 (1977): 211–18.

Arnheim, Rudolf. "On the Late Style of Life and Art." *Michigan Quarterly Review* 17 (Spring 1978): 149–56.

Berdes, Celia. "Winter Tales: Fiction about Aging." *The Gerontologist* 21 (1981): 121–25.

Blue, Gladys F. "The Aging as Portrayed in Realistic Fiction for Children, 1945–1975." *The Gerontologist* 18 (1978): 187–92.

Blythe, Ronald. *The View in Winter: Reflections on Old Age.* New York: Harcourt Brace Jovanovich, 1979.

Charles, D. C. "Literary Old Age: A Browse through History." *Educational Gerontology* 2 (1977): 237–53.

Clark, Kenneth. *The Artist Grows Old.* (Rede Lecture, 1970) New York: Cambridge University Press, 1972.

Clark, Martha. "The Poetry of Aging: Views of Old Age in Contemporary American Poetry." *The Gerontologist* 20 (1980): 188–91.

Cowley, Malcolm. *The View from Eighty.* New York: Viking Press, 1980.

Edel, Leon. "Portrait of the Artist as an Old Man." *The American Scholar* 47 (Winter 1977/78): 52–68.

Grene, David. *Reality and the Heroic Pattern: Last Plays of Ibsen, Shakespeare and Sophocles.* Chicago: University of Chicago Press, 1967.

Koch, Kenneth. *I Never Told Anybody: Teaching Poetry Writing in a Nursing Home.* New York: Random House, 1977.

Lefcowitz, Barbara F., and Allan B. Lefcowitz. "Old Age and the Modern Literary Imagination: An Overview." *Soundings* 59 (Winter 1976): 447–66.

Loughman, Celeste. "Novels of Senescence." *The Gerontologist* 17 (1977): 79–84.

Lyell, Ruth Granetz, ed. *Middle Age, Old Age: Short Stories, Poems, Plays, and Essays on Aging.* New York: Harcourt Brace Jovanovich, 1980.

Maduro, Renaldo. "Artistic Creativity and Aging in India." *International Journal of Aging and Human Development* 5 (1974): 303–29.

Morrow, Patricia, ed. *The Meanings of Old Age.* Columbia: Missouri Gerontology Institute, 1983.

Munsterberg, Hugo. *The Crown of Life: Artistic Creativity in Old Age.* New York: Harcourt Brace Jovanovich, 1983.

O'Connor, Francis V. "Albert Berne and the Completion of Being: Images of Vitality Extinction in the Last Paintings of a 96-year-old Man." In *Aging, Death, and the Contemplation of Being,* edited by David D. Van Tassel, 255–89. Philadelphia: University of Pennsylvania Press, 1979.

Riley, Matilda White, et al., eds. *Aging and Society.* Vol. 3, *A Sociology of Age Stratification.* New York: Russell Sage Foundation, 1972.

Sohngen, Mary. "The Experience of Old Age as Depicted in Contemporary Novels." *The Gerontologist* 17 (1977): 70–78.

———. "The Writer as an Old Woman." *The Gerontologist* 15 (1975): 493–98.

———, and Robert J. Smith. "Images of Old Age in Poetry." *The Gerontologist* 18 (1978): 181–86.

Thomas, Lloyd S. "Krapp: Beckett's Aged Narcissus." *CEA Critic* 39 (January 1977): 9–11.

Todd, Janet. *Gender and Literary Voice.* New York: Holmes and Meier, 1980.

Westbrook, F. "Death, Separation, and Autumn Imagery in Early Chinese Poetry." *Advanced Thanatology* 5, no. 1 (1980): 38–61.

Wiseman, Richard. "The Aging Genius." In *Wisdom and Age,* edited by John Raphael Staude. Berkeley: Ross Books, 1981.

Woodward, Kathleen M. *At Last, the Real Distinguished Thing.* Athens: Ohio University Press, 1980.

———. "Frailty and the Meanings of Literature." In *Vitalizing Long-term*

Care, edited by Stuart F. Spicker and Stanley Ingman, 128–37, New York: Springer, 1984.

———. "May Sarton and the Fictions of Old Age." In *Gender and Literary Voice,* edited by Janet Todd. New York: Holmes and Meier, 1980.

Zavatsky, William. "Journey through the Feminine: The Life Review Poems of William Carlos Williams." In *Uses of Reminiscence,* edited by Marc Kaminsky. New York: Haworth Press, 1984.

See also:

I. *History and Public Policy:* Carlton 1978.

II. *Philosophy:* Berg and Gadow 1978; Hustedde 1977.

IV. *Medicine, Nursing and Health Care:* Cole and Winkler 1985.

V. *Psychology:* Erikson 1976.

VII. *Gerontology:* Beauvoir 1972.

FURTHER SOURCES

Conrad, C. "Altwerden und Altsein in Historicher Perspektive. Zur neueren Literatur." *Zeitschrift fur Sozialisationforschung und Erziehungssoziologie* 2 (1982): 131–45.

———. "Geschicte des Alterns: Lebensverhaltnisse und sozialpolitische Regulierung." *Zeitschrift fur Sozialisationsforchung und Erziehungssoziologie* 4 (1984): 143–56.

Kondratowitz, Hans-Joachim von. "Societal and Administrative Definitions of Old Age: Continuities and Change in Germany from the 18th Century to the 20th Century." In *Old Age in a Bureaucratic Society: The Elderly, the Experts, and the State in American History,* edited by David Van Tassel and Peter Stearns. Westport, Conn.: Greenwood Press, 1986.

Contributors

W. ANDREW ACHENBAUM is Associate Professor in the Applied History and Social Sciences Program at Carnegie-Mellon University, Pittsburgh, and a consultant to the Institute of Gerontology in The University of Michigan, Ann Arbor. The author of *Old Age in the New Land* and *Shades of Gray*, he is completing a history of Social Security in America for The Twentieth Century Fund.

ROBERT A. BURT is the Southmayd Professor of Law at Yale University, where he is Co-Chairman of the Program in Law and Medicine. He is a member of the bars of the District of Columbia, Michigan, and the United States Supreme Court and is the author of *Taking Care of Strangers*.

CHRISTINE K. CASSELL, M.D., is Associate Professor of Medicine, University of Chicago Pritzker School of Medicine. She is coeditor of *Geriatric Medicine*.

THOMAS R. COLE is Assistant Professor of History and Medicine in the Institute for the Medical Humanities at The University of Texas Medical Branch in Galveston. His essays on aging and cultural history have appeared in *American Quarterly*, *The Gerontologist*, and the *Hastings Center Report*. He is completing a history of aging in American culture and working on a study of aging in American autobiography.

SALLY GADOW is a health care philosopher living in England. She has contributed to curriculum development in aging at the Johns Hopkins University, the University of Florida, and the University of Texas Medical Branch at Galveston. Her publications address issues in geriatric ethics and the phenomenology of aging.

WILLIAM F. MAY is the Cary M. Maguire Professor of Ethics, Southern Methodist University. As a Founding Fellow of the Hastings Center, he co-chaired its research group on death and dying. His most recent book is *The Physician's Covenant*.

HARRY R. MOODY is Deputy Director for Academic Affairs at the Brookdale Center on Aging of Hunter College in New York. A philosopher, his interests include reminiscence, late style in art, education and public policy for older people. His articles have appeared in *Thanatology and Aging* and *Educational Gerontology*.

DAVID W. PLATH is Professor of Anthropology and Asian Studies at the University of Illinois at Urbana-Champaign. The author of *Long Engagements*, he has concentrated in recent years on aging and the life cycle in modern Japan.

NATALIE ROSEL is Assistant Professor of Social Gerontology and Sociology at New College, University of South Florida in Sarasota. After completing her Ph.D. research on institutionalized elderly, she settled in a neighborhood of primarily older people, where she has been studying their relationships in preparation for a forthcoming monograph.

KATHLEEN WOODWARD is Director of the Center for Twentieth Century Studies and Associate Professor of English at the University of Wisconsin in Milwaukee. She is coeditor of *Aging and the Elderly* and author of *At Last, the Real Distinguished Thing: The Late Poems of Eliot, Pound, Stevens, and Williams*.

Notes

Introduction

1 G. Stanley Hall, *Senescence* (New York: D. Appleton, 1922), 403.
2 Carl G. Jung, "The Stages of Life," in *Modern Man in Search of a Soul* (New York: Harcourt Brace Jovanovich, 1933).
3 A. L. Vischer, *On Growing Old*, trans. G. Onn (Boston: Houghton Mifflin, 1967), 23.
4 Erik Erikson, "Human Strength and the Cycle of Generations," in *Insight and Responsibility* (New York: W. W. Norton, 1964), 132.
5 Irving Rosow, *Socialization to Old Age* (Berkeley: University of California Press, 1974), 148.
6 Leopold Rosenmayr, "Achievements, Doubts and Prospects of the Sociology of Aging," *Human Development* 23 (1980): 60.
7 Philip Rieff, *The Triumph of the Therapeutic* (New York: Harper and Row, 1966).
8 Mary Douglas and Steven M. Tipton, eds., *Religion and America* (Boston: Beacon Press, 1983).
9 Robert Nozick, *Philosophical Explanations* (Cambridge, Mass.: Harvard University Press, 1981), 574–75.
10 See Charles Taylor, "Interpretation and the Sciences of Man," and H. G. Gadamer, "The Problem of Historical Consciousness," in Paul Rabinow and William M. Sullivan, eds., *Interpretive Social Science* (Berkeley: University of California Press, 1979), 25–71, 103–160.
11 Herbert Fingarette, *The Self in Transformation* (New York: Harper and Row, 1977), 63–64.
12 Gerald N. Izenberg, *The Existentialist Critique of Freud* (Princeton: Princeton University Press, 1976).
13 Ronald Blythe, *The View in Winter: Reflections on Old Age* (New York: Harcourt Brace Jovanovich, 1979), 29.

Notes

The Meaning of Life and the Meaning of Old Age

1 M. C. Nelson, ed., *The Narcissistic Condition: A Fact of Our Lives and Times* (New York: Human Sciences Press, 1977).

2 Philip Rieff, *The Triumph of the Therapeutic* (New York: Harper and Row, 1966); Christopher Lasch, *The Culture of Narcissism* (New York: W. W. Norton, 1978).

3 Ludwig Wittgenstein, *Tractatus Logico-Philosophicus*, trans. D. F. Pears and B. F. McGuinness (London: Routledge and Kegan Paul, 1961), 149–51.

4 Elliot Jaques, "Death and Mid-Life Crisis,"' *International Journal of Psycho-Analysis* 46, no. 4 (1965): 502–12.

5 See Kenneth Boulding, *The Image* (Ann Arbor: University of Michigan Press, 1956). Boulding is heavily influenced by Fred Pollak, *The Image of the Future.*

6 Milton Munitz, *The Mystery of Existence* (New York: Appleton-Century-Crofts, 1966).

7 See Steven Korner, *Kant* (New York: Penguin Books, 1955). For more detail, see Alfred C. Ewing, *A Short Commentary on Kant's Critique of Pure Reason* (Chicago: University of Chicago Press, 1970).

8 Erik Erikson, "The Human Life Cycle," *International Encyclopedia of the Social Sciences* (1968). For an appraisal, see Paul Roazen, *Erik Erikson: The Limits of a Vision* (New York: Free Press, 1977).

9 David Ross, *Aristotle* (New York: Barnes & Noble, 1964); and John Herman Randall, Jr., *Aristotle* (New York: Columbia University Press, 1960). A reconstruction of the Aristotelian point of view applied to life span development can be found in David Norton, *Personal Destinies* (Princeton: Princeton University Press, 1976). Norton is one of the few American philosophers who has approached the concept of life stages as a significant philosophical problem.

10 John M. Rist, *The Stoic Philosophy* (New York: Cambridge University Press, 1969).

11 On the question of "rational suicide" based on declining quality of life in old age, see H. R. Moody, "Can Suicide on Grounds of Old Age Be Ethically Justified?" in Margot Tallmer, ed., *Thanatology and Aging* (New York: Columbia University Press, 1983).

12 See Erik Erikson, *Childhood and Society* (New York: W. W. Norton, 1950), and *The Life Cycle Completed: A Review* (New York: W. W. Norton, 1982).

13 Robert C. Peck, "Psychological Development in the Second Half of Life," in B. Neugarten, ed., *Middle Age and Aging* (Chicago: University of Chicago Press, 1968).

14 Robert J. Lifton, *The Broken Connection: On Death and the Continuity of Life* (New York: Simon and Schuster, 1979).

15 Charles Tart, *Transpersonal Psychologies* (New York: Harper and Row, 1977).

16 Rudolf Otto, *The Idea of the Holy*, trans. John W. Harvey (New York: Oxford University Press, 1923 [rpt., 1971]). On contemplation, see Frithjof Schuon, *The Transcendent Unity of Religions*, trans. Peter Townsend (New York: Harper and Row, 1975).

17 Raimundo Panikkar, "The Contemplative Mood: A Challenge to Modernity," *Cross Currents* 31 (Fall, 1981): 261–71.
18 Simone de Beauvoir, *The Coming of Age*, trans. Patrick O'Brien (New York: G. P. Putnam's Sons, 1972).
19 Thomas R. Cole, "The 'Enlightened' View of Aging: Victorian Morality in a New Key," *Hastings Center Report* 13 (June 1983): 34–40.
20 On the hegemony of the *vita activa* in the modern age, see Hannah Arendt, *The Human Condition* (Chicago: University of Chicago Press, 1958).
21 Frithjof Schuon, *Understanding Islam* (New York: Penguin Books, 1972), 35.
22 Karl Jaspers, *Man in the Modern Age* (London: Routledge and Kegan Paul, 1951).
23 Karl Britton, *Philosophy and the Meaning of Life* (New York: Cambridge University Press, 1969); W. D. Joske, "Philosophy and the Meaning of Life," *Australasian Journal of Philosophy* 52, no. 2 (1974): 93–104. Reprinted in E. D. Klemke, ed., *The Meaning of Life* (Cambridge, Mass.: Harvard University Press, 1981).
24 Robert Nozick, *Philosophical Explanations* (New York: Cambridge University Press, 1981).
25 Jacob Needleman, "Why Philosophy is Easy," *Review of Metaphysics* 22, no. 1 (September 1968): 3–14. More recently, Jacob Needleman, *The Heart of Philosophy* (New York: Alfred A. Knopf, 1982).
26 Viktor Frankl, *Man's Search for Meaning* (Boston: Beacon Press, 1963).
27 Robert N. Butler, "The Life Review: An Interpretation of Reminiscence in the Aged," *Psychiatry* 26 (1963): 65–76; "Successful Aging and the Role of the Life Review," in S. H. Zarit, *Readings in Aging and Death* (New York: Harper and Row, 1977). For a bibliography, see H. R. Moody, "Bibliography on Life-Review," in Marc Kaminsky, ed., *The Uses of Reminiscence* (New York: Haworth Press, 1984).
28 Sharan Merriam, "The Concept and Function of Reminiscence: A Review of the Research," *The Gerontologist* 20 (1980): 604–9.
29 Kurt Baier, "The Meaning of Life," in Klemke, ed., *The Meaning of Life*, 81–117.
30 Ibid., 115.
31 See Donald M. Frame, *Montaigne's Discovery of Man* (New York: Columbia University Press, 1955).
32 See Ludwig Wittgenstein, *Philosophical Investigations*, trans. G. E. M. Anscombe (New York: Oxford University Press, 1953). This is the source for the important idea of family resemblance as the key to the unity of concepts within a language game. Cf. Renford Bambrough, "Universals and Family Resemblances," *Proceedings of the Aristotelian Society* 61 (1960–61).
33 Stephen Pepper, *World Hypotheses* (Berkeley: University of California Press, 1942); and Thomas Kuhn, *The Structure of Scientific Revolutions* (Chicago: University of Chicago Press, 1970).
34 James Olney, *Metaphors of Self* (Princeton: Princeton University Press, 1973).
35 Lionel Trilling, *Sincerity and Authenticity* (San Diego: Harcourt Brace Jovanovich, 1980).

36 James Olney, *Autobiography: Essays Theoretical and Critical* (Princeton: Princeton University Press, 1980). See Olney's introductory essay for an account of what appears to be the cul-de-sac of the contemporary autobiographical consciousness, where linguistic acts abolish both self and history.

37 Janet Varner Gunn, *Autobiography: Toward a Poetics of Experience* (Philadelphia: University of Pennsylvania Press, 1982).

38 The examples of Augustine, Montaigne, Rousseau, and Kierkegaard are instances of philosophical thought which is at the same time personal and autobiographical. But in the history of philosophy it is possible to identify instances of what might be called pseudo-autobiography, such as Descartes's *Discourse on Method*. In our time philosophers such as Bertrand Russell, A. J. Ayer, or George Santayana can write elegant autobiographies which seem to have no explicit relation to their thought—another instance of the gulf between public and private worlds. The relation between the literary style and the conceptual intentions of philosophers remains an unwritten chapter in the history of ideas.

39 Cf. Mircea Eliade, *Cosmos and History: The Myth of the Eternal Return* (New York: Harper and Row, 1959).

40 Peter Berger, *The Homeless Mind: Modernization and Consciousness* (New York: Random House, 1973).

41 Michel Philibert, *L'Echelle des Ages* (Paris: Editions du Seuil, 1968); M. Philibert, "The Phenomenological Approach to Images of Aging," *Soundings* 57 (1974): 33–49.

42 David Stannard, *The Puritan Way of Death* (New York: Oxford University Press, 1977).

43 "We are witnessing now an attempt to eliminate the darker, more painful aspects of human living, no longer by rising above them (and thereby gaining in stature), but either by abolishing them—which is impossible since they lie in the nature of things—or by pretending they do not exist. It was possible for the men of other times to accept these conditions because life as such was situated in an infinitely wider context. They knew that however deeply involved they might be in the scenario of suffering and loss, they were not by nature totally submerged in it. Experience taught them to look elsewhere for peace and for perfection, and faith assured them that there are indeed other dimensions than those which seem to hem us in. Today most people are confined in a place that knows no 'elsewhere,' trapped with wild beasts that tear their flesh and from which they cannot escape. It is hardly surprising that they need to be drugged to be able to exist in such a situation." Gai Eaton, *King of the Castle: Choice and Responsibility in the Modern World* (London: The Bodley Head, 1977), 37.

44 See John-Raphael Staude, *Wisdom and Age* (Berkeley: Ross Books, 1981); Vivian Clayton and James Birren, "The Development of Wisdom Across the Lifespan: A Reexamination of an Ancient Topic," in Paul Baltes and Orville Brim, *Lifespan Development and Behavior* (New York: Academic Press, 1980).

45 On the concept of wisdom in the classical and medieval tradition, see James D. Collins, *The Lure of Wisdom* (Milwaukee: Marquette University Press, 1962).

46 Jean-Pierre Dupuy, "Myths of the Information Society," in Kathleen Woodward, ed., *The Myths of Information: Technology and Postindustrial Culture* (Madison: University of Wisconsin Press, 1980), p. 9.

47 David Hackett Fischer, *Growing Old in America* (New York: Oxford University Press, 1978), 232–69; and W. Andrew Achenbaum and Peter Stearns, "Old Age and Modernization," *The Gerontologist* 18 (June 1978): 307–12.

48 William Graebner, *A History of Retirement: Meaning and Function of an American Institution, 1885–1978* (New Haven: Yale University Press, 1980); Peter Townsend, "The Structured Dependency of the Elderly: Creation of Social Policy in the Twentieth Century," *Aging and Society* 1, no. 1 (March 1981): 5–28.

49 Peter Berger, *The Homeless Mind: Modernization and Consciousness* (New York: Random House, 1973).

50 Robert J. Lifton, "Protean Man," in his *History and Human Survival* (New York: Random House, 1970).

51 Marshall Berman, *All That Is Solid Melts into Air: The Experience of Modernity* (New York: Simon and Schuster, 1982). Berman is helpful in distinguishing between *modernization* as a politico-economic transformation and *modernity* as a cultural condition. This distinction is ignored in the gerontological literature, resulting in a confusion of the status and meaning of old age.

52 Edward Shils, *Tradition* (Chicago: University of Chicago Press, 1981); Huston Smith, *Forgotten Truth: The Primordial Tradition* (New York: Harper and Row, 1976).

53 Gerald J. Gruman, "Cultural Origins of Present-Day 'Age-ism': The Modernization of the Life Cycle," in Stuart F. Spicker, Kathleen M. Woodward, and David Van Tassell, eds., *Aging and the Elderly: Humanistic Perspectives in Gerontology* (Atlantic Highlands, N.J.: Humanities Press, 1978).

54 Richard Bolles, *The Three Boxes of Life* (Berkeley: Ten Speed Press, 1979). See also Fred Best, *Flexible Life Scheduling: Breaking the Education-Work-Retirement Lockstep* (New York: Praeger Publishers, 1980).

55 Alasdair MacIntyre, *After Virtue* (Notre Dame, Ind.: University of Notre Dame Press, 1981), 190.

56 Philippe Aries, *Western Attitudes Toward Death*, trans. P. M. Ranum (Baltimore: Johns Hopkins University Press, 1974); Jacques Choron, *Death and Western Thought* (New York: Collier Books, 1963).

57 Ernest Becker, *The Denial of Death* (New York: Free Press, 1973); Jacques Choron, *Death and Modern Man* (New York: Collier Books, 1964).

58 Compare Sally Moore and Barbara Myerhoff, eds., *Secular Ritual* (Amsterdam: Van Gocum, 1977), and Victor Turner, *The Ritual Process: Structure and Anti-Structure* (London: Routledge and Kegan Paul, 1969).

59 James O'Conner, *The Fiscal Crisis of the State* (New York: St. Martin's Press, 1970).

60 Daniel Bell, *The Coming of Post-Industrial Society* (New York: Basic Books, 1973). Bell argues that the economy and the culture of postindustrial society pull in diametrically opposite directions: the economy demands increased specialization and limits, while the culture promises indefinite augmentation of the self.

61 Bernice Neugarten, "Age Groups in American Society and the Rise of the

Young-Old," *Annals of the American Academy of Political and Social Science* 320 (1974): 187–98; and *Age or Need?* (Beverly Hills: Sage Publications, 1983).

62 Jurgen Habermas, *Knowledge and Human Interests* and *Legitimation Crisis* (Boston: Beacon Press, 1975). For an introduction, see Thomas McCarthy, *The Critical Theory of Jurgen Habermas* (Cambridge, Mass.: MIT Press, 1978).

63 Daniel Bell, *The Cultural Contradictions of Capitalism* (New York: Basic Books, 1976).

64 Neil Postman, *The Disappearance of Childhood* (New York: Delacorte, 1982); and Marie Winn, *Children Without Childhood* (New York: Pantheon, 1983).

65 See Klaus F. Riegel, "The Influence of Economic and Political Ideologies upon the Development of Developmental Psychology," *Psychological Bulletin* 78 (1972): 29–141; "On the History of Psychological Gerontology," in Carl Eisdorfer and M. Powell Lawton, eds., *The Psychology of Adult Development and Aging* (Washington, D.C.: American Psychological Association, 1973); "Toward a Dialectical Theory of Development," *American Psychologist* 31 (1976): 689–700.

66 Josef Bleicher, *Contemporary Hermeneutics* (London: Routledge and Kegan Paul, 1980); Lawrence C. Watson, "Understanding a Life History as a Subjective Document: Hermeneutical and Phenomenological Perspectives," *Ethos* 4 (1976): 95–131.

67 David Burrell and Stanley Hauerwas, "From System to Story: An Alternative Pattern for Rationality in Ethics," in H. Tristram Englehardt and Daniel Callahan, eds., *Knowledge, Ethics, and Belief* (Hastings on Hudson, N.Y.: Hastings Center, 1977), 111–52.

68 See C. G. Prado, "Aging and Narrative," *International Journal of Applied Philosophy* 1, no. 3 (Spring 1983): 1–14. What MacIntyre had termed the "narrative unity of a human life" constitutes, in essence, a regulative ideal for the meaning of old age. Yet the notion of narrative unity itself may not be consistent with the cultural mood of modernism. "One feature that links the [modernist] movements . . . is that they tend to see history or human life not as a sequence or history, not as an evolving logic. . . . Modernist works frequently tend to be ordered, then, not on the sequence of historical time or the evolving sequence of character, from history or story as in realism or naturalism; they tend to work spatially or through layers of consciousness, working toward a logic or metaphor or form."— Malcolm Bradbury and James McFarlane, *Modernism* (New York: Penguin Books, 1976), 50. The devaluation of character, sequence, and narrative has its counterpart in the destruction of ideals of virtue, wisdom, and meaning: all ingredients of the narrative unity of a human life.

69 Daniel Levinson, *The Seasons of a Man's Life* (New York: Alfred A. Knopf, 1978).

70 Albert W. Levi, *The Humanities Today* (Bloomington: Indiana University Press, 1970). On the humanities and gerontology, see David Van Tassell, ed., *Aging, Death and the Completion of Being* (Philadelphia: University of Pennsylvania Press, 1979).

71 See Paul Rabinow and William M. Sullivan, eds., *Interpretive Social Science* (Berkeley: University of California Press, 1979).

72 James W. Fowler, *Stages of Faith: The Psychology of Human Development and the Quest for Meaning* (New York: Harper and Row, 1981).

73 Henry Nouwen, *Aging: The Fulfillment of Life* (Garden City, N.Y.: Doubleday, 1974); Eugene C. Bianchi, *Aging as Spiritual Journey* (Los Angeles: Crossroads, 1982).

The Virtues and Vices of the Elderly

1 Ronald Blythe, *The View in Winter* (New York: Harcourt Brace Jovanovich, 1979), 22–23.

2 Ibid., 104.

3 David Gutmann, "The Premature Gerontocracy: Themes of Aging and Death in the Youth Culture," in Arien Mack, ed., *Death in American Experience* (New York: Schocken Books, 1973).

4 For a study of the Benedictines, see Blythe's chapter on the "Prayer Route," *The View in Winter*, 235–67.

5 Erik Erikson, *Identity, Youth and Crisis* (New York: W. W. Norton, 1968), 139–40.

6 Ibid.

7 Ibid.

8 Romans 8:38–39.

9 William Butler Yeats, *The Collected Poems of W. B. Yeats* (New York: Macmillan, 1976), 291.

The Meaning of Risk, Rights, and Responsibility in Aging America

1 Franklin Delano Roosevelt, "Objectives of the Administration," June 8, 1934, in *The Public Papers and Addresses of Franklin Delano Roosevelt*, comp. Samuel I. Rosenman (New York: Random House, 1938), 3: 291–92.

2 Ibid., 291.

3 For instructive historical interpretations, see Roy Lubove, *The Struggle for Social Security* (Cambridge, Mass.: Harvard University Press, 1968); and Carolyn L. Weaver, *The Real Crisis in Social Security* (Durham, N.C.: Duke University Press, 1982). For two eyewitness accounts of the various preferences of policymakers in 1934–1935, see Edwin E. Witte, *The Development of the Social Security Act* (Madison: University of Wisconsin Press, 1963), and J. Douglas Brown, *The Genesis of the American Social Security System* (Princeton: Princeton University Industrial Relations Section, 1969).

4 U.S. Senate, 74th Cong., 1st sess., Report of the Senate Finance Committee, no. 628: The Social Security Bill, p. 2. President Roosevelt transmitted the unanimous report of The Committee on Economic Security to Congress on January 17, 1935. Both houses then held hearings in January and February. The House passed H.R. 7260 on April 19. The discussion of "insecurity" and "risks" in each of these earlier documents is similar to that quoted here. In addition to Roosevelt's letter of transmittal, see also his "Annual Message," January 4, 1935, in *The Public Papers*, 4: 9.

5 Carole Haber, *Beyond Sixty-Five* (New York: Cambridge University Press, 1983).

6 W. Andrew Achenbaum, *Old Age in the New Land* (Baltimore: Johns Hopkins University Press, 1978), 128–30.

7 April 16, 1935, *Congressional Record*, 5789.

8 Social Security Board, *Social Security in America* (Washington, D.C.: U.S. Government Printing Office, 1937), 149, 154.

9 The views of William Green, president of the American Federation of Labor, are representative of the times. Green observed that, unlike the threat of unemployment, *all* workers risked financial insecurity in their later years.

10 Title I, *Social Security Act*, 49 Stat. 620 (1935), ch. 531.

11 Achenbaum, *Old Age*, 135.

12 J. Douglas Brown, *Essays on Social Security* (Princeton: Princeton University Industrial Relations Section, 1977), 28–31; Edwin E. Witte, "Old-Age Security in the Social Security Act" (1937) in *Social Security Perspectives: Essays by Edwin E. Witte*, ed. Robert J. Lampman (Madison: University of Wisconsin Press, 1962), 146. For an interpretation of the negative consequences of this decision, see Jerry R. Cates, *Insuring Inequality* (Ann Arbor: University of Michigan Press, 1983).

13 See Franklin D. Roosevelt's letter of transmittal of the report of the Committee on Economic Security, January 17, 1935; for more on the need for a centralized polity to administer a complex welfare state, see Wilensky, *The Welfare State and Equality*, chap. 2. See also Roosevelt's "Address to the Advisory Council of the Committee on Economic Security," November 14, 1934, in *Papers*, 3: 454; and Hearings before Senate Finance Committee on S. 1130, pp. 104–5.

14 April 19, 1935, *Congressional Record*, 6070.

15 U.S. Senate, 74th Congress, 1st sess., *Economic Security Act*, Hearings before the Senate Committee on Finance, p. 1337.

16 Social Security Board, *Social Security*, 381.

17 June 19, 1935, *Congressional Record*, 9636–37.

18 U.S. Senate Finance Committee, *Social Security Bill*, 27. The phrases quoted in the next sentence come from S. 1130 (The Economic Security Act), p. 1338.

19 Franklin D. Roosevelt, "Presidential Statement upon Signing the Social Security Act, August 14, 1935," in *Papers*, 4: 324.

20 June 17, 1935, *Congressional Record, Senate*, 9419. See also sections 208 and 1104 of the Social Security Act.

21 Franklin D. Roosevelt, "A Message on Social Security to Congress," January 17, 1935, in *Papers*, 4: 44.

22 Social Security Board, *Social Security in America*, 496.

23 Ronald D. Rotunda, *Modern Constitutional Law: Cases and Notes* (St. Paul: West Publishing, 1981), 227–32. It is worth recalling that this decision was rendered shortly after Roosevelt unsuccessfully attempted to "pack" the Supreme Court. Some constitutional scholars waggishly note that "a switch in time saved nine!"

24 Frank Bane, "Social Security Expands," *Social Service Review* 13 (December 1939): 608–9. Henceforth, benefits were to be available not just to the retired worker who had contributed to the system, but also to his wife upon her sixty-fifth birthday. Should an employee with a sufficient number of earned credits die before age sixty-five, his widow, dependent children,

and (in some circumstances) his dependent parents could claim a *right* to survivors' benefits.

25 *Report of the Advisory Council on Social Security,* December 10, 1938, 18.

26 J. Douglas Brown, "Economic Problems in the Provision of Security Against Life Hazards of Workers, *American Economic Review* 30 (March 1940): 67.

27 Reprinted in *The Papers and Addresses of Franklin Delano Roosevelt* (New York: Macmillan, 1941), 9: 411.

28 See Otis L. Graham, Jr., *Toward a Planned Society* (New York: Oxford University Press, 1976), chap. 2; E. Wright Bakke, "America and the Beveridge Plan," *Yale Review* 33 (June 1944): 644–57; Marion Clawson, *New Deal Planning* (Baltimore: Johns Hopkins University Press, 1981).

29 Franklin D. Roosevelt, "Message on the State of the Union," January 11, 1944, in *Papers,* 13: 41.

30 James Gilbert, *Another Chance: Postwar America, 1945–1968* (New York: Alfred A. Knopf, 1982).

31 Edwin E. Witte, "Social Security–1948" in Lampman, ed., *Social Security Perspectives,* 31. Witte reiterated this theme in a 1955 essay, "Changing Roles in the Quest for Security."

32 Brown, *Essays,* 53.

33 See Martha Derthick, *Policymaking in Social Security* (Washington, D.C.: Brookings Institution, 1979).

34 Brown, *Essays,* 58.

35 Ibid., 20.

36 There is nothing new in the use of chronological age as a criterion for public policies. In *Beyond Sixty-Five,* Carol Haber notes that age categorization gradually became an acceptable and accepted practice in late nineteenth-century America. Actually, there are precedents in Europe and the United States before then. See Peter N. Stearns, *Old Age in European Society* (New York: Holmes and Meier, 1977); John Demos, "Old Age in Colonial New England," in Michael Gordon, ed., *The Family in Social-Historical Perspective,* 2d ed. (New York: St. Martin's Press, 1978), 220–57; and W. Andrew Achenbaum, "The Evolution of Federal Old-Age Policies," in *The Wilson Quarterly* (Fall 1984).

37 "History of the Provisions of the Old-Age, Survivors, Disability, and Health Insurance Program," in *Social Security Bulletin,* Annual Statistical Supplement, 1983.

38 See David E. Stannard, "The Dilemmas of Aging in Bureaucratic America," in *Aging and the Elderly,* ed. David D. Van Tassel, Stuart Spicker, and Kathleen Woodward (Atlantic Highlands, N.J.: Humanities Press, 1978), 9–20; and W. Andrew Achenbaum, "Societal Perceptions of the Aged and Aging," in Robert H. Binstock and Ethel Shanas, eds., *Handbook of Aging and the Social Sciences,* 2d ed. (New York: Van Nostrand Reinhold, 1985).

39 Edwin E. Witte, "Changing Roles in the Quest" (1955), in Lampman, ed., *Social Security Perspectives,* 76.

40 Gaston V. Rimlinger, "Social Security, Incentives, and Controls in the U.S. and U.S.S.R.," *Comparative Studies in Society and History* 4 (1961–62): 108–9.

41 *Flemming* vs. *Nestor, Supreme Court Reporter* 80: 1372.

42 For more on this, see W. Andrew Achenbaum, "The Elderly's Social Security Entitlements as a Measure of American Life," to appear in a volume on historical gerontology edited by David D. Van Tassel and Peter N. Stearns.

43 Charles A. Reich, "The New Property," *The Public Interest*, 3 (Spring 1966): 86.

44 Archibald Cox, "The Supreme Court—Foreword," *Harvard Law Review* 80 (November 1966): 119.

45 Public Law 89–73, July 14, 1965.

46 And as I have tried to demonstrate elsewhere, this preamble is riddled with outmoded images of age and often works at cross-purposes. See Achenbaum, *Shades of Gray*, chaps. 4–5.

47 Samuel H. Beer, "Liberalism and the National Idea," *The Public Interest* 5 (Spring 1966): 82; but see also 78–80.

48 For an influential and prophetic essay representative of the genre, see Charles A. Reich, "Individual Rights and Social Welfare: The Emerging Legal Issues," *Yale Law Journal* 74 (June 1965): 1245–59.

49 397 U.S. 254 (1970).

50 Paul A. Samuelson, "Social Insurance," *American Economic Review* 54 (May 1964): 95.

51 John Kenneth Galbraith, *The Affluent Society* (Boston: Houghton Mifflin, 1958), 115.

52 J. Douglas Brown, "The American Philosophy of Social Insurance," *Social Service Review* 30 (March 1956): 3.

53 Brown, *Essays*, 31–32.

54 Brown, *Essays*, 22.

55 Yair Aharoni, *The No-Risk Society* (Chatham, N.J.: Chatham House, 1981), 1–2.

56 Robert J. Samuelson, "Social Insecurity," *National Journal* (May 29, 1982): 965. I have reversed the sentence order of the original.

57 James L. Athearn, "The Riskless Society," *The Journal of Risk and Insurance*, 45 (December 1978): 573. See also Aharoni, *No-Risk Society*, 35–36, 207.

58 Bernice L. Neugarten, "Policy for the 1980s," in *Age or Need?*, ed. Bernice L. Neugarten (Beverly Hills: Sage Publications, 1982), 25.

59 It is worth noting that even this argument provokes dissent within the ranks. Some of Social Security's loyal supporters stress that most gender discriminations have been eliminated from the system. See Robert J. Myers, *Social Security*, 2d ed. (Homewood, Ill.: Richard D. Irwin, 1981), 240–43.

60 *Weinberger* vs. *Wiesenfeld*, 420 U.S. 651.

61 *Mathews* vs. *DeCastro*, 429 U.S. 181, 185–87.

62 *Mathews* vs. *Eldridge*, 424 U.S. 319, esp. 321, 340–41. See also Lawrence H. Tribe, "Unraveling National League of Cities: The New Federalism and Affirmative Rights to Essential Governmental Services," *Harvard Law Review* 90 (April 1977): 1080–81; and Melvin Aron Eisenberg, "Participation, Responsiveness and the Consultative Process," *Harvard Law Review* 92 (December 1978): 421.

63 For a fine summary of the literature and issues that it raises for consti-

tutional law, see Peter Weston, "The Empty Idea of Equality," *Harvard Law Review* 95 (January 1982): esp. 540–41.

64 John Rawls, *A Theory of Justice* (Cambridge, Mass.: Harvard University Press, 1971), 303.

65 Marc Plattner, "The Welfare State vs. The Redistributive State," *The Public Interest* 55 (Spring 1979): 47–48.

66 For more on this, see Frank I. Michelman, "In Pursuit of Constitutional Welfare Rights: One View of Rawls's Theory of Justice," *University of Pennsylvania Law Review* 121 (1973): esp. 1002–03.

67 Robert Nozick, *Anarchy, State, and Utopia* (New York: Basic Books, 1974), 153.

68 Alasdair MacIntyre, *After Virtue* (Notre Dame, Ind.: University of Notre Dame Press, 1981), 231.

69 Marc Plattner, "The New Political Theory," *The Public Interest* 40 (Summer 1975): 128.

70 John Rawls, "A Well-Ordered Society," in *Philosophy, Politics & Society*, 5th ser., ed. Peter Laslett and James Fishkin (New Haven: Yale University Press, 1979), 6–9.

71 Nozick, *Anarchy, State, and Utopia*, 333–34.

72 Michael Sandel, *Liberalism and the Limits of Justice* (Cambridge: Cambridge University Press, 1982), 172–73.

73 See David W. Noble, *Historians against History* (Minneapolis: University of Minnesota Press, 1965); Ernest Lee Tuveson, *Redeemer Nation* (Chicago: University of Chicago Press, 1968); and Paul C. Nagel, *This Sacred Trust* (New York: Oxford University Press, 1971).

74 Robert N. Bellah, *The Broken Covenant* (New York: Seabury Press, 1975), 139.

75 Larry Atkins, "Refinancing Social Security: Implications for the Incomes of the Elderly," paper presented to the Western Economic Association, July 22, 1983. Atkins is a staff member of the U.S. Senate Special Committee on Aging.

76 For more on the difficulties with the concept, see the argument and notes in chap. 1 of Robert Wohl's *The Generation of 1914* (Cambridge, Mass.: Harvard University Press, 1979).

77 Peter Laslett, "The Conversation Between the Generations," in Laslett and Fishkin, eds., *Philosophy, Politics and Society*, 48.

78 Ibid., 51. I trust it will not be too churlish to note that Americans have not always responded to the poor with a wholehearted sense of "their universal obligation." See James T. Patterson, *America's Struggle Against Poverty, 1900–1980* (Cambridge, Mass.: Harvard University Press, 1981).

79 George F. Will, *Statecraft as Soulcraft* (New York: Simon and Schuster, 1983), 45. See also Morris Janowitz, *The Reconstruction of Patriotism* (Chicago: University of Chicago Press, 1983).

80 MacIntyre, *After Virtue*, 236.

81 *Report of the National Commission on Social Security Reform* (Washington, D.C.: U.S. Government Printing Office, 1983), p. 2–2.

82 Letter from Thomas Jefferson to Samuel Kercheval, July 12, 1816, in *The Writings of Thomas Jefferson*, ed. Albert Ellery Bergh (Washington, D.C.: The Thomas Jefferson Memorial Association, 1907), 15: 40–41. Sen. Jen-

nings Randolph quoted from this passage in the 1983 debate. See March
21, 1983, *Congressional Record*, S. 3488.

83 I use this word in the sense that it appears in the following passage from
    Glenn Tinder's *Community: Reflections on a Tragic Ideal* (Baton Rouge:
    Louisiana State University Press, 1980), 199: "Civility is the stance in
    which one consciously bears, in the sense of enduring and of supporting,
    the existence of multitudes of unpredictable and troublesome fellow
    humans."

Legal Reform and Aging

1   Age Discrimination in Employment Act of 1967, 29 U.S.C. secs. 621–634
    (1976 and Supp. IV 1980); Age Discrimination in Employment Act
    Amendments of 1978, Pub. L. No. 95–256, 92 Stat. 189 (codified at scat-
    tered sections of 5 U.S.C. and 29 U.S.C.).

2   Age Discrimination Act of 1975, 42 U.S.C. secs. 6101–7 (1976 and Supp.
    IV 1980).

3   For debate on the aptness of this analogy between blacks and elderly
    people, compare Schuck, "The Graying of Civil Rights Law: The Age Dis-
    crimination Act of 1975," *Yale Law Journal* 89 (1979): 27, with Alexander,
    "Shucking Off the Rights of the Aged: Congressional Ambivalence and
    the Exceptions to the Age Discrimination Act of 1975," *Chicago-Kent Law
    Review* 57 (1981): 1009.

4   See *Massachusetts Board of Retirement* vs. *Murgia*, 427 U.S. 307 (1976);
    Vance vs. *Bradley*, 440 U.S. 93 (1979); Eglit, "Of Age and the Constitu-
    tion," *Chicago-Kent Law Review* 57 (1981): 859.

5   Thomas R. Cole, "The 'Enlightened' View of Aging: Victorian Morality
    in a New Key," *Hastings Center Report* 13 (1983): 34.

6   See, for example, *In re Karen Quinlan*, 355 A.2d 647 (1976).

7   See Robert Burt, *Taking Care of Strangers: The Rule of Law in Doctor-
    Patient Relations* (New York: Free Press, 1979), 4–18.

8   David Hilfiker, "Allowing the Debilitated to Die," *New England Journal
    of Medicine* 308 (March 24, 1983): 716, 717.

9   *New York Times*, May 31, 1983, p. C3, col. 1.

10 See S. Rothman, *Woman's Proper Place* (New York: Basic Books, 1978),
    267–76.

11 Robert Burt, "Constitutional Law and the Teaching of the Parables," *Yale
    Law Journal* 93 (1984): 455, 489–500.

The "Enlightened" View of Aging

1   I am deliberately overgeneralizing about "critics of ageism" to make my
    point. For notable exceptions, see Richard A. Kalish, "The New Ageism
    and the Failure Models: A Polemic," *The Gerontologist* 19 (1979): 398–
    402; and Robert H. Binstock's 1982 Kent Lecture, "The Aged as Scape-
    goat," *The Gerontologist* 23 (April 1983): 136–43.

2   Robert N. Butler, "Age-ism: Another Form of Bigotry," *The Gerontologist*
    9 (1969): 243–46.

3   Robert N. Butler, *Why Survive?* (New York: Harper and Row, 1975).
    Butler's coauthored book with Myrna Lewis, *Aging and Mental Health:*

Positive Psychosocial Approaches (St. Louis: C. V. Mosby, 1973), has gone through several editions and is an influential textbook in gerontology.

4 Butler, *Why Survive?*, 11–12.

5 See Erdman B. Palmore, "Attitudes Toward the Aged," *Research on Aging* 4 (1982): 333–48, which summarizes the findings of over one hundred studies in this area.

6 See Butler, *Why Survive?*, chap. 1; Louis Harris and Associates, *The Myth and Reality of Aging in America* (Washington, D.C.: National Council on Aging, 1977).

7 One exception to this generalization is Jack Levin and William Levin, *Ageism: Prejudice and Discrimination Against the Elderly* (Belmont, Calif.: Wadsworth, 1980). These authors argue, with limited success, that prejudice and discrimination are based on the minority group status of the elderly.

8 See, for example, Clark Tibbitts, "Can We Invalidate Negative Stereotypes of Aging?" *The Gerontologist* 4 (1979): 10–20; or Harris and Associates, *Myth and Reality of Aging*.

9 See, for example, Anne Foner, ed., *Age in Society* (Beverly Hills: Sage Publications, 1976); Matilda White Riley, "Aging, Social Change, and the Power of Ideas," *Daedalus* 107 (1978): 39–52.

10 See, for example, Lawrence Fries and James Crapo, *Vitality and Aging* (San Francisco: W. H. Freeman, 1981); Alex Comfort, *A Good Age* (New York: Crown, 1976); Frances Tenenbaum, *Over 55 Is Not Illegal* (Boston: Houghton Mifflin, 1979).

11 This definition derives from Mark Schorer, "The Necessity of Myth," reprinted in Henry A. Murray, ed., *Myth and Mythmaking* (Boston: Beacon Press, 1968), 355–58.

12 For a fuller treatment, see Thomas R. Cole, "Past Meridian: Aging and the Northern Middle Class, 1830–1930" (Ph.D. dissertation, University of Rochester, 1980). My position differs from those of other historians who have addressed this question. See David Hackett Fischer, *Growing Old in America* (New York: Oxford University Press, 1977); W. Andrew Achenbaum, *Old Age in the New Land* (Baltimore: Johns Hopkins University Press, 1978); Gerald J. Gruman, "Cultural Origins of Present-Day Age-ism," in Stuart F. Spicker, Kathleen Woodward, and David D. Van Tassel, eds., *Aging and the Elderly* (Atlantic Highlands, N.J.: Humanities Press, 1978).

13 See, for example, Cortlandt Van Rensselaer, "Old Age: A Funeral Sermon" (Washington, D.C., 1841).

14 This was Cotton Mather's view of his own good health as an old man. See Mather, *The Angel of Bethesda* (1724), reprinted in Gordon W. Jones, ed., *The Angel of Bethesda* (Waltham, Mass.: American Antiquarian Society, 1972).

15 Nathaniel Emmons, "Piety: A Peculiar Ornament to the Aged," in *Works* (Boston: Congregational Board of Publications, 1842), 3: 501–2.

16 Joseph Lathrop, *The Infirmities and Comforts of Old Age* (Springfield, Mass., 1802), 12.

17 Fischer, *Growing Old in America*, chap. 1; Keith Thomas, "Age and Authority in Early Modern England," *Proceedings of the British Academy* 62 (1976): 204–48.

18 See Pamela T. Amoss and Stevan Harrell, eds., *Other Ways of Growing Old* (Stanford: Stanford University Press, 1981), introduction.
19 Thomas R. Cole, "The Ideology of Old Age and Death in American History," *American Quarterly* 31 (Summer 1979): 223–31.
20 See, for example, Stephen Nissenbaum, *Sex, Diet, and Debility in Jacksonian America* (Westport, Conn.: Greenwood Press, 1980); Martin C. Van Buren, "The Indispensable God of Health: A Study of Republican Hygiene and the Ideology of William Alcott" (Ph.D. dissertation, University of California at Los Angeles, 1977).
21 See Thomas R. Cole, " 'Putting Off the Old': Middle-Class Morality, Antebellum Protestantism, and the Origins of Ageism in America," in David D. Van Tassel and Peter Stearns, eds., *Old Age in a Bureaucratic Society: The Elderly, the Experts, and the State in American History* (Westport, Conn.: Greenwood Press, 1986).
22 For a fascinating critique of New England theology after Edwards, see Joseph Haroutunian, *Piety versus Moralism* (New York: Henry Holt, 1932).
23 William Alcott, *Forty Years in the Wilderness of Pills and Powders, or, The Cogitations and Confessions of an Aged Physician* (Boston: J. P. Jewett, 1859), 43.
24 See, for example, Charles G. Finney, "Reprobation," in *Sermons on Important Subjects* (New York: John F. Taylor, 1836); Lyman Beecher, "Six Sermons on Temperance," in *Sabbath and Temperance Manuals* (New York: The American Tract Society, n.d.).
25 William Alcott, *The Laws of Health* (Boston: J. P. Jewett, 1860), 9–10; also Russell Trall, *Sexual Physiology* (New York: Miller, Wood, 1866), 304.
26 Several historians have emphasized the declining status of old age in the late nineteenth century. See Achenbaum, *Old Age in the New Land*, chap. 3; Carol Haber, *Beyond Sixty-Five* (New York: Cambridge University Press, 1983); William Graebner, *A History of Retirement* (New Haven: Yale University Press, 1980).
27 See Robert Wiebe, *The Search for Order* (New York: Hill and Wang, 1966); Burton J. Bledstein, *The Culture of Professionalism* (New York: Norton Press, 1976); William R. Leach, *True Love and Perfect Union* (New York: Basic Books, 1980).
28 Ralph Waldo Emerson, "Old Age," reprinted in *Society and Solitude* (Boston: Houghton Mifflin, 1904), 320.
29 Frederick L. Hoffman, "The Art of Living a Hundred Years," *Sanitarian* 47 (1901): 238.
30 G. Stanley Hall, *Senescence* (New York: D. Appleton, 1922), 377.
31 During the 1870s Beard lectured on "Legal Responsibility in Old Age" and on "The Decline of the Moral Faculties in Old Age." These lectures were incorporated into *American Nervousness* (New York: G. P. Putnam's Sons, 1881).
32 See Graebner, *History of Retirement*, chap. 1.
33 For a lonely exception, see Felix Adler, *The Spiritual Attitude Toward Old Age* (New York: The New York Society for Ethical Culture, 1906).
34 See, for example, Lee Welling Squier, *Old Age Dependency in the U.S.*

(New York: Macmillan, 1912). Many social workers in this period preferred social casework (which required professional intervention) to old age pensions. See Brian Gratton, "Social Workers and Old Age Pensions," *Social Service Review* 57 (September 1983): 403–15.

35 Abraham Epstein, *The Challenge of the Aged* (New York: Alfred A. Knopf, 1928), 25.

36 See Ernest Burgess, *Aging in Western Societies* (Chicago: University of Chicago Press, 1960); Donald Olen Cowgill and L. D. Holmes, eds., *Aging and Modernization* (New York: Appleton, 1972).

37 George Lawton, *New Goals for Old Age* (New York: Columbia University Press, 1943), 32.

38 See Carroll Estes, *The Aging Enterprise* (San Francisco: Jossey-Bass, 1980).

39 See Henry J. Pratt, *The Gray Lobby* (Chicago: University of Chicago Press, 1976); Richard B. Calhoun, *In Search of the New Old* (New York: Elsevier–North Holland, 1978).

40 Bernice L. Neugarten, "Age Groups in American Society and the Rise of the Young-Old," *Annals of the American Academy of Political and Social Science* 415 (1974): 187–98.

41 Stephen Crystal, *America's Old Age Crisis* (New York: Basic Books, 1982).

42 See, for example, Spicker, Woodward, and Van Tassel, eds., *Aging and the Elderly;* David Van Tassel, ed., *Aging, Death, and the Completion of Being* (Philadelphia: University of Pennsylvania Press, 1979).

Introduction to Part II

1 John A. Prior and Jack S. Silberstein, *Physical Diagnosis: The History and Examination of the Patient* (St. Louis: C. V. Mosby, 1973), 1.

2 Oliver Sacks, *Awakenings* (New York: Vintage Books, 1976), 262.

3 Virginia Woolf, "On Being Ill," in *The Moment and Other Essays* (New York: Harcourt Brace Jovanovich, 1974), 11.

4 Sacks, *Awakenings*, 260.

5 T. S. Eliot, "East Coker," in *Four Quartets* (New York: Harcourt Brace Jovanovich, 1971).

6 John Berger and Jean Mohr, *A Fortunate Man* (New York: Pantheon, 1976), 99.

7 Oliver Sacks, "The Leg," *London Review of Books* 17 (1982): 3–5.

8 Sacks, "The Leg," 4.

9 D. H. Lawrence, *Apocalypse* (New York: Penguin Books, 1976).

Reminiscence and the Life Review

1 Samuel Beckett, *Krapp's Last Tape and Other Dramatic Pieces* (New York: Grove Press, 1960), 16.

2 Yashusi Inoue, *Chronicle of My Mother*, trans. Jean Odo Moy (Tokyo: Kodansha International, 1982), 33.

3 Ibid., 32–33.

4 Ibid., 26.

5 Ibid., 54.

6   Ibid.
7   Ibid., 55.
8   Marion Roach, "Another Name for Madness," *New York Times Magazine*, 16 January 1983, 22–31.
9   Ibid., 25.
10 Ibid., 22.
11 Ibid., 25.
12 Inoue, *Chronicle*, 105–6.
13 Carolyn Smith, "Watching the Clock in James Joyce's *Ulysses* and Virginia Woolf's *Mrs. Dalloway*," unpublished MS, 4.
14 Erik Erikson, "Identity Crisis in Autobiographic Perspective," in his *Life History and the Historical Moment* (New York: W. W. Norton, 1975), 21.
15 Ibid., 22.
16 Fredric Jameson, *The Political Unconscious: Narrative as a Socially Symbolic Act* (Ithaca: Cornell University Press, 1981).
17 Robert Butler, "The Life Review: An Interpretation of Reminiscence in the Aged," *Psychiatry* 26 (February 1963): 65–76.
18 Ibid., 66.
19 Pamela Babb de Ramon, "The Final Task: Life Review for the Dying Patient," *Nursing* (February 1983): 45–49.
20 Ibid., 46.
21 Ibid., 47.
22 Walter Benjamin, "The Storyteller" (1936), in his *Illuminations*, ed. Hannah Arendt, trans. Harry Zohn (New York: Harcourt, Brace and World, 1968), 94.
23 Ibid., 72.
24 We can also propose several theoretical objections to the life review. Indeed, although I have been referring to Butler's work as theoretical, this adjective is misleading. For while he advances an idea that is highly speculative, he does not map out in theoretical terms the mechanisms by which the life review actually might work. He postulates a catalyst for the life review—the biological fact of death—and he offers many examples of reminiscence in late life drawn from divergent domains ranging from his own clinical experience to the literary tradition of the West. But we are left with no idea of how the life review would operate. Butler had psychoanalytic training, yet Freud is mentioned nowhere in his essay. While Freud was concerned with developing a metapsychology of mind from topographical, dynamic, and economic points of view, Butler does not enlist his aid. He deliberately uses the language of psychoanalysis; he believes the life review is "characterized by the progressive return to *consciousness* of past experience, and, particularly, the resurgence of *unresolved conflicts*" (Butler, 66, italics mine); he notes the "counter transference concerns of the psychiatrists" and remarks that "the recovery of memories, the making the unconscious conscious, is generally regarded as one of the basic ingredients of the curative process" (Butler, 75). Thus we may well ask just *how* the fact of impending death will cause unconscious conflicts to emerge. What undoes repression? What unlocks the gate of censorship? How does the "patient" recognize the unconscious patterns that have characterized his life? What is the analyti-

cal process? But the analyst is for the most part absent in Butler's sketch, and in his place we find instead the psychiatrist, the therapist, the friend, or, perhaps, no one at all. (If to this Butler would respond that he is not following a Freudian psychoanalytic model, I would have to ask, why not?)

As for empirical research that has tested Butler's theory, with conflicting results, I will mention only one: Virginia Revere and Sheldon S. Tobin, "Myth and Reality: The Older Person's Relationship to His Past," *International Journal of Aging and Human Development* 12, no. 1 (1980–81): 15–26. In absolute contradiction to Butler's thesis that the elderly may see their lives with the clear eyes of truth as a result of life review, Revere and Tobin found that the elderly tend to *mythicize* their pasts rather than make sense of them and that the goal of mythicizing is *justification* rather than insight and responsibility. Where Butler suggests that the life review is normative, Revere and Tobin conclude that "while a realistic stance in relation to one's life may be adaptational, it is not normative. The reminiscences undoubtedly serve a life function, but rather than making sense of their lives in a way which involves acceptance of 'the way it was,' these aged persons have recast their memories to make the uniqueness of themselves vivid." (Revere and Tobin, 25.)

25 Butler, "The Life Review," 68.
26 Joyce Cary, *To Be a Pilgrim* (London: Michael Joseph, 1951), 80.
27 Ibid.
28 Ibid.
29 Ibid., 158–59.
30 T. S. Eliot, "The Dry Salvages," *Four Quartets*, in his *Complete Poems and Plays* (New York: Harcourt, Brace, 1952), 133.
31 Cary, *To Be a Pilgrim*, 158.
32 Ibid., 220.
33 Ibid., 220–21.
34 Ibid., 55.
35 Ibid., 221.
36 Marcel Proust, *The Past Recaptured*, trans. Frederick A. Blossom (New York: Modern Library, 1959), 192.
37 Cary, *To Be a Pilgrim*, 34.
38 Eliot, "The Dry Salvages," 125.
39 Cary, *To Be a Pilgrim*, 291.
40 Ibid., 220.
41 Ibid., 298.
42 Ibid., 299.
43 Ibid.
44 Ibid.
45 Ibid., 213.
46 Butler, "The Life Review," 71.
47 Henry James, "The Beast in the Jungle," in *The Ghostly Tales of Henry James*, ed. Leon Edel (New Brunswick, N.J.: Rutgers University Press, 1948), 678.
48 Ibid., 698.
49 Ibid., 718.
50 Ibid., 716–17.

51 Henry James, quoted in *The Ghostly Tales*, 667.

52 Butler, "The Life Review," 69.

53 Beckett, *Krapp's Last Tape*, 13.

54 Wallace Stevens, "The Rock," in his *The Palm at the End of the Mind*, ed. Holly Stevens (New York: Vintage Books, 1972), 362.

55 Ibid.

56 Beckett, *Krapp's Last Tape*, 25–26.

57 Frank Kermode, *The Sense of an Ending* (New York: Oxford University Press, 1967), 58.

58 Beckett, *Krapp's Last Tape*, 16.

The Wizard of Pilgrimage

1 Ray Bradbury, "Because, because, because of the wonderful things he does" (1974), in *The Wizard of Oz*, ed. Michael Patrick Hearn (New York: Schocken Books, 1983), 250.

2 L. Frank Baum, *The Wonderful Wizard of Oz* (Chicago: Henry Regnery, rpt. of original 1900 ed., 1956).

3 Henry M. Littlefield, "The Wizard of Oz: Parable on Populism" (1968), in Hearn, ed., *The Wizard of Oz*, 221–32.

4 John C. Tower, "Age and Oz," *The Baum Bugle* 8, no. 3 (1964): 15, quoting *The Tin Woodman of Oz*.

5 Baum, *The Wonderful Wizard of Oz*, 12.

6 Ibid., 18.

7 Ibid., 20.

8 Ibid.

9 Ibid., 49.

10 Ibid., 59.

11 Ibid., 122.

12 Ibid.

13 Ibid., 123.

14 Ibid., 133.

15 Ibid., 145–46.

16 Ibid., 180.

17 Ibid.

18 Ibid., 216.

19 Ibid., 231.

20 Ibid., 200–201.

21 C. Warren Hollister, "Oz and the Fifth Criterion" (1971), in Hearn, ed., *The Wizard of Oz*, 192–96.

22 Brian Attebury's essay in ibid., 295.

23 Ibid., 294.

24 Bernice Neugarten, "Dynamics of Transition from Middle Age to Old Age: Adaptation and the Life Cycle," *Journal of Geriatric Psychiatry* 4 (1970): 71–81.

25 Littlefield, "The Wizard of Oz: Parable on Populism," 221.

The Meaning of Health Care in Old Age

1 Suzanne G. Haynes and Manning Feinleib, eds., *Second Conference on the Epidemiology of Aging*, U.S. Department of Health and Human Services (Washington, D.C.: NIH Publication No. 80-969, 1980), 287–328.

2 Louis Harris and Associates, *The Myth and Reality of Aging in America* (Washington, D.C.: The National Council on Aging, 1975), 128–72.

3 Anne R. Somers and Dorothy R. Fabian, eds., *The Geriatric Imperative* (New York: Appleton-Century-Crofts, 1981), 1–38.

4 *Selected Poems of William Carlos Williams* (New York: New Directions, 1969), 94.

5 Nancy L. Mace and Peter V. Rabins, *The 36-Hour Day* (Baltimore: Johns Hopkins University Press, 1981).

6 E. M. Greenberg, "Epidemiology of Senile Dementia," in Haynes and Feinleib, eds., *Second Conference on the Epidemiology of Aging*.

7 Sally Gadow, "Frailty and Strength: The Dialectic in Aging," *The Gerontologist* 23 (1983): 144–47.

8 James J. Strain, "Noncompliance as a Diagnostic Issue," in D. J. Withering, ed., *Communication and Compliance in a Hospital Setting* (Springfield, Ill.: Charles C Thomas, 1980), 3–17.

9 Louis S. Baer, *Let the Patient Decide: A Doctor's Advice to Older Persons* (Philadelphia: Westminster Press, 1978).

10 The President's Commission on the Study of Ethical Problems in Medicine and Biomedical and Behavioral Research, *Making Health Care Decisions: Report* (Washington, D.C.: U.S. Government Printing Office, 1982), 1: 15–52.

11 Christine K. Cassel, "Ethical Issues in the Care of ALS Patients: Autonomy as Therapy," in Donald W. Mulder, ed., *Amyotrophic Lateral Sclerosis: Evaluation and Care* (Boston: Houghton Mifflin, 1980), 325–32.

12 Robert Kane, David Solomon, John Beck, and Emmett Keeler, "The Future Need for Geriatric Manpower in the United States," *New England Journal of Medicine* 302 (1980): 1327–32.

13 Evan Calkins, "Establishing an Academic Unit in Geriatric Medicine—An Internist's Point of View," in K. Steel, ed., *Geriatric Education* (Lexington, Mass.: Collamore Press, 1981), 93–94.

14 Simone de Beauvoir, *The Coming of Age* (New York: Warner Books, 1973).

15 V. George and A. Dundes, "The Gomer: A Figure of American Hospital Folk Speech," *Journal of American Folklore* 91 (1978): 568–81.

16 Ruth B. Purtilo and Christine K. Cassel, *Ethical Dimensions in the Health Professions* (Philadelphia: W. B. Saunders, 1980), 83–91, 211.

17 Muriel Gillick, "Is the Care of the Chronically Ill a Medical Prerogative?" *New England Journal of Medicine* 310 (1984): 190–93.

18 Christine K. Cassel and Andrew L. Jameton, "Dementia in the Elderly: An Analysis of Chronic Disease," *Annals of Internal Medicine* 94 (1981): 802–7.

19 Katherine M. Hunter, "The Satiric Image: Healers in *The House of God*," *Literature and Medicine* 2 (1983): 135–47.

20 Susan Sheehan, "Kate Quinton's Days," *New Yorker*, 21 November 1983, 58–138, and 28 November 1983, 56–104.

21 Thomas R. Cole, "The 'Enlightened' View of Aging: Morality in a New Key," *Hastings Center Report* (June 1983): 34–40.

22 David Rabin, "Compounding the Ordeal of ALS: Isolation from My Fellow Physicians," *New England Journal of Medicine* 307 (1982): 506–9.

23 Ronald Blythe, *The View in Winter: Reflections on Old Age* (New York: Penguin Books, 1979), 179.

24 John O. Urmson, "Saints and Heroes," in J. Feinberg, ed., *Moral Concepts in Medicine* (New York: Oxford University Press, 1970), 60–73.

25 Sidney Katz, Lawrence G. Branch, Joseph A. Papsidero, John C. Beck, and David S. Greer, "Active Life Expectancy," *New England Journal of Medicine* 309 (1983): 1217–23. See also B. J. McNeil, R. Weischelbaum, and S. G. Pauker, "Speech and Survival: Tradeoffs between Quality and Quantity of Life in Laryngeal Cancer," *New England Journal of Medicine* 305 (1981): 982–87.

26 Lewis Thomas, "Humanities and Science," in *Late Night Thoughts on Listening to Mahler's Ninth Symphony* (New York: Viking Press, 1983), 143–55.

27 Anne R. Somers, "Long-term Care for the Elderly and Disabled," *New England Journal of Medicine* 307 (1982): 221–26.

28 Michael Berman, *All That Is Solid Melts into Air: The Experience of Modernity* (New York: Simon and Schuster, 1982), 13–37.

29 Roger W. Evans, "Health Care Technology and the Inevitability of Resource Allocation and Rationing Decisions," *Journal of the American Medical Association* 249 (1983): 2213.

30 Robert M. Veatch, *A Theory of Medical Ethics* (New York: Basic Books, 1981), 43–49.

31 R. R. Kohn, "The Cause of Death in Very Old People," *Journal of the American Medical Association* 247 (1982): 2793–97.

32 Paul Starr, *The Social Transformation of American Medicine* (New York: Basic Books, 1983).

33 Robert L. Kane and Rosalie A. Kane, "Care of the Aged: Old Problems in Need of New Solutions," *Science* 200 (1978): 913–19.

Growing Old Together

1 Alfred Schutz, *Collected Papers I: The Problem of Social Reality* (The Hague: Nijhoff, 1962), 16–17.

2 James Agee and Walker Evans, *Let Us Now Praise Famous Men* (Boston: Houghton Mifflin, 1941), 236.

3 Maurice Natanson, *Phenomenology, Role and Reason* (Springfield, Ill.: Charles C Thomas, 1974), 44.

4 Yi-Fu Tuan, *Space and Place: The Perspective of Experience* (Minneapolis: University of Minnesota Press, 1977), 179.

5 Ibid., 199.

6 Graham Rowles, *Prisoners of Space? Exploring the Geographical Experience of Older People* (Boulder, Colo.: Westview Press, 1978), 165.

7 Walter Cain, personal communication.

8 Jennie Keith-Ross, *Old People, New Lives* (Chicago: University of Chicago Press, 1977), 27.

9   Bert Smith, *The Pursuit of Dignity: New Living Alternatives for the Elderly* (Boston: Beacon Press, 1977), 14.
10 Tuan, *Space and Place*, 199.
11 Roth.
12 Kai Erikson, *Everything in Its Path* (New York: Simon and Schuster, 1976), 187.
13 Ibid., 189.
14 See Gerald Caplan, *Support Systems and Community Mental Health* (New York: Behavioral Publications, 1974), and Helena Lopata, *Women as Widows: Support Systems* (New York: Elsevier, 1979).
15 Barbara Myerhoff, *Number Our Days* (New York: Simon and Schuster, 1978).
16 Marcel Mauss, *The Gift* (New York: W. W. Norton, 1967 [1925]), 11.
17 Carol Stack, *All Our Kin: Strategies for Survival in a Black Community* (New York: Harper and Row, 1974), 90.
18 Ronald Blythe, *The View in Winter: Reflections on Old Age* (New York: Penguin Books, 1979), 208.
19 Marjorie F. Lowenthal and Betsy Robinson, "Social Networks and Isolation," in Robert Binstock and Ethel Shanas, eds., *Handbook of Aging and the Social Sciences* (New York: Van Nostrand Reinhold, 1976), 432–56.

Frailty and Strength

1   Florida Scott-Maxwell, *The Measure of My Days* (New York: Penguin Books, 1979), 32.
2   John Berger, *About Looking* (New York: Pantheon, 1980), 14.
3   Edith Wyschogrod, "Empathy and Sympathy as Tactile Encounter," *The Journal of Medicine and Philosophy* 6 (1981): 30.
4   Scott-Maxwell, *The Measure of My Days*, 36.
5   Ray Bradbury, *Dandelion Wine* (New York: Bantam Books, 1964), 109.
6   Simone de Beauvoir, *The Coming of Age*, trans. Patrick O'Brian (New York: G. P. Putnam's Sons, 1972), 290.
7   Scott-Maxwell, *The Measure of My Days*, 32.
8   Ronald Blythe, *The View in Winter: Reflections on Old Age* (New York: Penguin Books, 1979), 212.
9   Friedrich Wilhelm Nietzsche, *Ecce Homo*, ed. and trans. Walter Kaufman, in *Basic Writings of Nietzsche* (New York: Modern Library, 1968; rpt. of 1908 ed.), 714.
10 Ibid., 678.
11 Ibid.
12 Scott-Maxwell, *The Measure of My Days*, 32.
13 Ibid., 33.
14 Ibid.
15 Ibid., 128.
16 Blythe, *The View in Winter*, 18.
17 Ibid., 120.
18 Scott-Maxwell, *The Measure of My Days*, 117.

Index

Library of Congress Cataloging-in-Publication Data
Main entry under title:
What does it mean to grow old?
Bibliography: p.
Includes index.
1. Old age—Addresses, essays, lectures. 2. Aged—
United States—Addresses, essays, lectures. I. Cole,
Thomas R., 1949–   . II. Gadow, Sally.
HQ1061.W44 1986   305.2'6   85–27406
ISBN 0–8223–0545–3